POLICE VEHICLES
OF THE WORLD

POLICE VEHICLES

OF THE WORLD

Roy D. Ingleton

LONDON

IAN ALLAN LTD

Contents

Introduction   5

Abbreviations   5

Part One: Cars and Vans   6

Part Two: Motorcylces   93

Part Three: Aircraft and Helicopters   129

Index   152

Front cover, top: *Aerospatiale Alouette 3 of the French Gendarmerie.*

Front cover, bottom: *Hestair Eagle of the Punjab Police.*

Back cover: *Mercedes-Benz L409 accident wagon.*

First published 1981

ISBN 0 7110 1015 3

Published by Ian Allan Ltd, Shepperton, Surrey; and printed by Ian Allan Printing Ltd at their works at Coombelands in Runnymede, England

Introduction

Transport, in the sense it is used in this book, has two meanings; on the one hand it is a means of moving men and materials from one point to another, on the other it is the mechanical means used by patrolling officers to carry out their duties more efficiently.

Ever since the first organised law-enforcement agencies were formed, the need for some form of transport has been recognised. Thus the Maréchaussée in France and the Bow Street Patrol in England were mounted on horses, the better to apprehend highwaymen and fleeting fugitives from justice. The police became 'mechanised' towards the end of the 19th century with the introduction of the bicycle which enabled the patrolling officer in sparsely-populated areas to cover a much larger 'beat'. His superior was, however, more likely than not to be seen visiting the men by horse and trap, at least in England. In other countries too, the horse remained supreme.

The advent of the horseless carriage made only a limited impression on police work for quite some time and it was not until after World War I that the automobile came to be accepted. The Chief of Police reluctantly exchanged his pony and trap for a Ford, a Renault or a bull-nose Morris and, as the number of motor vehicles grew on the roads, so the need for motorised patrols began to make itself felt. Many of the earlier traffic patrols were mounted on motorcycles — a means of transport which continues to prove its worth in most countries of the world. Not surprisingly it was in the United States that the motorcar first really came to be accepted for police work. Patrol cars did not make any great impression on British policing systems until after 1945 and, in France, there are still many more motorcycles used than patrol cars.

The history of airborne police follows very much the same pattern, with the United States leading the way, both in fixed wing aircraft and helicopters. In Great Britain, at the time of writing, no police force has its own aircraft although both types are readily hired for use as required. Similarly, in France the Police Nationale, despite the fact that it has a branch known as the 'Police de l'Air et des Frontières', has no aircraft of its own, although the Gendarmerie Nationale, being a branch of the armed forces, is well equipped in the aviation field.

This book contains details of most of the cars, motorcycles and aircraft known to be in use with the various police forces throughout the world. The references to particular police forces are not necessarily exhaustive but merely intended to be representative. Unlike the Armed Forces, the majority of vehicles and aircraft used by the police are civilian models, bought through normal commercial outlets. In some cases special police versions are available but these are usually normal products with modifications and equipment designed to assist in their police function. Most police transport is fitted with VHF (or UHF) radio these days and some of the terrestrial vehicles are fitted with a speed detection device such as 'Traffipax' (a camera linked to the patrol car's speedometer and which takes a photograph of the offending car with the recorded speed, date and time superimposed on it) or VASCAR (a device which computes the average speed of a vehicle between two points). Other 'police extras' include flashing lights (blue, red or orange) and sirens or two-tone air horns.

When one looks at the wide range of sophisticated machinery available to law enforcement officers today, it is evident that the profession has indeed come a long way since the horse and bicycle era of less than a century ago.

Abbreviations

A = amp

DIN = Deutsche Industrie Norm

G/clearance: = Ground clearance

h = hour

SAE = Standard Automotive Engineers

T/circle = Turning circle

Alfa Romeo   Italy

The Italian firm of Alfa Romeo has been known as the manufacturer of quality, high speed cars for many years. The principal factory and main offices are at — Alfa Romeo SpA, Via Gattemalata 45, 20149 Milano, Italy, but another factory near Naples produces the Alfasud models.

The reliability, good handling, rapid acceleration and high speed of Alfa Romeos make them ideal for certain types of police work, although the price rules them out in many countries.

Alfasud

Length: 12ft 11in
Width: 5ft 2.5in
Height: 4ft 6in
Tyres: 145SR × 13
Kerb weight: 870kg
Fuel tank: 11gal
Max speed: 95mph approx
Engine: 1,286cc four-cylinder horizontally opposed (Bore 80mm × Stroke 64mm) 68bhp (DIN). Compression ratio 8.8:1. Twin choke down draught carburettor
Transmission: Five-speed gearbox
Suspension: Front — Independent
Rear — Rigid axle with Watts linkage
Brakes: Servo assisted, dual circuit, discs on all wheels

A complete departure from the classic Alfa Romeos, the Alfasud is a high performance, volume-production car with a 1.3litre engine (there is also a 1.5litre sporting version). Manufactured in a huge, highly automated and State-sponsored factory, specially built for the purpose near Naples, the Alfasud has a remarkable performance for a small engined car, due in no small measure to its twin ohc, flat four-cylinder engine and five-speed gearbox driving the front wheels.

The Alfasud is used extensively by the police forces in Italy, including the Carabinieri as well as a number of Vigili Urbani for town patrol duties. It is also used by the Valais Cantonal Police in Switzerland.

Alfetta

Data: 1.8litre model
Length: 14ft 0.5in
Height: 4ft 8.5in
Wheelbase: 8ft 2.75in
G/clearance: 5in
T/circle: 33ft
Tyres: 165SR × 14
Kerb weight: 20.75cwt
Fuel tank: 10.7gal
Max speed: 111mph approx
Engine: 1,779cc four-cylinder twin ohc (Bore 80mm × Stroke 88.5mm) 140bhp (SAE). Compression ratio 9.5:1. Two twin choke carburettors
Transmission: Five-speed gearbox, all synchromesh
Suspension: Front — Independent torsion bars
Rear — Coil springs, de Dion axle with Watts linkage
Brakes: Servo-assisted, dual circuit discs, front and rear

Produced in the famous Milan factory, the Alfetta bears the name of the racing car which gave Fangio his first World Championship. In its original form it used the standard '1750' engine but a 2,000 was introduced later, as was a smaller 1,600cc engine. Both the 1,779cc and the 1,962cc models are used by the Italian Carabinieri and Pubblica Sicurezza and versions are in use with the Valais Cantonal Police in Switzerland, the Rijkspolitie in Holland and the Royal Malaysia Police.

Below: *Alfa Romeo Alfetta.*

Giulia

Length: 13ft 8in
Width: 5ft 1in
Height: 4ft 8in
Wheelbase: 8ft 3in
Tyres: 155SR15 (optional 165SR14)
Kerb weight: 2,288lb
Fuel tank: 10gal
Max speed: 107mph
Engine: 1,570cc four-cylinder twin ohc (Bore 78mm × Stroke 82mm) 116bhp SAE) at 5,500rpm. Two horizontal twin-choke carburettors.
Transmission: Five-speed gearbox with floor mounted gear shift
Suspension: Front — Independent by transverse A-arm
Rear — Coil springs

Brakes: Servo-operated, dual circuit disc brakes all round. Independent hand brake operating on drums on rear wheels.

The Giulia came in 1.3 and 1.6litre versions and proved highly successful in motor sport competitions in the 1960s and early 1970s. It was used in large numbers by both the Carabinieri and the Pubblica Sicurezza in its native Italy and a considerable number remain in active use as a compact, high speed patrol car. Production ceased in 1976 and the Giulia was replaced by the Giulietta.

Below: *Alfa Romeo Giulia.*

ARO   Romania

ARO vehicles are manufactured by Intreprinderea Mecanica Muscel, Str Vasile Roaita Nr 173, Cimpulung-Muscel, Romania and are exported under the trade name 'Auto-Dacia'.

Apart from use by police forces in Romania and other Warsaw pact countries (no details available), export models are used in some Mediterranean countries and in Africa.

ARO 240

Length: 13ft 2.7in
Width: 5ft 9.9in
Height: 6ft 6.3in
T/circle: 39ft 4.4in
Tyres: 6.50 × 16
Kerb weight: 1,550kg
Fuel tank: 25 US gal
Payload: 700kg
Max speed: 68mph approx
Engine: 2,495cc four-cylinder water cooled (Bore 97mm × Stroke 84.4mm) 80bhp at 4,200rpm. Compression ratio 8:1
Transmission: Single dry plate clutch, hydraulic

operation. Four-speed gearbox with two ratio transfer box.
Suspension: Front — Independent, helical springs, hydraulic telescopic dampers
Rear — Live axle and leaf springs with overload rubber springs. Hydraulic telescopic dampers
Brakes: Hydraulic drum brakes duplex (front) and simplex (rear). Mechanical handbrake operating on rear wheels

The ARO 240 is a rugged, four-wheel drive vehicle which has two doors, two front seats and a canvas top. A further six people can be accommodated on two rear benches or these can be folded up to provide carrying space. The ARO 240 has an 8in ground clearance and can traverse 2ft deep fords, climb high banks and cross over ditches 21in wide and negotiate 9in soft sand, mud or silt. It has a sturdy chassis with box-section side and cross members to withstand the roughest terrain.

It is reported (unconfirmed) that the ARO 240 is widely used for police work in Eastern European countries and it is known that they are in use in Cyprus and Greece by the Police and Gendarmerie. A van version is used by the Sierra Leone Police. The ARO 240 has a front engine, four-wheel drive, separate chassis and optional left or right drive.

Audi
West Germany

The West German firm of Audi combined with the former NSU and Auto Union companies after World War II to produce a small range of quality touring and sports saloons. The head office of the firm is located at — Audi NSU Auto Union AG, 8070 Ingolstadt, West Germany and it now produces two basic models known as the 80 and the 100.

Audi 80

Length: 13ft 9in
Width: 5ft 3in
Wheelbase: 8ft 1in
Tyres: 155SR13
Kerb weight: 857kg
Fuel tank: 9.8gal
Max speed: 100mph approx
Engine: 1,588cc four-cylinder ohc (Bore 79.5mm × Stroke 80mm) 85bhp (DIN).
Compression ratio 8.2:1. Twin choke down draught carburettor
Transmission: Maintenance free gearbox introduced in 1976

Originally produced in both 1.3 and 1.6litre versions, only the larger engined model is now generally available, the smaller engine being discontinued to meet the EEC exhaust emission controls without loss of performance. Not a particularly inexpensive car, its quality, speed and reliability are greatly appreciated by police forces, especially in Europe where they are used by several of the West German Länder police forces and in Sweden, Oslo City, Geneva and Zurich.

Below: *Audi 80*.
The Bavarian Minister of the Interior

Audi 100

Data: 2litre model
Length: 15ft 4.3in
Width: 5ft 9.5in
Height: 4ft 6.5in
Wheelbase: 8ft 8in

T/circle: 32ft
Tyres: 165SR14
Unladen weight: 1,135kg
Max speed: 105mph approx
Engine: 1,984cc four in line cylinders ohc (Bore

86.5mm × Stroke 84.4mm) 115bhp (DIN) at 5,500rpm. Compression ratio 9.3:1. Solex down draught two stage carburettor.
Transmission: Four-speed gearbox, single dry plate clutch
Suspension: Front — McPherson strut independent coil springs
Rear — Dead axle located by two trailing links and Panhard rod, coil springs
Brakes: Servo-assisted, dual circuit, discs (front) and drums (rear)

Big brother of the 80, the 100 uses a 2litre or 2.2litre engine and has proved to be extremely popular since its introduction in the late 1960s. A complete re-styling took place in 1976/7 when the 100 was offered with a wide range of luxury items as

standard equipment including dual-circuit brakes, halogen headlamps, underseal and radial tyres.

About the same time, the revolutionary 2.2litre five-cylinder model was introduced. This uses basically the same bodyshell as the four-cylinder version. The Audi 100 has a low waistline, large glass area and rather high seating position giving excellent visibility — a useful asset for police work. Audi 100s may be seen on police work in Schleswig Holstein and in Sweden and are also used by the West German Bundesgrenzschutz. For police work these cars are fitted with two-tone horns, revolving roof lamps and, in Germany, are painted in the normal police livery of green and white.

Below: *Audi 100.*

Austin   UK

One of the earliest British car manufacturers, Austin products were amongst the most popular in the 1930s when the tiny Austin Seven gained a well deserved reputation for economy and reliability. Following World War II, general difficulties in the motor manufacturing business led to Austin being involved in a number of amalgamations and take-overs, principally with Morris and others to form the British Motor Corporation and, more recently,

coming under the Government supported giant British Leyland. Currently the firm is located at Leyland Cars, Grosvenor House, Prospect Hill, Redditch B97 4DQ, England.

Two cars, the Allegro and the Maxi, are still marketed under the Austin name, plus the Sherpa small commercial vehicle and all three are used by police forces, mainly in the United Kingdom.

Austin Allegro

Data: 1,500cc model
Length: 12ft 7.5in
Width: 5ft 3.4in
Height: 4ft 6.3in
Wheelbase: 8ft 0.25in
T/circle: 32ft 9.7in
G/clearance: 7.5in
Tyres: 145 × 13
Kerb weight: 873kg
Fuel tank: 10.5gal
Max speed: 93mph approx

Engine: 1,485cc four-cylinder ohc (Bore 76mm × Stroke 81mm) 68bhp (DIN).
Compression ratio 9:1. SU carburettor
Transmission: Five-speed gearbox, automatic optional
Brakes: Servo-assisted discs (front) and drums (rear)

Introduced in 1973, the Allegro is available with a choice of engines from 1,100cc to 1,750cc. It uses a Hydragas, all-independent suspension developed from the Hydrolastic system used on the Mini range. The Allegro has a transverse engine driving the front wheels and is fitted with a four-speed gearbox on the 1,100 and 1,300cc versions and a five-speed gearbox on the 1,500 and 1,750cc models. Many Allegros are now being manufactured in Leyland's Belgian plant from parts made in England.

Allegros are widely used for routine urban and rural patrol work by police forces throughout the United Kingdom, including the Metropolitan Police in London.

Avia   Spain

The Spanish police use vehicles almost exclusively of the local Avia make, these appearing in three basic engine/chassis types — the 1250 squad car, the 4000 personnel carrier and the 2500 prison van. The latter two types are purchased in cab and chassis form and the required body is fitted according to the type of use planned. The manufacturers of these vehicles are Aeronautica Industrial SA, Plaza de las Cortes 2, Madrid 14.

Avia 2500

Length: 17ft 3in
Width: 6ft 7.6in (cab)
Height: 7ft 3in (cab)
Wheelbase: 8ft 2.4in
T/circle: 20ft 4in
Fuel tank: 75litre
Tyres: 600 × 16PR10
Engine: 4,203cc Perkins 71bhp (SAE).
Transmission: Four-speed (optional five-speed) gearbox
Suspension: Semi-eliptical leaf springs and with hydraulic dampers to the front
Brakes: Servo-assisted, double circuit, drum type.

(The 4000 is closely similar but most dimensions are somewhat greater.) The cabin seats three persons behind a wide and deep windscreen and is fitted with soundproofing, heater and demister and a high level of comfort. The special steel chassis is designed for the carrying of heavy loads and for easy maintenance.

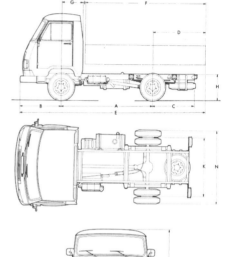

Right: *Avia 2500.*

Bedford   UK

Bedford have been making commercial vehicles since the early days of motoring and are still amongst the leaders in the light van field. Now a branch of Vauxhall Motors (itself part of the enormous General Motors combine), Bedford vans are produced by Bedford Commercial Vehicles, Vauxhall Motors Limited, Luton, Bedfordshire, England.

Bedford HA Van

Engine: 1,256cc, 52.8bhp at 5,400rpm
Transmission: Four-speed all synchromesh gearbox
Suspension: Front — Independent by coil springs
Rear — Semi-elliptic leaf springs

Brakes: Servo-assisted, dual circuit with 9.4in discs (front) and 7.9in drums (rear). Load sensing on rear brakes.

One of the smaller models produced, the Bedford HA has proved popular with police forces for use by dog handlers, scenes-of-crime officers and others who need a simple, utilitarian vehicle which offers reliability and a reasonable level of comfort for the driver.

Above: *Bedford HA van.*

Forces using HA vans include Cumbria and Staffordshire, plus the Cyprus police.

Bedford CF Van

Length: 14ft (short wheelbase)
15ft 8in (long wheelbase)
Width: 7ft 4in
Height: 6ft 6in (short)
6ft 11.5in (long)
Wheelbase: 8ft 10in (short)
10ft 6in (long)
G/clearance: 6in
Unladen weight: From 1.2 tons to 1.51 tons according to chassis body type
Fuel tank: 13gal
Engine: 1,759cc or 2,279cc four-cylinder ohc 67bhp at 5,200rpm, 80.5bhp at 4,600rpm. Compression ratio 7.3:1. Also optional four-cylinder

diesel 2,064cc engine.
Transmission: Four-speed all synchromesh gearbox (automatic gearbox optional)

Another useful and popular load/personnel carrier is the Bedford CF range which runs from 18cwt to 38cwt versions. One version or another is to be found in Belgium (Ghent City), Hong Kong, Leichtenstein, Malaysia, New Zealand, Botswana and Jamaica. It is, curiously, more popular abroad than it is in its country of origin so far as police work is concerned. The cab will take three persons and all instruments are contained is a clearly visible binnacle in front of the driver.

BMW   West Germany

The Bavarian firm of BMW (Bayerische Motoren Werke AG, Lerchenauerstrasse 76, München 13) makes superb quality cars which, despite their

(justifiably) high price, are used by a number of police forces.

BMW 2002/520

Length: 15ft 2in
Width: 5ft 6.5in
Height: 4ft 8in
Wheelbase: 8ft 8in
T/circle: 34ft 6in
Kerb weight: 24.25cwt
Max speed: 106mph approx
Engine: 1,990cc four-cylinder (Bore 89mm × Stroke 80mm) 100bhp. Compression ratio 9:1. Two Stromberg carburettors
Transmission: Four-speed gearbox

Brakes: Servo-assisted, twin dual circuit, disc (front) drum (rear)

A development of the BMW 2000, the 2002 was launched in the mid-1960s, using a four-cylinder power unit of 2litre capacity. In 1973 it was superseded by the current 520 models which used the same engine but developed to give increased power and a 'cleaner' exhaust. The front axle has an inclined spring damper strut system for improved lateral stability and reduced steering effort — factors

much appreciated by police drivers. The 520 incorporates increased brake servo-assistance headlamp and rearlamp output. The instruments are housed in a binnacle with aircraft-type lighting. The 520 has fuel injection using the Kugelfischer system.

Above: *BMW 520.*
The Bavarian Minister of the Interior

Versions of these cars are in use in Cyprus, Hamburg and Bavaria.

BMW 320

Length: 14ft 3.4in
Width: 5ft 3.3in
Height: 4ft 6.2in
Wheelbase: 8ft 4.9in
Tyres: 185/70HR × 13
Kerb weight: 1,025kg
Fuel tank: 11.4gal
Engine: 1,977cc four-cylinder ohc 125bhp (DIN). Compression ratio 9.3:1
Transmission: Four-speed gearbox or automatic
Suspension: Independent by spring struts all round
Brakes: Servo-assisted, dual circuit, discs (front) drums (rear)

First introduced in 1975, the 320 is handsome two-door saloon which handles superbly. The 2litre engine is similar to that used in the 520 and is also available with fuel injection.

Well suited to the roads and autobahns of Northern Europe, the 320 patrols North Rhine-Westphalia and also Holland, being used by the Rijkspolitie to detect cars exceeding the speed limit. Other 320s are to be found being used by the police in the bustling port of Rotterdam.

BMW 2500/525

Length: 15ft 3in
Width: 5ft 6in
Height: 4ft 8in
Wheelbase: 8ft 8in
G/clearance: 5.5in
T/circle: 34ft 5in
Tyres: 175HR × 14
Kerb weight: 2,976lb
Fuel tank: 15.5gal
Max speed: 114mph approx
Engine: 2,494cc six-cylinder ohc 150bhp (DIN). Compression ratio 9:1. Solex two-stage, twin-choke carburettor
Transmission: Four-speed all synchromesh gearbox
Suspension: Front — Independent, wishbones and trailing links with coil springs/damper struts
Rear — Independent trailing arms, coils springs/ damper units
Brakes: Hydraulic dual circuit with dual servo-

assistance with 11in ventilated discs (front) and 10.7in ventilated discs (rear). Handbrake operates a 6.3in drum at rear via mechanical linkage.

The 2500 was introduced in 1968 as a bigger and better version of the 2002 with a completely new engine with twin carburettors. In 1973 the 525 was launched as a replacement for the 2500, making its debut at the Frankfurt Motor Show. The bodyshell is identical to the 520 but using the bigger 2.5litre engine. The added power is appreciated by the police in Schleswig-Holstein and North Rhine-Westphalia who use these models for road patrol, whilst the 2500 is still in use in Cyprus.

Police versions include certified speedometer, zipped headlining and roof beacons. Police/stop signs, two-tone horns and high-visibility side markings are optional equipment.

BMW 528

Data: As for 525 except
Kerb weight: 3,108lb
Tyres: 195/70VR × 14
Engine: 2,788cc six-cylinder ohc (Bore 86mm × Stroke 80mm) 165bhp (DIN). Compression ratio 9:1. Solex carburettor or Bosch fuel injection.

The 528 uses the same basic bodyshell as the 520 and 525 but is equipped with the 2.8litre engine.

Apart from West Germany, where the Schleswig-Holstein and North Rhine-Westphalia police use them, 528s are to be found in Great Britain where they patrol the widely differing areas of West Mercia and Strathclyde.

BMW 728/730
BMW 2800/3.OS

Data: 3.0Si model
Length: 15ft 4.2in
Width: 5ft 9in
Height: 4ft 9in
Wheelbase: 8ft 10in
T/circle: 33ft 9.5in
Tyres: 195/70VR × 14
Kerb weight: 1,443kg
Max speed: 133mph
Engine: 2,985cc six-cylinder ohc (Bore 89mm × Stroke 80mm) 195bhp (DIN). Compression ratio 9:1 Fuel injection
Transmission: Four-speed gearbox

Suspension: Independent coil
Brakes: Servo-assisted. Discs front and rear

The 2800 was introduced in 1968 at the same time as the 2500 which it closely resembled. In 1971 the 3.0S (carburettor) and 3.0Si (fuel injection) came on to the market to replace the 2800. A few 2800 remain in use in Cyprus as well as the 3.0S and 3.0Si. The latter is also used by the Thames Valley Police in England. The 3.0 has now been superseded in its turn by the 7-series saloons but no information is currently available on the use of these for police work.

Chevrolet   USA

A branch of the giant General Motors organisation. Chevrolet have been noted for some years as the manufacturers of sound, fairly inexpensive cars in the United States. The company is Detroit based — General Motors Corporation, Chevrolet Division, Detroit, Michigan, USA and has important subsidiaries in Canada and South Africa.

The Chevrolet range is a popular one in North America and in one or two other countries, but this size and type of vehicle which is expressly manufactured for the prevailing road conditions in North America is seldom ideal elsewhere.

Caprice

Length: 17ft 8in
Width: 6ft 4in
Wheelbase: 9ft 8in
Max speed: 108mph
Engine: 5,733cc eight-cylinder
Transmission: Turbo Hydramatic automatic gearbox
Brakes: Disc (front) and drums (rear)

The Caprice is a full-sized, typical American saloon and is used by several American Police forces (eg Maricopa County Sheriff's Office, Arizona) and in the Punjab province of India. The Caprice handles well for a large car although reports suggest that the 5.5 litre engine is not really powerful enough to provide the sort of acceleration needed for police interception work on the open road.

Impala

Length: 17ft 8in
Width: 6ft 4in
Height: 4ft 8in
Wheelbase: 9ft 8in
T/circle: 38ft 8in
Engine: (I) 4.1litre (250cu in) six-cylinder in-line 115bhp at 3,800rpm (SAE) (II) 5litre (305cu in) V8 cylinder 130bhp at 3,200rpm (SAE) (III) 5.7litre (350cu in) V8 cylinder 170bhp at 3,880rpm (SAE)
Transmission: Turbo Hydramatic automatic gearbox

With its stable mates, the Nova and the Malibu, the Impala is a popular vehicle for police work in North America. A completely new version was introduced in 1977 and continued, with minor changes, the following years. Users include the Arizona Department of Public Safety, the Florida Highway Patrol and the Maricopa County (Arizona) Sheriff's Department. Among the reasons for its selection are the 116in wheelbase giving a tight turning circle, lighter weight than most longer vehicles, roomy and comfortable passenger compartment, capacious boot and impressive driving characteristics.

The standard Impala features include automatic transmission, power steering and power brakes and the Chevrolet 9C1 police chassis package and special police equipment option are also available. These include 8.5in ring gear rear axle, semi-metallic front brake pads, 11in × 2in 23lb rear drum brakes, 15in × 7in wheels, special police pursuit suspension, 4,000W (80A) battery, larger radiator, police speedometer, police service tyres etc.

Three engine sizes are available; 4.1litre, 5litre and 5.7litre the two larger sizes being the more popular.

Malibu

Length: 16ft 1in
Width: 5ft 11.5in
Height: 4ft 6in
Wheelbase: 9ft
T/circle: 37ft 2in
Engine: 3.3litre (200cu in) V6 cylinder 94bhp at 4,000rpm (SAE)
Transmission: Turbo Hydramatic three-speed automatic gearbox
Brakes: Power assisted discs (front) and drums (rear)

More compact than the Impala, the Malibu is the favoured patrol vehicle of the Virginia State Police and is rapidly finding favour amongst many of the other law-enforcement agencies in North America, its manoeuvrability making it popular for urban patrol work. Introduced in 1978 for the first time, the Malibu is intended as a replacement for the extremely popular Nova.

The police package offered by the manufacturers includes a reinforced chassis frame, semi-metallic brake linings front and rear, cast iron drums, 9.5in × 2in, 14in × 6in vented wheels, special body mounts, 4,000 watt battery, special suspension, higher capacity radiator, special balanced drive shaft, specific brake master cylinder and booster, police speedometer, special tyres, etc as well as the standard automatic gearbox, power steering and power brakes. Three engine versions are available, 3.3litre and the 5litre and 5.7litre versions as used in the Impala.

Below: *Chevrolet Malibu Patrol car.*

Bottom: *Chevrolet Nova patrol car of the Los Angeles County Sheriff's Dept.* Los Angeles County Sheriff

Nova

Length: 16ft 4.7in
Width: 6ft 0.5in
Height: 4ft 5.6in
Wheelbase: 9ft 3in
Engine and Transmission: As for Impala

One of the most popular cars for police work in the United States, where it is used by the Puerto Rico Police, the Sheriff's Departments in Los Angeles County and in Maricopa County (Arizona), the St Louis Police Department and the Virginia State Police, it is also to be found across the border in Canada where, in addition to the Royal Canadian Mounted Police, the Nova is used by the City Police

forces in Vancouver, Calgary, Halifax and Edmonton. In the Caribbean, the Bahamas Police and the Jamaican Constabulary also use Novas, as do the Belize Police and Greek Gendarmerie. Both marked cars (for patrol purposes) and plain cars (for detective work) are in use by the North American forces. Last produced in 1978 the Nova is now being superseded by the new Malibu police sedan. It was offered with a police package similar to that now available on the Malibu and came with the option of two engine sizes — 5 and 5.7litre. An adapted version of the larger engine is also available for use in California and in high altitude areas.

Chrysler   USA

One of the great American based motor manufacturers, Chrysler produce vehicles in a number of countries and under a variety of brand names, most of which have been acquired by take overs over the years. The list includes Dodge, Plymouth, Simca, Hillman, etc and, where vehicles are marketed under one of these names, as opposed

to the Chrysler family name, they have been shown under that name.

Under the Chrysler flag, the Chrysler Corporation offer just one police vehicle for the American market — the Chrysler Newport — although Coronets and Satellites have been used in Canada.

Newport

Engine: (I) 225cu in six-cylinder with single-barrel carburettor.
(II) 318cu in eight-cylinder with either two or four-barrel carburettor.
(III) 360cu in V8 cylinder with four-barrel carburettor.
Transmission: Manual transmissions are not available for heavy duty police work.

The Newport is a regular sized (185in wheelbase) hardtop which, although conforming to the stringent US exhaust emission laws, is capable of 120mph

and 0-60 acceleration within 10 seconds (using 360cu in engine). The police specification includes heavy duty seating, added chassis welds and reinforcements and an auxiliary transmission oil cooler. Also available is a three-speed Torque Flite automatic transmission, heavy duty suspension components for high-speed handling, pursuit tyres, maintenance free battery, heavy duty alternator, special brakes, wheels and shock absorbers, high capacity radiator, certified calibrated speedometer and firm-feel, pursuit-type power steering.

Chrysler   Australia

Chrysler (Australia) Limited, Box 1320F GPO, Adelaide, South Australia is a major subsidiary of the great American conglomerate, producing a small

range of saloons and coupés, some of which are used for police work in the Antipodes.

Below: *Chrysler Valiants of the Royal Hong Kong Police.* Royal Hong Kong Police

Valiant

The Valiant in its estate car form is used by the Royal Hong Kong Police as well as the South Australia Police. The latter force also uses a pickup version as well as saloons.

The Valiant is built on the lines of an American 'compact', with a powerful six-cylinder 4.3litre or a 5.2litre V8 engine to power a vehicle 16ft long (16ft 6in for estate) and 6ft 2.5in wide. The wheelbase is 9ft 3in.

Charger Coupe

Length: 15ft
Width: 6ft 2.5in
Wheelbase: 8ft 9in

Below: Chrysler Charger Coupe of the New South Wales Police driving school. NSW Police

Using the same 5.2litre engine as the Valiant, the Charger Coupe is more than a foot shorter with a steeply sloping roof making it essentially a 2 + 2 high speed tourer. The police in both South Australia and New South Wales use these vehicles for highway patrol work.

Chrysler   Spain

The busy Chrysler plant situated near Madrid is mainly occupied in producing parts for other vehicles

in Chrysler's European range but it is now the sole factory making the 180 and 2litre models.

180/2litre

Length: 14ft 8.3in
Width: 5ft 8in
Height: 4ft 8in
Wheelbase: 8ft 9in
G/clearance: 5.5in
T/circle: 33ft 1.6in
Tyres: 175HR × 14
Kerb weight: 1,130kg
Fuel tank: 14.3gal
Max speed: (I) 101mph (II) 103mph
Engine: (I) 1,812cc four-cylinder ohc (Bore 87.3mm × Stroke 75mm) 100bhp (DIN).
(II) 1,981cc four-cylinder ohc (Bore 91.7mm × Stroke 75mm) 100bhp (DIN).
Compression ratio 9.45:1. Weber twin-choke carburettor (both models).
Transmission: Four-speed gearbox (180) or automatic Torqueflite (2litre)

Suspension: Independent by coil springs
Brakes: Servo-assisted discs to all wheels.

A truly international product — manufactured by an American company to a British design, first in France and now entirely in Spain! The 180 first appeared in the United Kingdom as an import from Chrysler (France) in 1971 and was the first to be sold entirely under the Chrysler brand name. Two years later the 2litre came on the scene using the same bodyshell and a bored-out version of the 180 engine and with automatic transmission as standard. It is a handsome car with a vinyl roof and upholstery and trim in the limousine class and, perhaps for this reason (although it is not an expensive car to buy), it has had only limited appeal for police work. However, the Sussex Police, the Durham Constabulary and the Royal Ulster Constabulary have all found uses for it.

Chrysler   UK

The Chrysler badge is now worn by a range of cars which once bore the proud independent names of

Hillman, Humber, Sunbeam, Singer, etc and which, for some time after the takeover of the Rootes

Group, continued to be marketed under their old brand names. Today only the family name of Chrysler is used, although the British range is probably one of the largest in the company. The British subsidiary is to be found at Chrysler (UK) Limited, Ryton-on-Dunsmoor, Coventry, Warwickshire.

Chrysler cars from the UK firm are widely used by the various police forces of Great Britain and the company make efforts to provide police specification models to attract this type of customer.
(See also Hillman Imp.)

Alpine

Data: 1,300cc model
Length: 13ft 11.5in
Width: 5ft 6in
Height: 4ft 7.1in
Wheelbase: 8ft 5.4in
Tyres: 155SR × 13
Kerb weight: 1,052kg
Fuel tank: 13.25gal
Max speed: 94mph approx
Engine: 1,294cc four-cylinder transverse ohv (Bore 76.7mm × Stroke 70mm) 68bhp (DIN).
Compression ratio 9.5:1 Solex carburettor
Transmission: Four-speed, all synchromesh gearbox (automatic now available on 1,600cc)
Suspension: Front — Independent by torsion bars
Rear — Independent by coil springs
Brakes: Servo assisted, split circuit discs (front) and drums (rear)

The Alpine is the British made version of the French Simca 1307/1308/1309 with which it is, to all intents and purposes, identical. It has a good looking, five-door body with rear seats which fold away to give near estate car carrying capacity. It has front-wheel drive and all independent suspension giving a supple ride. 1,300cc and 1,450cc versions of the Alpine are currently in use with the Royal Ulster Constabulary but only in limited numbers.

Below: *Chrysler Alpine.*

Avenger

Length: 13ft 6in
Width: 5ft 3.6in
Height: 4ft 7.4in
Wheelbase: 8ft 2in
G/clearance: 5.7in
T/circle: 31ft 8.2in
Tyres: 155 × 13
Kerb weight: 863kg
Fuel tank: 9.8gal

Max speed: approx 80mph (1,300) and 86mph (1,600)
Engine: (1300) 1,295cc four-cylinder ohv (Bore 78.6mm × Stroke 66.7mm) 59bhp.
Compression ratio 8.8:1 Zenith carburettor
(1600) 1,598cc four-cylinder ohv (Bore 87.3mm × Stroke 66.7mm) 69bhp (DIN).
Compression ratio 8.8:1. Zenith carburettor

Transmission: Four-speed manual or automatic gearbox (1,600cc only)
Suspension: Front — Independent by torsion bars
Rear — Live axle four link and coil to rear
Brakes: Servo-assisted, dual circuit, discs (front) and drums (rear)

The Avenger was launched as the Hillman Avenger, in 1970 and it is now available in a number of variations of engine size and trim levels. All have electronic ignition and an estate version, which is extremely roomy, is also available.

Above: *Chrysler Avenger.*

Widely used by police forces in the UK (some 16 different forces from Grampian to Avon and Somerset, from Kent to the Northern Constabulary at the tip of Scotland, and from North Wales to Essex) the Avenger is also used in Bermuda and by the Garda Siochana in Eire. Both saloons and estate versions are employed, mainly on urban patrols and for CID work.

Sunbeam

Length: 12ft 6.75in
Width: 5ft 3in
Height: 4ft 7in
Wheelbase: 7ft 11in
G/clearance: 6.5in
T/circle: 31ft 6in
Kerb weight: 1,792lb
Max speed: 75mph approx
Engine: (930) 928cc four-cylinder ohc (Bore 70mm × Stroke 60.3mm) 42bhp (DIN). Compression ratio 9:1. Zenith/Stromberg carburettor. (For 1.3 and 1.6 engines see under Avenger)
Transmission: Four-speed (automatic available on 1.3 and 1.6litre models)
Suspension: Front — Independent by MacPherson struts and coil springs
Rear — Live axle located by four links, coil springs and shock absorbers.
Hydraulic telescopic shock absorbers front and rear
Brakes: Servo-assisted, dual circuit, 9.5in discs (front) and 8in drums (rear)

The Sunbeam comes in 930cc, 1.3litre and 1.6litre versions, the smaller of these using the updated version of the now discontinued Hillman Imp engine. Made of light alloy with overhead camshaft, this unit is a direct descendant of the Coventry-Climax racing engine. The larger two versions use the same engines as the Avenger.

The bodywork of all three versions is virtually identical with two doors and a lift-up rear window which, together with individually folding rear seats, provides a variety of load areas. Standard equipment includes electronic ignition, rear fog lamp, tell-tales for low oil level, loss of brake fluid and unclosed doors.

The Sunbeam is produced at the Linwood Plant in Scotland and first made its appearance in 1977 since when the police in Norfolk, Derbyshire and Avon and Somerset have taken it into use, usually as a marked police car for 'Panda' work (combined foot/motorised patrol by single policeman in urban areas), for which its compact size (the same as a Citroën 2CV) and ease of handling make it admirably suited.

Hunter

Length: 14ft
Width: 5ft 3.5in
Height: 4ft 8in

Wheelbase: 8ft 2.5in
G/clearance: 6.75in
T/circle: 36ft

Tyres: 155 × 13
Kerb weight: 18.75cwt
Fuel tank: 10gal
Max speed: 100mph approx
Engine: 1,725cc four-cylinder ohv (Bore 81.5mm × Stroke 82.55mm) 72bhp (DIN).
Compression ratio 9.2:1 Zenith/Stromberg carburettor
Transmission: Four-speed all synchromesh gearbox; automatic optional
Suspension: Front — Independent coil
Rear — Semi-elliptic
Brakes: Servo-assisted, discs (front) and drums (rear)

Originally known as the Hillman Hunter (a model name previously used by the now defunct Singer company), the Hunter is now marketed under the Chrysler brand name. It first appeared in 1966 and has changed little externally since and is thus sometimes looked upon as rather old fashioned. The mechanical specification has, however, been regularly updated and it is still a competitive vehicle. Over the years it has been a popular car for certain types of police work and is currently in use in South Yorkshire, Kent, Northumbria, Gloucestershire, Sussex, Essex, Durham, Norfolk and the Metropolitan Police in London. In Scotland, the Lothian and Borders, Central Scotland, Strathclyde and Northern Constabulary forces use Hunters, as does the Royal Ulster Constabulary.

Two engine versions are available, both of 1.7litre but the Super version having an aluminium head as opposed to the cast-iron head on the DL.

Citroën   France

The Citroën company has gained a reputation for building cars of very advanced design such as the famous 'Light Fifteen' or 'Traction avant' of the 1930s which endured until the introduction of the very exciting ID and DS models. At the other end of the scale, Citroën were responsible for the spartan but rugged 'Deux chevaux' with its 'corrugated iron' bodywork and canvas hammock seats.

The company's main offices and plant are to be found at SA Andre Citroën, 133 Quai Andre Citroën, Paris XV, but it has recently been involved in a merger with Peugeot and is also associated with Chrysler (France).

ID21/Super

Length: 15ft 10.5in
Width: 5ft 10.5in
Height: 4ft 10in
Wheelbase: 10ft 3in
G/clearance: 5.75in
T/circle: 36ft
Tyres: 185 × 15
Kerb weight: 26cwt
Fuel tank: 14gal
Max speed: 105mph approx
Engine: 2,175cc four-cylinder ohv (Bore 90mm × Stroke 85.5mm) 106bhp (DIN).
Compression ratio 8.75:1. Weber down draught carburettor
Transmission: Five-speed, all synchromesh manual by steering column lever
Suspension: Independent by self levelling, hydro-pneumatic, front and rear

Brakes: Servo-assisted, dual circuit, discs (front) and drums (rear)

The ID series, introduced in 1954 with the DS range, was revolutionary in its aerodynamic design and hydro-pneumatic suspension. Originally fitted with a 1,900cc engine, a bigger engined version appeared in 1968 with a 2litre power unit which was, in its turn, raised to 2,175cc in 1972. In the UK the ID series became known as the D series in 1969 although the original titles were retained in France. The English version of the ID21, introduced in 1972, was known as the D super. Production of this model ceased in 1974/5 but a number of examples remain in use with the Gendarmerie Nationale in France, mainly for patrolling the 'Autoroutes' and 'Routes Nationales'.

DS23   Below: *Citroën DS23.*

Data: As for ID21 except
Engine: 2,347cc four-cylinder ohv (Bore 93.8mm × Stroke 85.5mm) 115bhp (DIN).
Compression ratio 9:1. Weber carburettor or optional Bosch electronic fuel injection

The DS range was the luxury, more powerful version of the ID cars and included the extra-luxurious Pallas versions. The DS range originally used the 1,911cc engine but the DS23 was launched in 1972 with the bigger, five-bearing, 2,447cc motor. Production of the series ceased in 1974 but DS23s are still in use with the French Gendarmerie and for the personal conveyance of the Chief of Police in Liege, Belgium.

SM (Maserati)

Length: 16ft
Width: 6ft
Height: 4ft 4in
Wheelbase: 9ft 8in
T/circle: 34ft 6in
Kerb weight: 29.5cwt
Fuel tank: 20gal
Max speed: 140mph approx
Engine: 2,670cc V6 cylinder ohc (Bore 87mm × Stroke 75mm) 188bhp (SAE).
Compression ratio 9:1. Bosch electronic fuel injection
Transmission: Five-speed all synchromesh gearbox
Suspension: Hydro-pneumatic, self levelling interconnected front and rear
Brakes: Servo-assisted, dual circuit, discs all round

Introduced in 1971 and discontinued in 1975, the SM was a two-door four seat aerodynamic saloon with a new, light alloy V6 engine designed by Maserati. Originally fitted with triple Weber twin-choke carburettors, these were replaced by Bosch fuel injection. The front wheel drive was via a five-speed gearbox and the fast-back body boasted six quartz-iodine driving lamps, the outer pair of which swivelled with the steering. A few of these super-fast (over 140mph), highly sophisticated vehicles are used by the French Gendarmerie for high speed interception work on main roads and motorways.

CX2400

Length: 15ft 3.5in
Width: 5ft 8in
Wheelbase: 9ft 4in
T/circle: 10.2m
Tyres: Front — 185SR × 14
Rear — 175SR × 14
Kerb weight: 1,240kg
Fuel tank: 15gal
Max speed: 112mph approx
Engine: See DS23
Suspension: Independent hydro-pneumatic
Brakes: Servo-assisted, dual circuit, discs all round

The CX range was introduced in 1974 as a replacement for the DS range with a choice of 1,985cc and 2,175cc engines. In 1976 the CX2400 was introduced to supplement the CX2000 and CX2200, using the well tried 2,347cc power unit from the DS23.

The CX body has been described as the best-streamlined, volume-production, four-door car in the world (CX is the French term for drag coefficient) and is now being taken into use by the French Gendarmerie to replace the ID and DS models currently in use for high speed patrol work on the main roads of France.

Fourgon

Citroën vans and personnel carriers are used by both the Police Nationale and the Gendarmerie Nationale in France and also by the police in Geneva. In particular, the police Nationale use Citroën vehicles (as well as Peugeot's of same type) for their emergency 'Police-Secours' service in the main towns and cities.

Right: *Citroën Fourgon of the Paris Police emergency response service.* Prefecture de Police, Paris

Colt (Mitsubishi)

Vehicles produced by the Mitsubishi Motor Corporation in Tokyo are marketed under the brand name of Colt in the United Kingdom. In Australia they are sold by the Chrysler car company.

Galant/Galant Sigma

Data: Sigma
Length: 14ft 2.5in
Width: 5ft 5.2in
Height: 4ft 5.5in
Wheelbase: 8ft 3in
G/clearance: 6.5in
T/circle: 37ft 8.7in
Tyres: 165SR × 13
Kerb weight: 1,053kg
Fuel tank: 13.2gal
Max speed: 100mph approx
Engine: (2000) 1,995cc four-cylinder ohc (Bore 84mm × Stroke 90mm) 85bhp (DIN). Compression ratio 8.5:1. Down draught twin-barrel carburettor
Transmission: Five-speed gearbox (automatic optional)
Suspension: Front — Independent coil
Rear — Four link coil
Brakes: Servo-assisted, discs (front) and drums (rear)

The Galant made its appearance in the United Kingdom market in 1974 in both 1,600 and 2,000cc versions, and both saloon and estate car body styles. Like many Japanese products, the Galant has been adopted by a number of police forces throughout the world, including the Greek Gendarmerie, the Guyana Police, the Singapore Police and the South Australia Police.

In 1976 the body style was updated and the model became the Galant Sigma or simply the Sigma.

Below: *Colt Galant Sigma of the South Australia Police.* South Australia Police

Lancer

Length: 13ft 1.5in
Width: 5ft 0.5in
Height: 4ft 5.5in
Wheelbase: 7ft 8.25in
G/clearance: 6.5in
T/circle: 9.6m
Tyres: 155SR × 13
Fuel tank: 11gal
Max speed: 96mph approx

Engine: (1400) 1,439cc four-cylinder ohc (Bore 73mm × Stroke 86mm) 68bhp (DIN). Compression ratio 9:1. Single down draught twin-barrel carburettor
Transmission: Four-speed gearbox (automatic optional)
Suspension: Front — Independent strut type
Rear — Asymmetrical semi-elliptical leaf spring
Brakes: Discs (front) and drums (rear)

Also introduced into the UK in 1974, the Lancer has since made a name for itself in international rallies, testimony to its rugged reliability. The current range comprises 1,200 and 1,400cc saloons, 1,400cc estate and 1,600cc sports and examples may be found in service with the police in Bermuda (CID work), Guyana and Singapore (patrol).

Daihatsu   Japan

One of the smaller, less-well known Japanese motor manufacturers, the four-wheel drive models would be of interest to any police or military authority which needs a rugged, cross-country vehicle.

Daihatsu FZO

Length: 11ft 6in
Width: 4ft 9in
Height: 6ft 1in
Wheelbase: 6ft 8in
T/circle: 35ft 6in
Kerb weight: 2,450lb
Engine: 1,587cc 67bhp at 5,200rpm (SAE).
Transmission: Four-speed, all synchromesh gearbox, plus high/low and two or four-wheel drive
Brakes: Dual circuit, drums front and rear

This 'Jeep-type', cross-country vehicle has a powerful 1,600cc engine which will run happily for hours at high revs. On leaving the highway it shows great climbing ability and lasting tenacity and is ideal for even the toughest roads and sand, mud or rock trails. The FZO comes in two body versions — hardtop or canvas tilt, the latter having a roll-bar for driver protection. Both have six seats (four folding in the rear). FZOs are used by the Singapore Police for dog handlers' transport.

Datsun   Japan

Datsun vehicles are manufactured by the Nissan Motor Company Limited, 17-1, 6-chome, Ginza, Chuo-Ku, Tokyo, one of the most important car firms in that country. In recent years Datsuns have been exported in large numbers and have gained a reputation for reliability and a high level of standard equipment.

160B/180B (Bluebird)

Length: 13ft 11in
Width: 5ft 4.2in
Height: 4ft 6.7in
Wheelbase: 8ft 2.4in
G/clearance: 6.9in
T/circle: 31ft 1in
Tyres: (160B) — 5.60 × 13-4PR
(180B) — 6.45 × 13PR
Kerb weight: 995kg
Fuel tank: 60litre
Max speed: 103mph approx
Engine: 160B — 1,595cc four-cylinder ohc (Bore 83mm × Stroke 73.7mm) 100bhp (SAE).
180B — 1,770cc four-cylinder ohc (Bore 85mm × Stroke 78mm) 105bhp (SAE)
Compression ratio 8.5:1

Transmission: Four-speed manual or three-speed automatic
Suspension: Front — Independent by coil springs and damper struts
Rear — Rigid axle with four-link coil springs with telescopic, double action dampers
Brakes: 160B — 9in drums front and rear
180B — 9.65in discs (front) and 9in drums (rear). Anti-skid NP valve.

The 160B was introduced in the early 1970s, together with its larger brother, the 180B, both of which use the same body shell. An estate version is also available. The Kenya Police use 160Bs in both saloon and estate versions and the Bermuda Police use the larger engined 180B saloons for uniform patrol work.

160J Violet

Length: 13ft 6in
Width: 5ft 2in
Height: 4ft 6.7in
Wheelbase: 8ft 4.6in
G/clearance: 6in
T/circle: 30ft 5in
Tyres: 165 × 13

Kerb weight: 957kg
Fuel tank: 11gal
Max speed: Over 100mph
Engine: See 160B
Suspension: See 160B
Brakes: See 160B

Also using the 1,595cc power unit as found in the Bluebird, the 160J is the bigger engined version of the 1,400cc 140J which also made its appearance in the early 1970s. A completely redesigned Mk III version was introduced in 1978 with a lower waistline giving more glass area and a crisper appearance. Interior space was increased with more extensive sound insulation. The 160J is used by Singapore Police as a patrol and staff car.

200GT Skyline

Length: 14ft 7.5in
Width: 5ft 7.5in
Height: 4ft 7in
Wheelbase: 8ft 7in
T/Circle: 35ft
Tyres: 175 × 14
Kerb weight: 23.5cwt
Fuel tank: 12.1gal
Max speed: Over 100mph
Engine: 1,998cc ohc (Bore 78mm × Stroke 69.7mm) 108bhp (DIN). Compression ratio 8.6:1. Twin-choke Hitachi carburettor
Suspension: Front — Independent coil
Rear — Four-link coil
Brakes: Servo-assisted, discs (front) and drums (rear)

Above: *Datsun 200GT Skyline of the Japanese Police.*

The Skyline was introduced on to the UK market in 1973, using a 2.4litre engine and known as the 240K GT. It is no longer available and the smaller engined 200GT has never been imported. It is, however, widely used by the Japanese Police for patrol work, thanks to the sports car performance, good handling and aerodynamic styling.

240C/260C/280C

Length: 15ft 4.6in
Width: 5ft 6.5in
Height: 4ft 8.7in
Wheelbase: 8ft 9in
G/clearance: 7.1in
T/circle: 39ft 5in
Kerb weight: 3,042lb
Max speed: 100mph plus
Engine: 260C — 2,565cc six-cylinder ohc (Bore 83mm × Stroke 79mm) 118bhp (DIN). Compression ratio 8.6:1.
280C — 2,753cc six-cylinder ohc (Bore 86mm × Stroke 79mm) 139bhp (SAE). Compression ratio 8.6:1. Two-barrel down draught carburettor
Transmission: Column-mounted three-speed manual, floor mounted four-speed or automatic gearbox
Suspension: Front — Independent, double wishbones, coil springs

Rear — Semi-elliptic leaf springs. Hydraulic double-acting shock absorbers
Brakes: Servo-assisted, dual circuit, with anti-skid NP valve. Discs (front) and drums (rear)

The 240C was introduced in the late 1960s and was replaced by the 260C in 1972, using a larger engine. In its turn the 260C was superseded by the 280C in 1977.

The C series — now referred to as the Custom Deluxe — is described as a vehicle with 'inspired styling, performance and luxury' and the 280C is the top model in this well-appointed series, although the lines are somewhat American to European eyes.

One version or the other is currently in use with the Royal Malaysia Police, the Guyana Police and the Punjab Provincial Police in India.

Dodge   USA

One of the early American motor manufacturers, Dodge is now a division of the giant Chrysler car firm, located at The Chrysler Corporation, Dodge Division,

PO Box 1919, Detroit, Michigan. A number of Dodge products are in use with various law enforcement agencies in North America.

Aspen

Length: 16ft 7.5in
Width: 6ft 0.75in
Wheelbase: 9ft 4.75in

Below: *Dodge Aspen patrol car of the City of Scottsdale (Arizona) Police Dept.*

A special police version of the Aspen is available, one of the reasons why this 'compact' car is used by the Royal Canadian Mounted Police, the Vancouver City Police, the City of St Louis (Missouri), the Sacramento County Sheriff and the Puerto Rico Police amongst others. Details of the engine options and police package features may be found under Chrysler Newport.

St Regis

Length: 18ft 4in
Width: 6ft 5in
Wheelbase: 9ft 10.5in

A new model, complete with 'police package', the St

Regis is a full sized saloon which is being taken into use by police forces in the United States.

The power unit for the St Regis is the same as that for the Chrysler Newport with the powerful V8, 360cu in engine.

Emergency One Inc

USA

Police Protection Vehicle

Length: 13ft 6in
Width: 6ft 8in
Height: 7ft 7in
Wheelbase: 7ft 10in
G/clearance: 1ft 5in
Fuel tank: 90litre
Max speed: 30mph approx
Body: 0.25in armour plate, glass 1.187in laminated. 300 or 500gal water tank
Engine: 346cu in six-cylinder Mercedes-Benz OM352 diesel (Bore 97mm × Stroke 128mm) 80bhp at 2,550rpm (SAE)
Transmission: Six forward and two reverse gears. Two- or four-wheel drive
Brakes: Drum type on all wheels

Right: *Emergency One riot control vehicle.*

Unusually, this vehicle has been expressly designed and manufactured for the Police market.

Built by Emergency One, Inc, of 1701 SW 37th Avenue, Ocala, Florida 32670, for the purpose of riot control, escort duty, tactical manoeuvring, aid at fires, relief during dangerous weather or any hazardous situation, the PPV has a bullet-proof body constructed of high tensile armour plate. Access is by two roof doors and it has slatted windows fitted with bullet resistant glass which fold down to allow use of weapons. It also has a water cannon fed from a rear-mounted water tank. A bulldozer blade may be fitted to clear barricades, etc. So far it is not known whether any police forces will be taking these vehicles into regular use, but a number are known to be taking an interest in this development.

Fiat   Italy

One of Italy's principal car manufacturers, Fiat have been making cars since the early days of motoring. Today they offer a full range from the tiny 126 to the prestigious 132 as well as the futuristic wedge-shaped sports X1/9. The firm is located at Fiat SpA, Corso G Marconi, 10 Turin.

127

Length: 11ft 9.5in
Width: 5ft
Height: 4ft 6 in
Wheelbase: 7ft 4in
T/circle: 31ft 5in
Tyres: 135SR × 13
Kerb weight: 780kg
Fuel tank: 6.6gal
Max speed: 87mph approx
Engine: 1050 model — 1,049cc four-cylinder transverse ohc (Bore 76mm × Stroke 57.8mm) 50bhp (DIN)
Compression ratio 9.3:1. Weber or Solex carburettor

Transmission: Four-speed gearbox
Suspension: Front — Independent coil
Rear — Independent transverse leaf
Brakes: Split circuit, discs (front) and drums (rear)

A front wheel drive, four/five-seater saloon, the 127 was introduced in 1971 to replace the 850. Originally it was powered by the well tried 843cc engine but this was later up-rated to 900cc and a 1,050 version introduced. A useful car for getting through traffic, it is used by the Italian Carabinieri and also the Dutch Rijkspolitie.

128

Length: 12ft 7.7in
Width: 5ft 2.5in
Height: 4ft 8in
Wheelbase: 8ft 0.5in
G/clearance: 5.7in
Tyres: 145SR × 13
Kerb weight: 827kg
Fuel tank: 8.75gal
Max speed: 95mph approx
Engine: 1300 — 1,290cc four-cylinder ohc (Bore 86mm × Stroke 55.5mm) 60bhp (DIN).
Compression ratio 9.2:1. Weber or Solex carburettor

Suspension: Front — Independent coil
Rear — Transverse leaf
Brakes: Servo-assisted, dual circuit, discs (front) and drums (rear)

The 128 was born in the late 1960s with a front mounted transverse 1,100cc engine. A 1,300cc model followed and both were revised in 1976, being given a new grille with rectangular headlamps and moulded resin bumpers. 128s are currently in use with the Italian Carabinieri.

131 Mirafiori

Length: 13ft 11.7in
Width: 5ft 5in
Height: 4ft 7in
Wheelbase: 8ft 2in
T/circle: 34ft 1.4in
Tyres: 155 × 13
Kerb weight: 1,013kg
Fuel tank: 10.9gal
Max speed: 95mph approx
Engine: 1,585cc four-cylinder ohv (Bore 84mm × Stroke 71.5mm) 75bhp (DIN).
Compression ratio 9.2:1. Weber carburettor
Transmission: Five-speed gearbox

Suspension: Front — Independent coil
Rear — Rigid axle, coil springs
Brakes: Split circuit, discs (front) and drums (rear)

The 131 comes in 1,300cc and 1,600cc versions and was launched in 1975. It represents Fiat's middle range and is named after the Turin district where it is made. Like many Italian products, the 131 is a lively, economical car which handles well. The 1,600cc version is used by the Italian Carabinieri and also the Policia de Seguranca Publica of Portugal for general police work.

132

Length: 14ft 5in
Width: 5ft 4.5in
Height: 4ft 7.7in
Wheelbase: 8ft 4.5in
G/clearance: 8in
T/circle: 34ft 9.3in
Tyres: 175/70SR
Kerb weight: 1,100kg
Fuel tank: 12.3gal
Max speed: 105mph approx
Engine: 1,995cc four-cylinder twin ohc (Bore 84mm × Stroke 90mm) 112bhp (DIN). Compression ratio 8.1:1. Weber twin-choke carburettor, electronic ignition
Transmission: Five-speed manual or automatic gearbox
Suspension: Front — Independent coil
Rear — Live axle coil springs
Brakes: Servo-assisted, split circuit, discs (front) and drums (rear)

The 132 was launched on the European market in 1972/3 in 1,600cc and 1,800cc forms to replace the 125. It incorporated high comfort levels for long distance cruising and proved very popular. In 1977 the 2,000cc engine was introduced and the smaller power units were discontinued. With the larger engine, the existing body shell was updated with new lamp clusters, new grille with twin headlamps and sidelamps mounted in the plastic bumpers.

The classical lines and excellent handling, coupled with a lively engine have proved attractive to a number of police forces including the Greek Gendarmerie, the Oslo City Police, the Sierra Leone Police, the Kenya Police, the Schutzpolizei in North Rhine-Westphalia as well as the Carabinieri in its native Italy.

Below: *Fiat 132 Supermirafiori.*

900 Citivan

Length: 12ft 2.75in
Width: 4ft 10.5in
Height: 5ft 5.5in
Wheelbase: 6ft 6.5in
T/circle: 29ft 6in
Tyres: 5.60 × 12
Kerb weight: 16.34cwt
Fuel tank: 7gal
Max GVW: 29.5cwt
Engine: 903cc ohv (Bore 65mm × Stroke 68mm) 35bhp at 4,800rpm (DIN). Compression ratio 7.9:1. Single down draught, single choke carburettor

Suspension: Front — Wishbones and coil springs
Rear — Semi-trailing arms and coil springs
Brakes: Drums all round

Smallest of Fiat's commercial vehicles, the 900 is a useful urban runabout. It is also available in a Multicar version which seats seven people including the driver. With a maximum payload of 11.8cwt and a carrying capacity of 93.5cu ft added to its great manoeuvrability it is understandable that the Italian Carabinieri as well as some of the Vigili Urbani have adopted the 900 for a variety of purposes.

FORD MOTOR COMPANY

One of the most famous makes of car in the world; everyone has heard of Henry Ford and the cars he brought to the masses by the use of modern production methods and assembly lines. 'Model T', 'Tin Lizzy' — names which evoke rather ramshackle vehicles used by hill-billy farmers scarcely do justice to the modern Ford range which, as well as simple, inexpensive cars, also includes superbly engineered and finished limousines. So far as the police are concerned, probably no single make is used by as many police forces as is Ford.

The principal factories are at Detroit, Michigan in the United States but there are important factories in Great Britain, Germany (Ford Werke AG, 5 Köln-Deutz 1) and in Australia.

Ford   USA

Unlike the European versions, the American Fords are typical of North American cars - large, with engines to match, built for long distances on straight roads, or rugged cross-country versions for desert and mountain tracks.

Bronco

Length: 15ft
Height: 6ft 3.5in
Wheelbase: 8ft 8in
Fuel tank: 25 US gal (32gal tank available)
Engine: The standard engine is the Ford 5.8litre V8 but a 6.6litre V8 is also available
Suspension: Standard suspension includes a front stabiliser bar, front coil and rear leaf springs with double acting, telescopic shock absorbers. For more rugged work a quad shock-absorber option is available with two heavy duty, gas filled units at each front wheel on both sides of the axle. Heavy duty shock-absorbers and a rear stabiliser bar may also be added.

The Bronco, as its name suggests, is a rugged 'work-horse' of a car, excellent for agile manoeuvrability on rough, off-the-road terrain but also giving unstressed motorway cruising. Equipped with four-wheel drive, two suspension options are available for police work. An automatic gearbox version is available with either the standard 'part-time' four-wheel drive or a permanently engaged four-wheel drive. The rear seat folds forward to provide more luggage space or can be entirely removed for maximum carrying capacity. The Bronco is justly popular with those US Sheriff's Departments which have expanses of open country to police, for example the Maricopa County Sheriff's Department in Arizona. The Puerto Rico Police also use Broncos.

Below: *Ford Bronco.*

Custom 500

Length: 18ft 8in
Width: 6ft 7.5in
Height: 4ft 6in
Wheelbase: 10ft 1in
Fuel tank: 24 US gal
Engine: (I) 460cu in V8 (Bore 4.36in × Stroke 3.85in) four-barrel carburettor with automatic choke (II) 400cu in V8 (Bore 4in × Stroke 4in). Two-barrel carburettor with automatic choke; solid state ignition (III) 351cu in V8 (Bore 4in × Stroke 3.5in). Two-barrel carburettor with automatic choke; solid state ignition
All engines designed to operate on unleaded fuels only
Transmission: Select shift Cruise-O-Matic three-speed gearbox with first gear lock-out
Suspension: Coil springs
Brakes: Dual system, discs (front) and 11in flared drums (rear). Special 'Police' booster. Foot operated parking brake with automatic release

A standard sized car, the Custom police car was discontinued in 1977 but a number are in use throughout North America, especially Canada, where the Vancouver City Police Department and the Royal Canadian Mounted Police both use them. Four versions or 'packages' were offered with three engines ranging from the 351cu in to the 460cu in, the latter also powering the fourth 'interceptor' package. A station wagon version was also available.

Econoline Vans & Club Wagons

Engine: 4.9litre six-cylinder, 5litre V8, 5.8litre V8 or 7.5litre V8
Transmission: Four-speed manual gearbox or Cruise-O-Matic automatic.

Similar to their European counterpart, the 'Transit', Econoline vans and club wagons (personnel carriers) have been used widely throughout North and South

Below: *Ford Econoline van of the Chilean Carabineros rural highway patrol.*
Los Carabineros de Chile

America for police purposes. Four models are offered — E100, E150, E250 and E350 with a choice of sliding or swing-open side cargo doors. The body styles include a plain cargo van, a display van with windows in the right side and rear doors, and a window van with windows all round. The Club Wagon offers a choice of from five to 12 passenger seating arrangements and 'privacy glass' can be fitted to the windows behind the front doors to give added privacy. Both the van and club wagon are available in long (138in) or short-wheelbase (124in) versions.

Fairmont

Length: 16ft 3in
Width: 5ft 11in
Wheelbase: 8ft 9.5in
Fuel tank: 16 US gal
Engine: 3.3litre (200cu in) six-cylinder, hydraulic valve adjusters or 5litre (302cu in) V8 Hydraulic valve adjusters. Compression ratio 8.5:1/8.4:1
Transmission: Automatic
Fuel consumption: 3.3litre — 19mpg (urban) 26mpg (open road)
5litre — 16mpg (urban) 23mpg (open road)

The Fairmont was introduced in 1978 as a compact car with a police package availability and found immediate acceptance with a number of law-enforcement agencies, including the Maricopa County Sheriff's Department in Arizona, the Royal Canadian Mounted Police, the Puerto Rico Police and the St Louis City Police. The Police package includes heavy duty unitised body construction with extra reinforcements for rough road durability and special front and rear springs, stabilisers and unique front struts and rear shock absorbers. Both 3.3litre and

5litre engines are available and other special items include a 77A/h battery, transistorised voltage regulator, heavy duty front seats, calibrated speedometer, map light, heavy duty wheels and tyres and power-assisted brakes with organic linings (discs front, drums rear) with lining wear indicators for the front discs, a foot operated parking brake, anodised aluminium bumper.

Above: Ford Fairmont (police version).

Road tests indicated a good acceleration from standstill with excellent, fade-free braking. The power steering is very sensitive and gives a tendency to oversteer. The low price is perhaps reflected in the reports of excessive road noise but the seats are firm and comfortable and the car handles well.

LTD

Length: 18ft 7.5in
Width: 6ft 5.5in
Wheelbase: 9ft 6in
The earlier models were slightly larger

The LTD has been available for a number of years, during most of which a police package has been available. It is a full-sized saloon (a station wagon version also being available) with seats for six adults and either two or four doors. The police package offers power steering, power front disc brakes, Cruise-O-Matic transmission, police radial tyres, front bumper guards and power ventilation. The LTD was completely redesigned in 1979 with a choice of two engines — 5litre and 5.8litre. The 5litre version

provides police departments with the benefits of a full-sized car with a thrifty 5litre (302cu in) V8 engine. It is ideal for light duty police work, such as personnel transport and routine investigations where rapid acceleration is not required. The 5.8litre model has a brisker performance, making it suitable for many duty assignments.

Up until 1978, a 6.6 litre, a 7.5litre and a 7.5litre interceptor engine option was available in addition to the 5 and 5.8litre versions.

The LTD is used by a great many police agencies in North and South America, including the Texas Department of Public Safety, the Florida Highway Patrol, the Winnipeg City Police, the Puerto Rico Police and Los Carabineros de Chille.

LTD II

Length: 17ft 11.5in (two door)
18ft 3.5in (four door)
Width: 6ft 6in (two door)
6ft 6.5in (four door)
Wheelbase: 9ft 6in (two door)
9ft 10in (four door)
Fuel tank: 21 US gal

The LTD II was introduced in 1977 as a mid-sized pursuit car — a scaled down version of the LTD. Available as a two or four door saloon with a choice of 5litre and 5.8litre V8 engines, the police version includes automatic transmission with auxiliary oil cooler, power brakes (front disc, rear drum with 11in semi-metallic anti-fade front pads and organic

29

linings), heavy duty chassis, power steering with oil cooler, heavy duty handling package (heavy duty springs, stabilisers and shock absorbers all round), maximum cooling system with adjustable fan, 70A alternator, 77A/hour battery, heavy duty front seats, calibrated speedometer, dual beam map lights,

remote control boot lid, heavy duty wheels and tyres. Solid state ignition is a standard feature. Amongst the police users of the LTD II are to be found the Quebec Provincial Police, the Royal Canadian Mounted Police, the Halifax (Nova Scotia) Police, the Houston City Police and the Puerto Rico Police.

Maverick

Length: 18ft 9.5in
Width: 6ft 8in
Wheelbase: 10ft 1in
Fuel tank: 21 US gal
Engine: 250cu in six-cylinder, seven bearing crankshaft
Brakes: Front — discs
Rear — 10in × 2in flared drums

The Maverick was in production from 1970 to 1977 and a police package was available for the latter part of this time. The Maverick was ideally suited for special duty city or suburban non-pursuit assignments with its small turning circle and easy

manoeuvrability in traffic or congested areas. A number of law-enforcement agencies use Mavericks, including a number of City Police forces, and it is also used by the Belize Police.

The special police package included a modified Cruise-O-Matic automatic transmission with an auxiliary, externally mounted transmission cooler; improved cooling; power steering oil cooler (when optional power steering is ordered); 60A alternator and heavy duty battery; heavy duty suspension, transistorised voltage regulator; solid state ignition; calibrated speedometer; heavy duty front bench seat; special wheels and tyres.

Torino

Introduced in the late 1960s, the Torino remained in the Ford range until 1976. For much of this time a police package of this popular medium sized car was available in four engine versions — 351cu in V8, 400cu in V8, 460cu in V8 and an 'Interceptor' tuned version of the 460cu in. The two smaller engines were popular with City Police forces, whilst the larger engined versions were more suitable for suburban areas and general highway patrol. Users include the Englewood City Police Department, the Metropolitan Police in Washington DC and the Virgina State Police.

Standard equipment or options for police package vehicles included solid state ignition with transistorised voltage regulator; heavy duty battery, frame, wheels, front seat, suspensions, brakes, rear axle; improved cooling system; stainless steel/aluminium exhaust system; special brake booster; power steering with forward mounted fluid cooler; calibrated speedometer and 'Police Special' non-steel radial ply tyres.

Below: *Ford Torino of the Englewood Police Dept, Ohio.* Englewood Police Dept

Ford   Australia

The Australian subsidiary of the Ford Motor Company is located at Private Mail Bag 6, Campbellfield, Victoria 3061, where a limited range of cars and commercial vehicles is produced. These are quite different from the European and American

ranges, although versions of the US power units are used. The body styles are completely different but the names are often the same as those used for the US market, which can prove somewhat confusing.

Falcon Sedan

Data: Falcon 500
Length: 15ft 11.5in
Width: 6ft 3in
Height: 4ft 6in
Wheelbase: 9ft 4in
Tyres: 185SR × 14BSW
Fuel tank: 79.5litre
Engine: 4.1litre six-cylinder ohv (Bore 93mm × Stroke 99mm) 172bhp at 3,700rpm. Compression ratio 8.9:1
Transmission: Automatic or three-speed gearbox (column change in both cases)
Suspension: Front — Angle-poised ball joint type, heavy duty coil springs with hydraulic shock absorbers
Rear — Semi-elliptic asymmetrical, longitudinally-mounted leaf springs with diagonally mounted shock absorbers. Rubber bushed shackles
Rubber bushed shackles

Above: *Ford Falcon of the Queensland Police.*
Queensland Police

Brakes: Dual circuit, self-adjusting hydraulic. 10in × 1.75in drums (rear) floating caliper power disc turbo-cooled 11.25in diameter (front)

Falcon Sedans have been produced for over 10 years, the body styles and engine options being changed from time to time. Models currently in use include the 351GT which is used in Western Australia and New South Wales, the XC, with the smaller 5litre V8 engine, which is in use in Queensland, and the 500, which is used by the Australian Capital Territory Police, the Queensland Police, the Northern Territory Police, the New South Wales Police and also in Guyana. Of these, only the 500 Sedan is currently in production.

Falcon Wagon and Utility

Length: 16ft 6in
Width: 6ft 3in
Height: 4ft 7.25in
Wheelbase: 9ft 8in
T/circle: 41ft 2in
Fuel tank: 72.7litre (wagon) 67litre (utility)
Engine: See Sedan
Suspension: See Sedan
Brakes: See Sedan

Based on the Sedan, Falcon Wagons and Utility (pick-up) trucks are also widely used by the police in Australia. Wagons are used by the Victoria Police Dog Squad and Utilities are used in New Zealand for the same purpose. The Victoria and Northern Territory Police also use Utilities.

F100

Below: *Ford F100 four-wheel drive.*

The F100 is a rugged, four-wheel drive, cross-country pick-up truck, based on the Ford 'Bronco' and using the same powerful 5.8litre V8 engine.

Rather longer than the 'Bronco', the main specifications are closely similar or identical.

Ford   UK

The British subsidiary of the Ford Motor Company has been in existence for many years and is now one of the principal car manufacturers in Great Britain. It is based at Eagle Way, Brentwood, Essex, and works in close liaison with other European branches of the Ford empire, especially that in West Germany.

Capri

Length: 14ft 4in
Width: 5ft 7in
Height: 4ft 5in
Wheelbase: 8ft 5in
T/circle: 30ft 3in
Kerb weight: 1.410kg
Max speed: 98mph
Engine: 1,998cc four-cylinder ohc 98bhp at 5,200rpm (DIN). Compression ratio 9.2:1 Twin-choke carburettor
Transmission: Four-speed manual gearbox
Suspension: Front — Independent MacPherson struts with anti-rollbar
Rear — semi-elliptic leaf springs with anti-rollbars
Brakes: Hydraulic dual line vacuum servo-assisted. Self adjusting discs (front) and drums (rear)

The sleek, low lines of the Capri made something of a sensation when it was introduced in 1969. A Series II was announced five years later incorporating a new body styling with a opening tailgate. In 1978 a Series III was launched in UK with new grille incorporating a four-shot headlamp system. Four principal engine options are available — 1,300cc, 1,600cc, 2,000cc and 3,000cc but, as a general rule, only the 2,000cc is used by the police. Principal users in the UK include the Greater Manchester Police, the Sussex Police, the Thames Valley Police, the Hampshire Constabulary, the Humberside Police, the Norfolk Constabulary and the Strathclyde Police. Capris are also used by the Dutch Rijkspolitie. Options available for police work include heavy duty suspension and battery, calibrated speedometer, zipped headlining.

Cortina (Taunus)

Data: 2000GL
Length: 14ft 6.5in
Width: 5ft 7in
Height: 4ft 4in
Wheelbase: 8ft 5.5in
T/circle: 32ft 6in
Kerb weight: 1,525kg
Fuel tank: 12gal
Max speed: 104mph approx
Engine: 1,993cc four-cylinder ohc 98bhp at 5,200rpm (DIN). Compression ratio 9.2:1 Twin-choke carburettor

Suspension: Front — Independent, short and long arms with coil springs
Rear — Four bar link
Variable rate coil springs. Anti-rollbars and telescopic shock absorbers front and rear
Brakes: Hydraulic dual line. Vacuum servo-assisted, self-adjusting 9.75in discs (front) and 9in drums (rear)

Below: *Ford Cortina of the Taiwan Police.*
Taiwan Police

The Cortina was introduced in the early 1960s and saw a number of body changes as it progressed from the Mark I to the current Mark IV model which appeared in 1976. The latest body shell is identical to the German built Taunus and some of the engines are also built in that country.

The Mark IV Cortina has a similar mechanical specification to its predecessors, including the smaller three engine sizes (the German 2.3litre engine only appeared in 1977), but the body provides greater window area.

The 1,600cc and the 2,000cc versions are the ones mostly favoured by the police, although the newer 2,300cc engine is also beginning to be adopted. How popular the Cortina has proved may be judged by the fact that 41 out of 52 police forces in the United Kingdom use saloon or estate car versions of this economical and reliable vehicle. Other forces throughout the world include the Bahamas Police, the Belize Police, the Botswana Police, the Cyprus Police, the Garda Siochana

(Ireland), the Greek Gendarmerie, the Hong Kong Police, the Royal Malaysia Police and the Singapore Police. The German built Taunus version is used by the Austrian Police, the Belgian Gendarmerie, the Danish State Police, the Eindhoven City Police and the Hague City Police in Holland, the Ghent City Police in Belgium, the Oslo City Police, the Schleswig Holstein and West Berlin Police in West Germany, the Valais and the Vaud Cantonal Police in Switzerland and the Dutch Rijkspolitie.

A police package is available which comprises a calibrated speedometer, $5\frac{1}{2}$J steel wheels with Michelin ZX185/70SR × 13 tyres, three zips in headlining, 66Amp/h battery, heavy-duty suspension, door mirror on passenger side.

The Cortina is also manufactured in Taiwan (Republic of China) by the Ford Lio Ho Motor Company Limited, Chung Li, where it is the main mobile unit of the Taiwan Police Department for city and highway patrol (1,600cc models).

Escort

Data: 1300
Length: 13ft 0.5in (Saloon)
13ft 3.75in (Estate)
Width: 5ft 2.25in (Saloon)
5ft 1.75in (Estate)
Height: 4ft 4.75in (Saloon)
4ft 5.75in (Estate)
Wheelbase: 7ft 11in
T/circle: 24ft 2in
Tyres: 155SR13 radial ply
Fuel tank: 9gal
Max speed: 88mph approx (94mph Sport/Ghia)
Engine: 1,298cc four-cylinder ohv 57bhp at 5,500rpm (DIN). Compression ratio 9.2:1
Single choke carburettor
Suspension: Front — Independent with MacPherson struts and a stabiliser bar
Rear — Semi-elliptic leaf springs with stabiliser bar
Brakes: Hydraulic dual line, discs (front) and drums (rear)

Below: *Ford Escort of the Taiwan Police.*
Taiwan Police

Britain's best selling small car, the compact Escort is as popular a vehicle for police work as the Cortina, albeit for different types of duty.

The Escort is well suited for the role of 'Panda' car, CID vehicle, supervisory officer's car and general purposes. The estate version can carry an astonishing amount of equipment in the rear with the back seat folded down — over 54cu ft — and is therefore widely used as an emergency response car, especially in congested urban areas. An economy version, known as the Escort Popular, is also available. In the UK 36 different police forces use the Escort saloon (mostly the 1,300cc engined version, although the Merseyside Police use the rally-bred RS2000 and the 1,600cc Sport) and 22 use the estate version. The Escort saloon, which is also manufactured in West Germany, Taiwan, Australia and New Zealand, is used by the Australian Capital Territory Police (Canberra), the Bremen City Police, the Eindhoven City Police and the Hague City Police (Holland), the Policia de Segurança Publica (Portugal), the Seychelles Police, the Singapore Police (Ghia 1600 version), the Taiwan Police

Department and the Canton of Vaud Police (Switzerland). The Escort Estate is also used in Brussels.

For police work a number of special options are available including Lagoon Blue paintwork (with or without white doors), 6in Police lettering, zipped headlinings, heavy duty alternator and battery, heavy duty suspension, a roof bow (necessary when fitting roof sign and/or flashing beacon).

Escort 35 and 45 Vans

Data: 45L
Length: 13ft 3.5in
Width: 5ft 1.5in
Height: 5ft 2.25in
Wheelbase: 7ft 10.75in
Tyres: 155SR × 13 reinforced radial ply
Kerb weight: 1,870lb
Max speed: 84mph approx
Engine: 1,298cc four-cylinder ohv (Bore 80.98mm × Stroke 62.99mm) 56bhp at 5,500rpm (DIN). Compression ratio 9:1. Single choke carburettor
Suspension: Front — Independent coil springs
Rear — Semi-elliptical springs
Telescopic dampers front and rear
Brakes: Dual line system, disc (front) and drums (rear) with servo-assistance

Based on the Escort Saloon and Estate, the van is a useful utility vehicle which has found favour with

many police forces for use as a dog van, scenes-of-crime van and general purpose load carrying vehicle. It is currently used by 34 of the 52 police forces in the United Kingdom and also by the Belize Police and the New Zealand Police. Two versions are available — the 35 with an 1,100cc engine, and the 45 with the 1,300cc engine. Both provide 72.4cu ft of load space and are offered with a number of special police options including Lagoon Blue paintwork with or without white doors, 6in Police lettering, zipped headlining, heavy duty alternator, battery and suspension, tubular steel full bulkhead and rear window mesh guards.

Below: *Ford Escort van of the Kent County Constabulary.* Kent County Constabulary

Fiesta

Data: 1100
Length: 11ft 8.5in
Width: 5ft 1.75in
Height: 4ft 3.75in
Wheelbase: 7ft 6in
Tyres: 145SR12
Kerb weight: 1,160kg
Luggage space: 42.6cu ft with rear seats folded
Max speed: 90mph approx
Engine: 1,117cc four-cylinder ohv 53bhp at

5,700rpm (DIN). Compression ratio 9:1. Single choke carburettor
Transmission: Four-speed manual gearbox
Suspension: Front — MacPherson struts with coil springs
Rear — Five-bar link comprising trailing arms, coil springs, beam axle with Panhard rod
Telescopic dampers front and rear
Brakes: Servo-assisted, diagonally split, dual line system with 8.7in diameter discs (front) and self-adjusting 7in drums (rear)

The newest and smallest addition to the Ford range, the Fiesta has already found favour with the Humberside Police in England, the Canton of Valais Police in Switzerland and the Rijkspolitie in Holland. It is a three-door hatchback with folding rear seats, a transverse engine and front wheel drive. It combines safe handling with a surprising amount of space and remarkable economy. Engine options range from 950cc to 1,100cc with a 1,300cc engine available for the 'S' model. For police work a number of special options are available including zipped headlining, heavy duty (43A/h) battery, 45A alternator, heavy duty suspension, 6in Police lettering in blue and a roof bow (necessary when fitting a roof sign and/or beacon).

Transit

Length: 14ft 11in (short wheelbase)
Width: 6ft 4.25in
Height: 6ft 5.25in
Wheelbase: 8ft 10in
G/clearance: 7.5in
T/circle: 34ft
Kerb weight: 2,734lb
Max speed: 75mph approx
Engine: (2litre) 1,993cc four-cylinder ohc 78bhp at 4,500rpm (DIN). Compression ratio 8.2:1. Ford down draught carburettor
Transmission: Four-speed gearbox
Suspension: Front — Single leaf springs with shock absorbers
Rear — Three-leaf springs with shock absorbers
Brakes: Hydraulic dual circuit with vacuum servo-assistance. 10.6in discs (front) and 9in drums (rear)

Introduced in 1965, the Transit has built a world-wide reputation for reliability and versatility. The most recent re-styling was unveiled in 1978 but the vehicle remains essentially the same as the original versions apart from a longer bonnet which enables all the engine options to be accommodated in a basic bodyshell. Two bodies are available — a short wheelbase version and a long wheelbase one — powered by a choice of three engines — 1.6litre, 2litre or 3litre. Body styles also range from vans to personnel carriers. Users of Transit include practically every police force in the United Kingdom, the Belgian Gendarmerie and the Brussels Police, the CRS of the French Police Nationale (reconnaissance car), the Monaco Police (personnel carrier and ambulance), the Oslo Police, the Eindhoven and Hague City Police in Holland, the Vaud, Valais and Zurich Police in Switzerland, the Hong Kong Police, the Royal Malaysia Police, the Singapore Police, the Cyprus Police, the Jamaica Police and South Australian, Northern Territory and Queensland Police in Australia. Uses include personnel transport, motorway accident unit, accident prevention and rescue, CID, prisoner conveyance and general purposes.

Below: *Ford Transit of the South Australia Police Accident Rescue Unit.* South Australia Police

Ford

West Germany

The principal models manufactured by the West German branch at the Ford Werke AG, 5 Köln-Deutz 1, are the Taunus, which is identical to the British built Cortina (and dealt with under that name) and the Granada.

Granada

Data: 2.8GL
Length: 15ft 2.5in
Width: 5ft 10.5in
Height: 4ft 6.5in
Wheelbase: 9ft 1in
Tyres: 175 × 14 radial ply
Kerb weight: 1,880kg
Max speed: Over 100mph
Engine: 2,792cc V6 cylinder ohv 160bhp at 5,700rpm (DIN). Compression ratio 9.2:1. Electronic ignition
Transmission: Automatic standard, manual gearbox optional. Power assisted steering
Suspension: Front — Independent with double wishbone isolated by rubber mountings. Coil springs, sub frame mounted anti-rollbar
Rear — Independent semi-trailing arm/coil spring. Gas shock absorbers
Brakes: Hydraulic dual line servo-assisted, 10in ventilated discs (front) and 8.58in diameter drums (rear)

Below: *Ford Granada of the Danish Police.*
Danish National Police

Flagship of the Ford of Europe fleet, the large and luxurious Granada offers a blend of performance, comfort, safety and economy. It is extremely popular with police forces in Europe, used mainly as a highway patrol and rapid intervention radio car. In Germany it is used by the North Rhine Westphalia police and the Bremen, Hamburg and West Berlin City Police. In Belgium the City Police of Brussels and Antwerp use Granadas, as do the police in Cyprus, Northern Ireland, Vaud Canton (Switzerland) Oslo, Denmark and Sweden. In England 32 police forces plus all eight forces in Scotland and the South Wales Police all use Granada saloons and, in some cases, estate versions as well.

The Granada comes in three engine sizes — 2litre, 2.3litre and 2.8litre. (The 3.0litre version was dropped in 1977 when the latest series was launched.) A 2.1litre diesel engine version is also available.

Police options include a calibrated speedometer, three zips in headlining, 66 or 88A/h battery. 70A alternator, heavy duty suspension, map reading lamp and second interior rear view mirror. The Granada is also manufactured in Taiwan by the Ford Lio Ho Motor Company Limited, Chung Li, Taiwan, and has been chosen by the Republic of China (Taiwan) Freeway Police Bureau for freeway (motorway) patrol.

Hestair

Wheelbase: 11ft 3in (550gal model)
13ft (750gal model)
Engine: 133bhp (petrol)
98bhp (diesel)
Pump rating: 500gal/min
Ground sweep nozzles: 6 (550)
10 (750)

Hestair Eagle is a small, specialist body builder, using basic commercial chassis and engines to form the basis of highly specialised vehicles. One such vehicle, built at the works at The Saltisford, Warwick, is a police riot control vehicle which has been supplied to the police in Pakistan, India and several Middle East countries. Based on the Bedford KD chassis with

Below: *Hestair Eagle of the Punjab Police.*

135in wheelbase, it comes with either a diesel or petrol engine, a four-speed gearbox and air brakes. The conversion includes a front mounted water pump, water tank and crew cab with roof mounted water monitors. The entire vehicle is designed to be difficult to climb on to and the windows are protected by mesh grilles. The skirt of the vehicle is fitted with ground sweep water spray nozzles to discourage approach to the vehicle. The two turret mounted water monitors cover 360° around the vehicle with overlap areas to front and rear. The water tank holds 550gal. All anti-riot functions of the vehicle are controlled from the spacious cab which can hold up to 12 people.

A newer, larger model, based on the Bedford M series chassis, with four wheel drive and a 750gal water tank was introduced at the end of 1978. The water supply is pumped by a separate cab controlled petrol engine.

Hillman

The Hillman Car Company, formerly part of the Rootes Group, is now part of Chrysler (UK) Limited and models previously marked under the Hillman badge, now carry the Chrysler brand name. However,

production of the Hillman Imp ceased before the change of name and it was never known as the 'Chrysler Imp'.

Imp

Length: 11ft 7in
Width: 5ft
Height: 4ft 5.9in
Wheelbase: 6ft 9.9in
G/clearance: 6in
T/circle: 30ft 6.1in
Tyres: 155 × 12
Kerb weight: 696kg
Fuel tank: 6gal
Max speed: 80mph approx
Engine: 875cc four-cylinder ohc (Bore 68mm × Stroke 60.35mm) 37bhp (DIN). Compression ratio 10:1. Solex carburettor
Transmission: Four-speed all synchromesh gearbox
Suspension: Independent coil springs front and rear
Brakes: Drums all round

The Imp was in production from 1963 to 1976 and was the lowest priced car made in Britain. This little rear-engined saloon has an economical light alloy, overhead camshaft engine of advanced design and a deceptively roomy body with an opening rear window to facilitate loading.

The Imp was very popular with British police forces as a 'unit beat policing' (Panda) car and is still in use in a number of forces, including the Kent County Constabulary, the Northumbria Police, the Avon and Somerset Constabulary, the Norfolk Constabulary and the Strathclyde Police.

Below: *Hillman Imp 'Panda' cars.*

Holden
Australia

The name Holden goes back to 1854 when a leather business of that name was established in Adelaide. It was not until 1917, when Holden's Motor Body Builders Limited was formed that the name became associated with motor vehicles.

General Motors had been represented in Australia prior to 1917 and, in 1923, General Motors Corporation negotiated an agreement for Holden's to

manufacture GM cars in Australia. In 1931 General Motors (Australia) Pty Limited merged with Holdens to become General Motors - Holdens Limited. After World War II GMH tackled the need for an Australian car and in 1948 the 48-215 Holden Sedan was introduced. The registered office is located at 241 Salmon Street, Port Melbourne 3207, Australia.

GTS

Length: 15ft 10.75in
Width: 6ft 2in
Height: 4ft 7in
Wheelbase: 9ft 3in

T/circle: 12.3m
Tyres: 205 × R14 steel belted radials on 7in rally wheels
Fuel tank: 75litre

Engine: 4.2litre V8 cylinder
Transmission: Turbo-hydramatic gearbox with floor change
Suspension: Radial tuned coil springs
Brakes: Four wheel power-assisted discs

So far as is known, the GTS is used for police work only in Brunei, where the Sultan keeps a fleet of black painted models, which are air-conditioned, as his personal escort and pursuit cars. With a very small population and only about 400km of roads one may wonder at the need for such a large powerful car but the Sultan is a man of adventure and keeps a stable of fine cars including Ferraris and

Lamborghinis. Most afternoons he goes for a drive in one of these and the police have to provide unobtrusive but tight security — a task made more difficult by the fact that they have no knowledge of the Sultan's proposed route. The Commander of the Royal Brunei Police considers the GTS to be the only production vehicle with the performance and handling for this work, combined with the strength and reliability needed in these demanding conditions.

Equipment includes four quartz halogen headlamps, dual exhausts, full sports instrumentation, front and rear air spoilers and power steering.

Gemini

Length: 13ft 6.7in
Width: 5ft 1.8in
Height: 4ft 4in
Wheelbase: 7ft 10.6in
Tyres: 13 × 450
Weight: 920kg
Fuel tank: 52litre
Engine: 1,600cc four-cylinder ohc, 82bhp at 5,200rpm. Compression ratio 8.7.1
Transmission: Four-speed manual or three-speed automatic
Suspension: Coil springs, radial tuned
Brakes: Dual circuit hydraulic, discs (front) and drums (rear)

The Victoria Police use the Gemini in several roles and it has used a small car (by Australian standards) for several years. It is used by the policewomen in welfare work and by the force generally as a 'file car' or 'commuter car' for transporting personnel and paperwork. It is also a useful 'Q' car for traffic surveillance as it is unmarked.

The Gemini was developed jointly by General Motors and Isuzu Motors of Japan for the international small car market and was launched in 1975 as the Gemini TX. In 1977 it underwent some restyling and became the Gemini TC. The current TD model is identical except for the GM Radial tuned suspension which is designed around steel belted radial tyres and gives superb handling.

Below: *Holden Gemini of the Victoria Police.*

Kingswood

Data: 3.3litre SL
Length: 15ft 10.75in (wagon 16ft)
Width: 6ft 2.5in
Height: 4ft 7in
Wheelbase: 9ft 3in (wagon 9ft 6in)
T/circle: 39ft 8in
G/clearance: 6.8in
Tyres: ER78S14
Kerb weight: 1,369kg (wagon 1,445kg)
Fuel tank: 75litre
Engine: 3,298cc six-cylinder (Bore 92mm × Stroke 82.5mm). Compression ratio 9.4:1
Transmission: Three-speed manual gearbox with column change or optional four-speed manual or Tri-matic automatic
Suspension: Front — Independent long and short arms with specially rated coil springs and shock absorbers

Top: *Holden Kingswood of the New Zealand Police.*
New Zealand Police

Above: *Holden Kingswood HX of the Victoria Police.*

Rear — Four-links with specially rated coil springs and calibrated shock absorbers
Brakes: Power assisted discs (front) and duo-servo drums (rear)

The first Kingswood sedans and station sedans were introduced in 1968, together with the luxury Premier and low priced Belmont models, and represented the popular model with a high degree of equipment. Three engine options are available — a 3.3litre six-cylinder, a 4.2litre and 5litre (both V8s). The Victoria Police use 4.2 Kingswood for patrol work, traffic operations, crime cars and normal police work. Unmarked vehicles are used by the CIB and special traffic operations. Station wagons are used for Dog

Squad, Breathalyser Squad and Accident Appreciation Squad. Other users in Australia include the Australian Capital Territory Police (utilities for property officers and frogmen), South Australia (patrol cars and pickup trucks), New South Wales, Western Australia, Tasmania and Northern Territory Police forces. Abroad, the Kingswood is used by the Royal Malaysia Police, the Cyprus Police, the Jamaica Police and the New Zealand Police. Like all the current Holden range, the latest Kingswoods have the 'Radial Tuned Suspension' which is computer calculated from the road up around steel-belted radial-ply tyres on 6in wheel rims. There is a deeper four-coil suspension and front and rear stabilising bars. The shock absorbers are specially calibrated and the whole system gives improved steering response and handling, better road holding and cornering and improved riding comfort.

Torana

Tyres: 4.50/5.50 × 13
Fuel tank: 55litre
Engine: 2,850cc six-cylinder ohv 105bhp at 4,000rpm. Compression ratio 9.4:1
3,300cc six-cylinder ohv 110bhp at 4,000rpm Compression ratio 9.4:1
4.2litre V8 cylinder 175bhp at 4,800rpm. Compression ratio 9:1
5 litre V8 cylinder 250bhp at 5,000rpm. Compression ratio 9.7:1
Transmission: Three-speed manual column shift or Trimatic console shift (sixes). Heavy duty four-speed manual floor shift or Trimatic console shift (V8s)
Suspension: Radial tuned
Brakes: Dual system hydraulic, four-wheel drums or power assisted discs (front)

Holden moved into the small car range (1,150cc) in 1967 with the Torana (Torana is an Aboriginal word meaning 'to fly'). Gradually the Torana grew in size and power, the 1,150 engine being dropped in 1974. The latest (LX) model is powered by 2.8-5litre engines, and comes in both sedan and hatchback coupé versions.

Apart from domestic police use (eg South Australia Police) the Torana is also used by the Fiji Police. (Some of these are powered by the 1,900cc engine which is no longer available.) The Tasmania and Australian Capital Territory Police use the 5litre V8s.

Below: *Holden Torana of the South Australia Police.*
South Australia Police

Holden/Kingswood Vans and Pickups

Length: 16ft 2.5in
Width: 6ft 2.25in
Wheelbase: 9ft 6in
T/circle: 40ft 6in
Tyres: 195SR14 textile belted radials
Fuel tank: 15.5gal
Engine: 3,298cc six-cylinder (Bore 92mm × Stroke 82.5mm) Compression ratio 9.4:1
Transmission: Three-speed manual gearbox, column change
Suspension: Radial tuned
Front — Independent coil springs

Rear — Semi-elliptic leaf springs
Brakes: Front — Power assisted discs
Rear — Drums, duo-servo

General Motors/Holden make two versions of a light van based on the Kingswood sedan. Known as the Holden van and the Kingwood van respectively, they are basically identical, the Kingswood version offering more refinement. Both are built on a full length box chassis with a solid steel floor and double steel lower sidewalls. A six-cylinder 3.3litre engine is standard but 4.2 and 5litre V8 power units may be

specified for either version. A feature of these vans is the car type interior with a comfortable bench seat and carpets in the front.

The Victoria Police base their divisional van on the 3.3litre engined Holden van. It has a custom rear door and the interior of the rear compartment is reinforced with wire mesh. The South Australian Police also use these vans for the same type of work.

In addition to the vans, GMH produce a pick-up truck or 'Ute' (utility) as it is known in Australia. This,

Above: Holden 3.3 litre divisional van of the Victoria Police, fitted with security cage.

too, is available as a Holden or Kingswood model and with the same choice of engines as the van. Unmarked pick-ups are used for general transport work by the South Australian Police.

In addition to the forces previously mentioned, vans and pick-ups are used by a number of other Australian forces and the New Zealand Police.

One Tonner

Data: As for Holden/Kingswood vans except
Wheelbase: 10ft
T/circle: 42ft

Holden's versatile workhorse, the One Tonner, has a full length box-section steel chassis on which a wide variety of bodies can be fitted behind a comfortable, car-type cab. For police work some of these have

been adapted for prisoner transport by the South Australian Police. The standard power unit is the six-cylinder 3.3litre ohv engine as used in the Kingswood.

Below: Holden one-ton divisional van of the South Australia Police.

Honda
Japan

Famous for its motorcycles the Honda Motor Company Limited (located at 5 Yaesu 5-Chome, Chuo-Ku, Tokyo) also produces a limited range of cars. These were mostly low-powered, 'town cars' using converted versions of the well-tried motor cycle engines. Honda's true entry into the motor car market dates from the introduction of the Civic, and consolidated with the Accord. Only the former is known to be used for police work although the Accord is likely to attract attention in the future.

Civic

Length: 11ft 11.9in
Width: 4ft 11.25in
Height: 4ft 4.4in
Wheelbase: 7ft 5.7in
G/clearance: 6.7in
Tyres: 155SR × 12
Kerb weight: 750kg
Fuel tank: 8.8gal
Max speed: Over 85mph
Engine: 1,238cc four-cylinder ohc (Bore 72mm × Stroke 76mm) 44bhp (DIN). Compression ratio 8.1:1. Keihin twin-choke carburettor
Transmission: Four-speed manual gearbox or two-speed automatic
Suspension: Independent by coil springs

Brakes: Servo-assisted, tandem circuit, discs (front) and drums (rear)

Honda's two-door compact saloon was introduced in the early 1970s with a choice of 1,169cc or 1,238cc, four-cylinder, aluminium, water-cooled ohv engines. In 1975 the 1,500cc four-door saloon was launched and the whole range up-dated. The compact dimensions and outstanding economy of these little urban run-abouts have proved a boon to several city and island police forces where sheer power can be unnecessary or even a downright embarrassment. These include Liège in Belgium, Rotterdam in Holland, the Bahamas and the Seychelles.

International Harvester
Australia

Although essentially an American, Chicago based manufacturer of (mainly) commercial vehicles, the only International Harvester product known to be in current service with the police is the D1610. At one time the Puerto Rico Police used Club Wagons, pick-up trucks and vans produced by this company, but as production of these ceased between 1969 and 1973 it may be assumed that these are now obsolescent if not completely obsolete.

The Australian Company (International Harvester Australia Limited) is located at PO Box 4305, Melbourne, Victoria 3001.

D1610

The Australian Capital Territory Police have used the D1610 chassis/cab on which to base their Search and Rescue and also their communications vehicles. The D series is a range of three lively lightweight, intermediate trucks with four-wheel drive built in Australia. The D1610 is the largest of the three and uses the International 6-281 142bhp or the V-345 177bhp power unit. The GVW is 20,000lb and the GCW 30,000lb.

Below: *International Harvester D1610 of the Australian Capital Territory Police Search & Rescue Section.* ACT Police

Jaguar   UK

Between the two world wars, the name of 'SS' was known as the manufacturer of fine, thoroughbred sporting cars. Over the years the name 'Jaguar' was added and, eventually the original SS prefix was dropped. Since 1945 Jaguar has been in the forefront of comparatively inexpensive sports cars and sports saloons, achieving considerable success on the race tracks in the 1950s. The XK120 and its successor, the E type are classics of their type whilst the big, powerful, luxurious saloons are the first choice of many senior executives in industry and commerce. Only the XJ saloons are currently used for police work.

XJ6/XJ4.2/XJ3.4

Length: 16ft 2.7in
Width: 5ft 9.9in
Height: 4ft 6.1in
Wheelbase: 9ft 4.8in
G/clearance: 7in
Tyres: E70/VR × 15SP
Kerb weight: 1,686kg
Fuel tank: 20gal
Max speed: (3.2) 115mph approx
(4.2) 120mph approx
Engine: (3.4) 3,442cc six-cylinder twin ohc (Bore 83mm × Stroke 106mm) 161bhp (DIN).
Compression ratio 7.8:1
(4.2) 4,235cc six-cylinder twin ohc (Bore 92mm × Stroke 106mm) 180bhp (DIN).
Compression ratio 8.5:1
Transmission: Four-speed manual with overdrive or automatic

Suspension: Independent by coil springs all round
Brakes: Servo-assisted discs all round

Originally known as the XJ6, the model was renamed XJ4.2 or XJ3.4, according to the size of the engine, in 1975. Both types are in use with British police forces as high-speed main road and motorway patrol cars, current users including the Avon and Somerset Constabulary, the Durham Constabulary, the Staffordshire Police, the Thames Valley Police, the South Wales Police, the Central Scotland Police and the Dumfries and Galloway Police.

The slightly less opulent (and therefore cheaper) 3.4 uses the six-cylinder engine in its original 'unstretched' size which many enthusiasts maintain is still the best version ever produced. The 4.2 engine has an increased bore to provide that little extra bit of power and the car has full luxury refinements.

Jeep   USA

One of the most famous names to come out of World War II, the 'Jeep' (named after its descriptive initials 'GP' or 'general purpose') won a place in the heart of many an ex-serviceman. Produced originally as a purely military vehicle, the success of the ex-service models on the civilian market after the war ensured their continued production. The manufacturers are the American Motors Corporation (14250 Plymouth Road, Detroit 32, Michigan, USA) but a number of subsidiaries and licensees also produce Jeeps so they may be found marketed under such names as Renault Argentina, Kaiser, IKA (Argentina), or simply as Jeep. It has therefore been thought prudent to include the Jeep range under the latter, generic heading.

The original, very basic Jeep is still available in only slightly refined form, but a number of other Jeep models offer a degree of sophistication and comfort the GIs never dreamed of.

CJ Range

Length: 12ft 3.75in
Width: 4ft 11.75in
Height: 5ft 7.75in
T/circle: 37ft 7in
G/clearance: 7in
Kerb weight: 2,734lb
Fuel tank: 13gal
Engine: 4,229cc six-cylinder ohc 110hp at 3,500rpm (SAE). Compression ratio 8:1.
Single choke down draught carburettor with cold start device. Electronic ignition
Transmission: Three-speed manual gearbox with full time four-wheel drive
Suspension: Longitudinal, multi-leaf, semi-elliptic springs to front and rear

Brakes: Split hydraulic system with ventilated 11.75in discs (front) and self adjusting 11in drums (rear)

The nearest thing to the original military version, the CJ range combines gutsy six-cylinder power units on a basic 93.5in wheelbase chassis. A set of factory options that include automatic transmission, hard top and special trim change the basic, mud-plugging utility into an advanced town-and-country car. All cars in the CJ range have four-wheel drive and electronic ignition, making them functional, weather proof, load or personnel carriers, suitable for a number of police purposes. Users include the Geneva Police and the Vaud Cantonal Police in Switzerland,

the Brussels City Police, the Hague Police in Holland, the Bahamas Police, the Punjabi Police, the Carabineros de Chile, the Nicaragua National Guard, the Ecuador Police, the Puerto Rico Police and the Argentine Federal Police. In Africa the Zaire and Côte d'Ivoire Gendarmeries use CJ6s while the Moroccan Gendarmierie use CJ5s with 84in wheelbase. The

Above: *Jeep CJ6 of the Puerto Rico Police.*

usual models are the CJ7 or the long wheelbase CJ6, both of which use the 4.2 engine, although one or two forces still use the now obsolete CJ5 which had a smaller 3.7litre engine.

Cherokee

Length: 15ft 3.5in
Width: 6ft 6.75in
Height: 5ft 7.75in
Wheelbase: 9ft 0.5in
T/circle: 39ft 5in
G/clearance: 8.75in
Kerb weight: 3,880lb
Fuel tank: 18.3gal
Engine: 5,900cc V8 ohv 175bhp at 4,000rpm (SAE). Twin choke down draught carburettor with automatic cold start device.
Transmission: Three-speed automatic gearbox with fulltime four-wheel drive

Suspension: Longitudinal multi-leaf, semi-elliptic front and rear
Brakes: Servo-assisted split hydraulic system with ventilated discs (front) and self adjusting drums (rear)

The Cherokee range offers a degree of comfort and refinement which might not be associated with the name of Jeep. The Cherokee Chief and Cherokee S are rugged but comfortable four-wheel drive estate cars with optional air-conditioning, tinted glass, power steering, electric tailgate window and luggage rack. The Cherokee is used by the Belize Police.

Wagoneer

Kerb weight: 3,912lb
Fuel tank: 81litre
Engine: 4,229cc six-cylinder. Compression ratio 8:1.
Transmission: Three-speed gearbox
Suspension: Longitudinal semi-elliptic leaf springs and rear
Brakes: 12in discs (front) and 11in drums (rear) Foot operated parking brake

Similar to the Cherokee, the Wagoneer uses a smaller 4.2litre engine as in the CJ range. Standard features include front and rear arm rests, bright aluminium bumpers, electronic ignition, carpets, and H78 × 15 polyester tyres. Wagoneers fitted with heavy duty cooling, heavy duty suspension and a fuel tank skid plate are used by the Belize Police.

Dispatcher 100

Tyres: CR78 × 15B
Engine: 3.7litre six-cylinder
Transmission: Three-speed automatic
Brakes: Drums

Based on the CJ range and using the smaller, 3.7litre engine, the Dispatcher is used in considerable numbers by the US Post Office Department and some urban police departments in the United States

45

1977 Jeep

(eg Dallas, Texas) employ them for duty such as parking control. The police specification includes two sliding doors and a rear door in the hard-top cab.

Above: *Jeep Dispatcher of the Dallas Police Dept.*

J20

Tyres: 8.75 × 16.5
Kerb weight: 4,146 — 4,267lb
Fuel tank: 70litre
Payload: 4,133lb
Engine: 4.2litre six-cylinder. Compression ratio 8:1. Electronic ignition
Transmission: Four-speed manual gearbox with silent type transfer case, high range 1:1, low range 2.03:1 and neutral power take off

Suspension: Dual leaf springs front and rear
Brakes: 12.5in power discs (front) and 12in × 2.5in drums (rear)

The Honduras 'Fuerza de Seguridad Publica' use J20 pick-up trucks with 8,400lb GVW for general duties. These have standard specifications apart from heavy duty suspension, battery and alternator.

Lada

USSR

The Russian built Lada, manufactured by the V/O Avtoexport, Smolenskaja P132-34, Moscow G200, uses an identical body to the Fiat 124 but with a Russian designed ohc engine. It is available in 1,200cc, 1,300cc, 1,500cc and 1,600cc versions.

Lada 1500

Length: 13ft 6in
Width: 5ft 3.5in
Height: 4ft 8in
Wheelbase: 7ft 9in
T/circle: 34ft 6in
Tyres: 165 × 13
Kerb weight: 1,018kg
Fuel tank: 8.5gal
Max speeds: Over 95mph
Engine: 1,452cc four-cylinder ohc (Bore 76mm × Stroke 80mm) 75bhp (DIN). Compression ratio 8.8:1. Twin choke compound carburettor

Transmission: Four-speed manual gearbox
Suspension: Front — Independent coil
Rear — Live axle with coil springs and Panhard rod
Brakes: Servo-assisted, dual circuit, discs (front) and drums (rear)

The 1500 was introduced in 1976, using a completely new Russian designed power unit. This version has been chosen by the the Cyprus Police and also the Greek Gendarmerie for general police work, as it is made for hard work under tough conditions.

Leyland

This government supported British car manufacturing giant was formed by the amalgamation of the former British Motor Corporation with Leyland Motors. It now produces Austin, Daimler, Jaguar, MG, Morris, Rover, Triumph and Vanden Plas vehicles, mostly marketed under their original names. The Mini, originally produced jointly by Austin/Morris and sold under the two 'marques', is now marketed under the British Leyland flag, as is the Princess and several commercial vehicles.

Mini

Length: 10ft
Width: 4ft 7.1in
Height: 4ft 5.1in
Wheelbase: 6ft 8.3in
T/circle: 28ft 6.5in
G/clearance: 5.9in
Tyres: 145 × 10
Kerb weight: 635kg
Fuel tank: 5.5gal
Engine: (850) 848cc four-cylinder ohv (Bore 62.9mm × Stroke 68.3mm) 33bhp (DIN).
Compression ratio 8.3:1. SU carburettor
Suspension: Independent rubber cone (replaced Hydrolastic suspension in 1971)
Brakes: Drums all round

The revolutionary and phenomenally successful Mini made its debut in 1959. The Alec Issigonis design incorporated a transverse 850cc engine driving the front wheels and the 'wheel at each corner' design gave an unexpected amount of space in a very small car. Other engines were introduced, up to the 1275cc GT (formerly Cooper S) as were estate and van body versions. For police work, the Mini in its 850cc and 1,000cc guise is used by probably half the police forces in England and Wales and by at least two in Scotland as well as by the Royal Ulster Constabulary, mainly for urban patrol work (Panda cars) for which its small size, economy and ease of parking made it admirably suitable. Mini vans are also widely used for a variety of purposes throughout the United Kingdom and the 'Jeep' type, open Mini-Moke is in use in the Bahamas and Seychelles.

Maxi

Length: 13ft 2in
Width: 5ft 4in
Height: 4ft 7in
Wheelbase: 8ft 8in
T/circle: 33ft 9in
G/clearance: 5.5in
Tyres: 165 × 13
Kerb weight: 19.75cwt
Fuel tank: 9gal
Engine: (1750 model — for 1500 model see under Allegro.)
1,748cc four-cylinder ohc (Bore 76.2mm × Stroke 95.75mm) 91bhp (DIN).
Compression ratio 9.5:1. Two SU carburettors
Transmission: Five-speed gearbox
Brakes: Servo-assisted, discs (front) and drums (rear)

The phenomenal success of the Mini was bound to result in a 'stretched' version and so, in the late 1960s, the Maxi made its appearance. A compact, five-door carry-all, the Maxi is available with a choice of 1,500 or 1,750cc engine and uses the same Hydragas suspension and transverse engine driving the front wheels as the Allegro. The near estate car carrying capacity of the Maxi, coupled with its saloon car handling make it an obvious choice for certain types of police work, such as an emergency response area car, equipped to deal with most normal types of accident or other emergency. Maxis are widely used in England, in South Wales, Central Scotland and by the RUC in Northern Ireland. Abroad, Maxis may be found in Cyprus and in the British Virgin Islands.

Princess

Length: 4ft 6.7in
Width: 5ft 8.1in
Height: 4ft 7.5in
Wheelbase: 8ft 9.2in
T/circle: 37ft 1in
G/clearance: 6.5in
Tyres: 135/70SR × 14
Kerb weight: 1,196kg
Fuel tank: 16gal
Engine: (2200 model) 2,227cc six-cylinder ohc. (Bore 76.2mm × Stroke 81.3mm) 110bhp (DIN).

Compression ratio 9:1. Two SU carburettors
Transmission: Four-speed, all synchromesh gearbox, automatic optional
Suspension: Hydragas interconnected front and rear
Brakes: Servo-assisted, dual-circuit, discs (front) and drums (rear).

The wedge shaped Princess was introduced in 1975, using the prefixes Austin, Morris and Wolseley but these have been dropped in favour of the plain

'Leyland' banner to avoid confusion with the previous 1800/2200 range. These vehicles are in use in about a dozen British Police forces, mostly the 2200 version, and employed on road patrol and CID work.

Sherpa

Length: 15ft 2in (van)
15ft 8in (bus)
Width: 6ft 6.75in
Height: 7ft 6in
Wheelbase: 9ft 6in
Tyres: 165 or 185 reinforced radial ply
Fuel tank: 11gal
Engine: 1,700cc four-cylinder ohc (Bore 84.45mm × Stroke 75.87mm) 61bhp at 4,100rpm. Compression ratio 7.8:1. Single SU carburettor. Diesel engine available
Transmission: Four-speed manual or automatic gearbox
Suspension: Semi-elliptic leaf springs front and rear
Brakes: Divided hydraulic servo-assisted system with two leading-shoe 10in drums (front) and leading/trailing shoe 9in drums (rear).

The Sherpa is British Leyland's answer to increasing demand for a mid-weight van and mini-bus. A variety of body styles are available, the most usual being the plain van (payload 22cwt) and the Minibus and Crewbus. The Minibus seats seven forward-facing passengers and four inwards-facing passengers as well as the driver. The Crewbus has a two seat, upholstered bench beside the driver, the whole of the rear being occupied by two, full length, inwards facing benches of slatted wood construction. Sherpas are to be found in use with the police in South Yorkshire, Kent, Cleveland and Cumbria in England, South Wales and North Wales and in Central Scotland, Tayside, Strathclyde and Northern Constabulary areas north of the border. Abroad, the Valais Canton Police in Switzerland and the Singapore Police also use Sherpas. Some buses are converted to take prisoners.

Below: *Leyland Sherpa prison van.*
Kent County Constabulary

Mazda

Japan

Mazda cars are manufactured by Toyo Kogyo Company Limited, 6047 Fuchu-Machi, Aki-Gun, Hiroshima, Japan and are exported worldwide. Like many other modern Japanese products, Mazda cars have a reputation for good engineering, reliability and economy and it is not surprising that several of them have been chosen by police forces outside Japan.

616

Length: 14ft 2.5in
Width: 5ft 3in
Height: 4ft 9.5in
Wheelbase: 8ft 3in
T/circle: 9.4m
G/ clearance: 6.75in
Tyres: 165SR × 13
Kerb weight: 970kg
Fuel tank: 11gal
Max speed: 97mph approx
Engine: 1,586cc four-cylinder ohc (Bore 78mm × 83mm) Compression ratio 8.6:1. Two-barrel down draught carburettor
Transmission: Four-speed all synchromesh gearbox
Suspension: Front — Independent coil

Rear — Four-link coil with positively located rear axle
Brakes: Servo-assisted, discs (front) and drums (rear)

The 616 is a 1,600cc saloon which appeared around 1971. Like most Japanese products it is extremely well-equipped with heated rear window, reversing lights, electric clock and laminated windscreen as standard equipment. The lines are cleaner than many Japanese cars and it has a vaguely Italian look. The front-end treatment, with full-width grille and four headlamps, is reminiscent of the Triumph 2000. The 616 is currently in use with the island forces in Bermuda and Cyprus for uniformed patrol work.

1300

Length: 12ft 10in
Width: 5ft 1.5in
Height: 4ft 7.5in
Wheelbase: 7ft 6.5in
T/circle: 4.2m
G/clearance: 6in
Tyres: 6.15 × 13
Kerb weight: 836kg
Fuel tank: 8.8gal
Max speed: Over 90mph
Engine: 1,272cc four-cylinder ohc (Bore 73mm × Stroke 76mm) 66bhp (DIN) Compression ratio 9.2:1. Twin-choke down draught carburettor

Transmission: Four speed manual gearbox
Suspension: Front — independent coil
Rear — Semi-elliptic leaf springs
Brakes: Dual circuit, discs (front) and drums (rear)

The 1300 saloon was introduced in 1974 and replaced an earlier 1,300cc model. The body is the same as that used for the 1000 saloon and has reclining front seats with head restraints as standard, as is a laminated windscreen. These nippy little saloons are in use with the Cyprus police.

1800

Length: 14ft 4in
Width: 5ft 4in
Height: 4ft 8in
Wheelbase: 8ft 2in
T/circle: 32ft 2in
G/clearance: 7in
Tyres: 6.45 ×14
Kerb weight: 20.5cwt
Fuel tank: 11gal
Max speed: Over 95mph
Engine: 1,796cc four-cylinder ohc (Bore 78mm × Stroke 94mm) 104bhp (SAE) Compresssion ratio 8.6:1. Hitachi carburettor
Transmission: Four-speed manual or automatic gearbox

Suspension: Front — Independent coil
Rear — Semi-elliptic leaf springs
Brakes: Servo-assisted system, discs (front) and drums (rear)

Like the 616, the 1800 had Italian lines, which is not surprising when one considers that the body styling was by Bertone. The four-door body had plenty of glass area and excellent visibility. The 1800 was in production between 1969 and 1974 when it was phased out with the introduction of the 929. A few examples still remain in service with the Cyprus Police.

929

Length: 14ft 2in
Width: 5ft 5in
Height: 4ft 7in
Wheelbase: 8ft 4in
T/circle: 10m
G/clearance: 7in
Tyres: 175SR × 13

Kerb weight: 1,095kg
Fuel tank: 14.3gal
Max speed: 100mph approx
Engine: 1,769cc four-cylinder ohc (Bore 80mm × Stroke 88mm) 83bhp (DIN).
Compression ratio 8.6:1. Two barrel down draught carburettor

Above: *Mazda 929 saloon.*

Transmission: Four-speed manual or automatic gearbox
Suspension: Front — Independent coil springs
Rear — Semi-elliptic leaf springs
Brakes: Servo assisted, discs (front) and drums (rear)

The 929 was launched in 1974 as a replacement for the 1800 and is available in saloon, coupé and estate car versions. All are fitted out to a high standard with laminated windscreen (with built in aerial), heated rear window, tachometer, clock, etc as standard equipment. The body was completely restyled in 1975 and 1976. The 929 is currently in use with the Punjabi Police, the Fiji Police and the Cyprus Police.

RX Series

Length: 14ft 2in
Width: 5ft 2in
Height: 4ft 6in
Wheelbase: 8ft 3in
T/circle: 32ft 10in
G/clearance: 6.5in
Tyres: 195/70HR × 13
Kerb weight: 20.5cwt
Fuel tank: 14.3gal
Max speed: Over 100mph
Engine: Twin-rotor 2 × 654cc (2.6litre) 115bhp (DIN). Compression ratio 9.2:1.Two stage four-barrel carburettor
Transmission: Five-speed manual or automatic gearbox
Suspension: Front — Independent coil springs
Rear — Semi-elliptic leaf springs
Brakes: Servo-assisted, dual circuit, discs (front) and drums (rear

The RX Series used the Wankel rotary engine and began with the RX2 in 1971. This was a 4/5 seater saloon with four doors, similar to the 616 saloon. The twin rotor Wankel engine had a displacement of 573cc per rotor, carbon apex seals and two sparking plugs to each rotor. The RX2 was discontinued in 1974. In 1972 the RX3 was launched to replace the original rotary engined Mazda, the R100. The RX3 came as a four-door saloon and estate or a two-door coupé. Standard equipment included front discs, laminated screen, reclining front seats and heated rear window. The body shell was almost identical to that of the 818. Production of the RX3 ceased in 1976.

The RX4 came on the scene in 1973, using the same engine as the RX2. The body versions available were a four-door saloon, an estate and a two-door coupé. JATCO automatic transmission was an optional extra. Production of the model also ceased in 1976. All the RX models are, or have been, in use with the Cyprus Police.

Mercedes-Benz

West Germany

The Stuttgart firm of Mercedes-Benz, located at 7000 Stuttgart 60 (Untertürkheim) West Germany, is the manufacturer of one of the world's classic cars. Since the early days of motoring the names of Benz, Daimler and, later, Mercedes Benz have been associated with fine cars. The present day's products

are no exception and range from 2litre saloons, through sleek, powerful sports cars to 7litre limousines. For police work the saloons are naturally favoured and these consist of two basic body sizes and styles with a range of engines and finishes.

200

Length: 15ft 6in
Width: 5ft 10.25in
Height: 4ft 8in
Wheelbase: 9ft 2in
T/circle: 11.29m
Tyres: 175SR × 14
Kerb weight: 1,340kg
Fuel tank: 16.5gal
Max speed: 96mph
Engine: 1,988cc four-cylinder ohc (Bore 87mm × Stroke 83.6mm) 94bhp (DIN). Compression ratio 9:1. Stromberg carburettor
Transmission: Four-speed manual or three or four-speed automatic
Suspension: Independent by coil springs all round
Brakes: Servo-assisted, dual circuit, with discs all round

Smallest, lowest-powered and most basic of the Mercedes-Benz range, the 200 is, however, no sluggard utility model. Its four-cylinder, 2litre engine propels a body with a high degree of finish and comfort at speeds of over 95mph. The accurately balanced suspension elements give excellent smooth road-holding, optimum manoeuvrability with wide safety reserves. There are many good reasons why the 200 has been chosen by a number of police forces, including the Jordan Police, the Sierra Leone Police, the Policia de Seguarança Publica of Portugal, the Royal Malaysia Police, the Hague City Police, the Bundesgrenzschutz (West German Federal Border Police) and the provincial police in North Rhine-Westphalia. The police in Portugal and the Hague also use diesel engined versions of the 200 (200D) and the slightly bigger engined 220D.

230/250

Data: As for the 200 except
Engine: (230) 2,307cc four-cylinder ohc (Bore 93.75mm x Stroke 83.6mm) 109bhp at 4,800rpm (DIN). Compression ratio 9:1. Stromberg carburettor (250) 2,525cc six-cylinder ohc (Bore 86mm × Stroke 72.45mm) 129bhp at 5,500rpm (DIN). Compression ratio 8.7:1. Twin-choke Solex Type 4A1 carburettor

The 230 uses a virtually identical body to the 200, as does the 250, the essential difference being the increased engine size — the 230 having a 2.3litre motor and the 250 a 2.5litre power unit.

One or the other of these models (sometimes both) are used by the West German 'Landpolizei' in Baden-Württemberg, Bremen, Schleswig-Holstein and North Rhine-Westphalia and also by the Oslo Police in Norway, the Greek Gendarmerie and the Punjab Police in India.

280/280E

Dimensions: As for the 200 except
Fuel tank: 91.5litre
Tyres: 195/70HR14
Max speed: 115mph (280) and 120mph (280E)
Engine: 2,746cc six-cylinder ohc (Bore 86mm × Stroke 78.8mm). Compression ratio 8.7:1 (280 and 280E), 9:1 (280E and SE). 156bhp at 5,500rpm (DIN) (280 and S), 185bhp at 5,800rpm (DIN) (280E and SE). 'E' models have Bosch petrol ignition, others have twin-choke Solex 4A1 carburettor
Suspension: As for 200
Brakes: As for 200

The 280 and its fuel-injected counterpart, the 280E are the most powerful of the basic Mercedes models. Like the 230 and 250 they use the same body shell as the 200 but with 2.8litre engine. Users include the Baden-Württemberg police, the North Rhine-Westphalia police and the Singapore Police. For all models up to and including the 280E a Radio Patrol Car (Funkstreifenwagen) kit is available as a factory-fitted option and includes additional instrument panel, tunnel covering and tachograph mounting bracket, radio-telephone mountings, kick plates on inside of rear doors, blue flashing lamp, roof aerial and special indicator units, heavy-duty battery, halogen headlamps. (All the 200-280 range body has four round headlamps.)

280S/280SE

Length: 16ft 3.25in
Width: 6ft 1.5in
Height: 4ft 9.5in
Wheelbase: 9ft 4.75in
T/circle: 11.5m
Tyres: 185HR14
Kerb weight: 1,610kg
Fuel tank: 109litre
Max speed; 115mph (280S) and 120mph (280SE)
Engine: As for the 280 and 280E

Suspension: As for the 200
Brakes: As for the 200

The bigger, more luxurious bodied Mercedes are known as the 'S' series and include, at the bottom of the range, the 280S and the fuel injected 280SE. The engine, performance and mechanical specifications are the same as for the 280 and the 280E but the body has a visual relationship to the SL sports-tourers with a wide, shallow radiator, wrap-

around lights with rectangular headlamps and body fluting to keep windows clean. Police users include the Kenya Police and the Gambia Police.

Above: *Mercedes-Benz 280SE.*

350SL/450SL

Length: 14ft 5in
Width: 5ft 11in
Height: 4ft 3.5in
Wheelbase: 8ft 1.5in
T/circle: 10.3m
Tyres: 205/70 VR14
Kerb weight: 1,580kg
Fuel tank: 103litre

Max speed: 120mph (350SL) and 125mph (450SL)
Engine: 3,499cc V8 cylinder ohc (Bore 92mm × Stroke 65.8mm) 195bhp at 5,500rpm (DIN). Compression ratio 9:1. Bosch fuel-injection
Transmission: Four-speed manual or automatic

Below: *Mercedes-Benz 350SL.*

Suspension: Independent by coil springs all round
Brakes: Servo-assisted, dual circuit, discs all round, drum parking brake

The sleek 350SL, and its bigger engined twin, the 450SL, are two-seaters with optional hardtops and 3.5 or 4.5litre V8 engines. The engine is fuel-injected and has transistorised ignition. The advanced heating/ventilation system also warms (or cools) the inner panels of the doors for ultimate comfort. At the time of writing a number of German police forces are carrying out trials with a specially equipped police version but no information is currently available as to any forces actually taking 350SL-450SLs into regular service.

L207

The L207 is a useful, medium sized vehicle, used by the West German police for accident investigation. The interior of the vehicle is set out as a small office with seating, a table, cupboards and other storage facilities for the items of equipment needed at the scene of an accident. The L207 is powered by a petrol engine producing 70bhp (DIN) and has an 8ft wheelbase.

Right: *Mercedes-Benz L207.*

L408/L409

Wheelbase: 9ft 8.1in (L408)
11ft 5.8in (L409)
T/circle: 35ft 5.2in (L408)
41ft (L409)
Tyres: 600 × 16C tubeless
Kerb weight: 2,245kg (L408)
2,565kg (L409)
Interior height: 1,600mm, 1,750mm or 1,900mm

Payload: 1,245-2,035kg
Engine: 2,277cc (Bore 93.75mm × Stroke 83.6mm) 90bhp (DIN). Compression ratio 8:1

Below: *Mercedes-Benz L409 of the Bavarian Police.* Bavarian Minister of the Interior

Larger than the L207, the L408 and L409 are still compact, manoeuvrable vehicles, popular with the West German police for a variety of duties including autobahn accident work (for which special, hydraulic lighting masts are fitted to illuminate the scene at night), communications/command vehicle, prison van and personnel carrier. Two wheelbase lengths are available with three interior heights. The same engine is used regardless of size of body — the robust M115 petrol engine.

Right: *Mercedes-Benz L409 accident wagon.*

L508D/L608D

Wheelbase: 11ft 5.8in
Fuel tank: 60litre
Max speed: 93km/h
Engine: 3,782cc four-cylinder (Bore 97mm × Stroke 128mm) 85bhp at 2,800rpm (DIN). OM314 direct injection diesel
Transmission: Five-speed gearbox

Developed particularly for use by the police, the L508D has a 3,500mm (11ft 2in approx) wheelbase

and is powered by an 85bhp diesel engine. It has 11 seats plus driver and co-driver, additional warm water heating (independent of the engine) weapon racks, two-tone horn and blue flashing lamps on the roof. Several West German police forces (eg West Berlin, Bundesgrenzschutz) use these vehicles, as do the Nigerian Police. The L608D is similar but has a greater permissible gross vehicle weight (5.6 tonnes instead of 3.49).

Miscellaneous

Below: *Mercedes-Benz 1210D personnel bus.*

Other Mercedes Benz vehicles used by the police include the 1210D bus (in Guyana as well as West Germany), the 1113-based riot control vehicle with two water-cannons and a special, armoured riot vehicle based on a Mercedes-Benz chassis, also with two water-cannons.

Right: *Mercedes-Benz based riot control vehicle.*

Mercury

The Lincoln Mercury Company is now a division of the giant Ford Motor Company (Lincoln-Mercury Division, Ford Motor Company, 300 Renaissance Center, PO Box 43322, Detroit, Michigan 48243). The Division markets a limited range of cars including the Marquis, Zephyr, Cougar, Bobcat, Monarch and Capri (not to be confused with the European Ford Capri) all of which feature advanced engineering concepts.

Cougar

Length: 18ft 3.5in
Width: 6ft 6.5in
Height: 4ft 5.5in
Wheelbase: 9ft 10in
Tyres: HR78 × 14
Kerb weight: 3,972lb
Fuel tank: 21gal US
Engine: 5litre V8 cylinders 134bhp at 3,400rpm (SAE). Compression ratio 8.4:1
Transmission: Automatic
Suspension: Front — Independent by helical coil, rubber insulated springs
Rear — Four-link, rubber insulated, by coil springs
Brakes: Dual system, power assisted, 10.8in discs (front) and 11in drums (rear)

The Cougar is a medium sized car, currently favoured by several Canadian police forces including the Royal Canadian Mounted Police, the Regina Police Department and the Quebec Provincial Police. The standard engine is a 5litre (302cu in) V8 unit but an optional 5.8litre (351cu in) powerplant is available. Both feature an electronic voltage regulator.

A 'police package' is available including heavy duty suspension, high capacity cooling system, 70 or 100A alternator, heavy duty front seat, calibrated speedometer, transistorised ignition, special tyres, etc. Special equipment options include spotlights, special paint jobs, hand throttle control, oil pressure and temperature gauges, ammeter, dome lights, Vascar split cable, rear window blower defogger, roof reinforcement and roof light wiring.

Monarch

Length: 16ft 5.75in
Width: 6ft 2in
Height: 4ft 5.25in
Wheelbase: 9ft 2in
Tyres: DR 78×14
Kerb weight: 3,246lb
Fuel tank: 18gal US
Engine: 4.1litre (250cu in) six-cylinder (5litre optional)
Transmission: Four-speed manual gearbox with overdrive or optional automatic
Suspension: Front — Helical coil springs

Rear — Hotchkiss semi-elliptic leaf springs
Hydraulic telescopic shock absorbers to front and rear
Brakes: Dual hydraulic system, 11in discs (front) and 10in drums (rear)

Introduced in 1976, the Monarch is described as a 'precision-sized' car (9ft 2in wheelbase). Although not currently offered with a 'police package' the Monarch is in use with the Royal Canadian Mounted Police for such duties as require a compact car.

Zephyr

Length: 16ft 3.75in
Width: 5ft 11in
Height: 4ft 5.5in
Wheelbase: 8ft 9.5in
Tyres: 195/70 HR14
Kerb weight: 2,701lb
Fuel tank: 16gal US
Engine: 2.3litre four-cylinder/3.3litre six-cylinder/5litre V8 cylinder
Transmission: Four-speed manual gearbox with overdrive or automatic
Suspension: Coil springs all round
Brakes: Dual hydraulic 10in discs (front) and 9in drums (rear)

The Zephyr is Mercury's popular compact, introduced in 1978, and offered with a 'police package', similar to that for the Cougar. Three engine sizes are available — the standard 2.3litre and optional 3.3 or 5litre. Standard options include power seats, windows and door locks, speed control, electric boot release and performance instrumentation (tachometer, trip odometer, engine gauges). Police users of the Zephyr include the Royal Canadian Mounted Police.

Marquis

For 1979 the Lincoln-Mercury Division are offering the new Marquis with a 'police package'. Although 17in shorter and over 800lb lighter than earlier models, the new Marquis offers more interior room and remains what the Americans regard as a full-sized car. New suspension and steering add to the car's manoeuvrability. Standard engine is a 5litre (302cu in) V8 with a 5.8litre (351cu in) as an option. The latter features a second generation Electronic Engine Control system that uses a small computer to control six of the engine functions.

Because of its newness no details of police users are available at the time of writing and a full specification is not yet available.

MG UK

The MG car company established a sound reputation for itself in the immediate pre and postwar periods as the manufacturer of inexpensive, well-engineered, comparatively fast sports cars. The company had considerable success in motor-racing but its road cars lived up to the firm's slogan of 'Safety Fast'.

Like many small companies, the postwar years were very difficult for MG and it was eventually taken over by the British Motor Corporation which, in its turn, was absorbed into the British Leyland giant.

Two cars are still marketed under the MG badge, the Midget and the MGB (also sold in the MGB GT version).

MGB GT

Length: 12ft 9in
Width: 5ft
Height: 4ft 7in
Wheelbase: 7ft 8.5in
Tyres: 165SR×14
Kerb weight: 1,025kg
Fuel tank: 12gal
Max speed: 105mph approx
Engine: 1,798cc four-cylinder ohv (Bore 80.3mm×Stroke 88.9mm) 97bhp (DIN). Compression ratio 9:1. Twin SU carburettors
Transmission: Four-speed gearbox with overdrive
Suspension: Front — Independent by coil springs Rear — Semi-elliptic leaf springs

The GT is the 2+2 coupé version of the MGB two-seater sports car, both of which have had considerable success in the United States. To comply with North American regulations, the height has been increased slightly in recent years and rubbery, body-blended bumpers have been added — items which have offended many purists. The power unit is the well tried British Leyland 'B' engine which is used in the whole of the company's 1.8litre range, albeit with modifications in the case of the MGB.

The fast, manoeuvrable coupé with its rapid acceleration (0-60 in under 12 sec), coupled with good fuel consumtpion (25-30mpg) make it a useful motorway and main road patrol car and is used as such by the Sussex Police. The principal drawback of this type of vehicle for police work (and the same applies to the Porsches used on the Continent) is lack of space for carrying the multifarious items of equipment needed for accident intervention on fast roads.

Morris UK

Like the MG car company, Morris was one of the early car manufacturers, specialising in this case in cars for the masses rather than sports cars, and like MG, Morris is now part of the British Leyland firm. Only one car is currently sold under the Morris badge — the Marina.

Marina

Length: 14ft 0.75in
Width: 5ft 4.25in
Height: 4ft 6.5in
Wheelbase: 8ft
T/circle: 9.4m
G/clearance: 4.75in
Tyres: 155×13
Kerb weight: 937kg
Fuel tank: 11.5gal
Max speed: 95mph approx
Engine: 1,798cc four-cylinder ohv (Bore 80mm×Stroke 89mm) 72bhp (DIN). Compression ratio 9:1. SU carburettor

Transmission: Four-speed manual or automatic gearbox
Suspension: Front — Independent by torsion bars Rear — Semi-elliptic leaf springs
Brakes: Discs (front) and drums (rear)

The Marina was introduced in 1971 with a 1.3litre and a 1.8litre engine choice. In 1978 the 1.8 was replaced by the Marina 1700. In addition to a selection of saloons with varying degrees of finish and comfort, there are estate car and van versions, plus a coupé. All of these are used by one or more police forces: for example, the saloon is used by 27 forces in Great Britain and also by the police in Bermuda, the Bahamas and Guyana. Both 1,300cc and 1,800/1,700 models are used. Estate car versions are used by the Royal Ulster Constabulary, the Durham Police, Kent County Constabulary and South Wales Police, whilst coupés by the North Wales Police and the Lothian and Borders Police in Scotland. Marina vans are used by 13 British police forces and also by the Jamaica Police.

Opel

West Germany

Once one of the principal private motor manufacturers in Germany, Opel suffered the fate of many of the smaller firms and became absorbed into one of the international giants, in this case the American General Motors Corporation. Many of the present-day Opel products bear a close resemblance to those of its British sister company, Vauxhall. The headquarters of the company is at Adam Opel AG, 6090 Ruesselsheim (Main), West Germany.

Ascona

Length: 14ft 2in
Width: 5ft 5in
Height: 4ft 6.25in
Wheelbase: 8ft 3in
T/circle: 9.15m
Tyres: 165SR×13
Kerb weight: 985kg
Fuel tank: 11gal
Max speed: 87mph approx
Engine: (1.6) 1,584cc four-cylinder ohc (Bore 85mm×Stroke 69.8mm) 60bhp (DIN) Compression ratio 8:1. Down draught Solex carburettor
Transmission: Four-speed, all synchromesh (automatic optional)

Suspension: Front — Independent coil springs Rear — Two link coil springs
Brakes: Servo-assisted, dual circuit, discs (front) and drums (rear)

The Ascona dates from 1970/71 and was originally produced in 1.6litre form only. Later a 1.9litre and a 2litre version were added. The Ascona is of conventional design but with striking good looks. It features a front air dam for high speed stability and a large glass area for excellent visibility. Asconas are used by the police in Rhineland-Pfalz, North Rhine-Westphalia and also in Eindhoven (Holland).

Commodore

Length: 15ft 1.5in
Width: 5ft 8in
Height: 4ft 8in
Wheelbase: 8ft 9in
T/circle: 10.1m
G/clearance: 6in
Tyres: 175HR×14
Kerb weight: 1,268kg
Fuel tank: 15.5gal
Max speed: 115mph approx
Engine: 2,784cc six-cylinder ohv (Bore 92mm×Stroke 69.8mm) 142bhp (DIN) Compression ratio 9.5:1. Two Zenith carburettors
Transmission: Four-speed all synchromesh gearbox or optional automatic
Suspension: Front — Independent coil Rear — Four link coil
Brakes: Servo-assisted, dual circuit, discs all round

The Commodore is Opel's six-cylinder version of the Rekord, but with more luxury and equipment. The power unit is Opel's 2.8litre in-line six-cylinder which is noted for smooth running coupled with impressive output. The bold styling is enhanced by a vinyl roof and a broad, plated sill at the base of the body sides. The rectangular headlamps have electric wash/wipe equipment.

Commodores are in use with a number of European police forces including the West German police in Schleswig-Holstein and North Rhine-Westphalia, the Swiss police in the Vaud, Basel and Geneva cantons and also the Greek Gendarmerie. In most cases the Commodore is used for patrolling main roads where its power and speed can be used to good effect.

Kadett

Length: 13ft 6.5in
Width: 5ft 2.25in
Height: 4ft 6in
Wheelbase: 8ft 0.75in
T/circle: 9.7m

Tyres: 175/70SR×13
Kerb weight: 1,697kg
Fuel tank: 9.75gal
Max speed: Over 85mph
Engine: 1,196cc four-cylinder ohc (Bore

79mm × Stroke 61mm) 55bhp (DIN)
Compression ratio 7.8:1. Solex down draught
carburettor
Transmission: Four-speed manual gearbox
(automatic optional)
Suspension: Front — Independent coil
Rear — Two link coil
Brakes: Dual circuit, discs (front) and drums (rear)

The smallest of the Opel range, the Kadett was
launched in 1967 but entirely redesigned in 1973
and offered in saloon, estate and coupé form, all with
choice of 1litre or 1.2litre engines. In 1978 an
Economy version of this already thrifty little car was
introduced returning around 40mpg when driven
hard. On the other hand, the eye-catching, sporting
coupé will reach over 90mph.

For police work, the Kadett is used by the Austrian
police and also by the Rotterdam City Police in
Holland.

Kadett City

Length: 12ft 9in
Width: 5ft 2in
Height: 4ft 6in
Wheelbase: 7ft 10in
T/circle: 9.4m
Tyres: 185/70SR × 14
Kerb weight: 1,122kg
Fuel tank: 13.5gal
Max speed: 85mph approx
Engine: 1,196cc four-cylinder ohv (Bore
79mm × Stroke 61mm) 55bhp (DIN)
Compression ratio 7.8:1
Transmission: Four-speed manual gearbox or
automatic

Suspension: Front — Independent coil springs
Rear — Live axle with coil springs
Brakes: Servo-assisted, dual circuit, discs (front)
and drums (rear)

The City was introduced in 1975, using the same
bodyshell as the Vauxhall Chevette, which had
appeared in the spring of that year, apart from the
frontal area. The City is a hatchback which comes in
DL or S trim; both have folding rear seats and
carrying capacities almost equal to an estate car. An
automatic gearbox is available on S models. The
Dutch Rijkspolitie use the Kadett City for police work,
mainly for CID surveillance duties.

Manta

Length: 14ft 8.5in
Width: 5ft 4.5in
Height: 4ft 4.5in
Wheelbase: 8ft 4.5in
T/circle: 9.15m
Tyres: 165SR × 13
Kerb weight: 1,020kg
Fuel tank: 11gal
Max speed: Over 100mph
Engine: 1,979cc four-cylinder ohc 100bhp (DIN).
Zenith carburettor
Transmission: Four-speed manual gearbox or
automatic
Suspension: Front — Independent by coil springs

Rear — Two link coil springs
Brakes: Servo-assisted, dual circuit, discs (front)
and drums (rear)

The Manta is the sporting, two-door 2+2 version of
the Opel Ascona, using the same underpan structure
but with an even more wind-cheating shape.
Originally offered in both 1.6 and 1.9litre versions,
the 1.6litre engine is no longer available and the
1.9litre power unit has been up-rated to 2litre. Police
users of the Manta include the North Rhine-
Westphalia police in West Germany and the Dutch
Rijkspolitie, the latter using them with 'Traffipax'
photographic speed detector equipment.

Rekord

Length: 15ft 1in
Width: 5ft 8in
Height: 4ft 8in
Wheelbase: 8ft 10.5in
T/circle: 10.8m
Tyres: 175SR × 14
Kerb weight: 1,122kg
Fuel tank: 14gal
Max speed: Over 100mph
Engine: 1,979cc four-cylinder ohv (Bore
95mm × Stroke 59.8mm) 100bhp (DIN)
Compression ratio 9:1. Zenith carburettor
Transmission: Four-speed manual or automatic
Suspension: Front — Independent by MacPherson
struts and coil springs

Rear — Rigid axle and five link coil springs
Brakes: Servo-assisted, dual circuit, discs (front)
and drums (rear)

The original Rekord appeared wayback in 1967 but
was completely redesigned in 1972. This Mark II
version had a great success for about six years when
the Rekord III appeared with a new, wedge-shaped
body giving high-speed stability, notable fuel
economy and quiet running. Clever designing gave
more internal space without changing the external
dimensions. The engine is Opel's 'cam-in-head' four-
cylinder unit of 2litre capacity. (Two diesel engines
are also available). Halogen headlamps, laminated
screen and adjustable head restraints are fitted to all

models, while the Berlina models also have headlamp wash/wipe, rear fog lamp, electric windows and sun roof. The Rekord is popular with European police forces, being in use with the Vaud, Geneva and Basle Cantonal Police in Switzerland, the Oslo City Police, the Austrian and Danish State Police and the West German police in North Rhine-Westphalia. Uses include radar checks, supervision and general duties.

Peugeot France

One of the earliest car manufacturers in the world, the Peugeot firm (Automobiles Peugeot, 75 Avenue de la Grande Armée, 75116 Paris) is now merged with Citroën and works in close collaboration with other car manufacturers, both in France and abroad.

J7

A rugged, reliable van/personnel carrier, the J7 has been chosen by a number of police forces in Europe, including Brussels (property surveillance, criminal police, traffic control, technical police and personnel transport), Monaco, Vaud Canton (Switzerland) (mobile command post,) Rotterdam (General Purpose vans), Geneva, Utrecht (mobile units) and the French National Police (emergency 'Police Secours' vehicle).

Below: *Peugeot J7 of the Utrecht City Police.* Gemeentepolitie Utrecht

204

Length: 13ft 1in
Width: 5ft 2in
Wheelbase: 8ft 6in
Engine: 1,130cc four-cylinder, all aluminium
Suspension: Front — MacPherson struts
Rear — Trailing arms, coil springs
Independent all round
Brakes: Discs (front) and drums (rear)

The 204 was launched in 1965 as a four-door saloon with a transverse, all-aluminium, single ohc engine driving the front wheels. It has independent suspension all round, a thermostatically controlled fan for the engine cooling system and radial tyres. An estate car version was also introduced. Production of these lively little cars ceased in 1976 but a number remain in use with the French Gendarmerie

Nationale, both in saloon and estate forms, in French Territories overseas as well as in Metropolitan France. Another user is the Luxembourg Police.

Above: *Peugeot 204 of the Luxembourg Police.* Corps de la Police Luxembourgoise

304

Length: 13ft 7in (Saloon)
13ft 1in (Estate)
Width: 5ft 2in
Wheelbase: 8ft 6in
Tyres: 145SR × 14
Kerb weight: 952kg
Fuel tank: 11gal
Max speed: Over 90mph
Engine: 1,290cc four-cylinder, aluminium, ohc (Bore 78mm × Stroke 67.5mm) 65bhp (DIN).
Compression ratio 8.8:1. Solex carburettor
1,127cc is available for the estate model
Suspension: Independent all round with anti-roller front and rear
Brakes: Servo-assisted, discs (front) and drums (rear)

The 304 first appeared in 1969, using an enlarged version of the 204 aluminium, transverse engine driving the front wheels, and the same basic bodyshell. It has excellent ride and handling characteristics. An estate car version is available and with the demise of the 204, the 304 range was increased to two saloons and two estate cars. All have the engine inclined 20° to reduce bonnet height.

The 304 is used by the Oslo City Police in Norway, the French Gendarmerie (saloon and estate) both at home and overseas, the Utrecht Police in Holland (with engines adapted to run on LP gas) and the Nigerian Police.

Below: *Peugeot 304 of the Utrecht City Police.* Gemeentepolitie Utrecht

305

Length: 13ft 11in
Width: 5ft 4in
Height: 4ft 8in
Wheelbase: 8ft 9in
T/circle: 10.1m
Tyres: 145SR × 14
Kerb weight: 916kg
Fuel tank: 9.4gal
Max speed: Over 90mph
Engine: 1,290cc four-cylinder (Bore 78mm × Stroke 67.5mm) 65bhp (DIN). Compression ratio 8.8:1. Solex carburettor
Suspension: Independent by MacPherson struts (front) and trailing arms (rear)
Brakes: Servo-assisted, dual circuit, discs (front) and drums (rear)

One of the latest Peugeots, the 305 only appeared in 1977. Three versions are available — GL and GR with 1,290cc engines and SR with a 1,472cc unit. The 305 has front wheel drive and all-round independent suspension. Like the 204/304 models the engine is located transversely and tilted 20° to reduce bonnet height. The fuel tank is mounted between the rear wheels for safety and the body has a supplementary cross member for added passenger protection. An estate version is currently in use with the Ghent City Police in Belgium.

Below: *Peugeot 305SR.*

404

Length: 14ft 7in
Width: 5ft 4in

Below: *Peugeot 404 of the BSA Police (Rhodesia).*
British South Africa Police

Engine: 1,618cc four-cylinder 62bhp
Transmission: Four-speed manual gearbox
Suspension: Front — MacPherson struts
Rear — Live axle with coil springs, torque tube and
Panhard rod
Brakes: Servo-assisted, discs (front) and drums
(rear)

Probably the most popular of the Peugeot range, the
404 was in production for around 15 years from
about 1960 to the mid-1970s. Powered by a 1.6litre
engine tilted at 45°, the 404 came in both saloon
and estate car versions, although the latter was
discontinued in 1971.

Police users of the 404 include the Ghent City
Police and Brussels City Police in Belgium as well as
the Belgian Gendarmerie, the British South Africa
Police in Rhodesia, the Sierra Leone and Nigerian
Police and the Policia de Seguranca Publica in
Portugal

504

Length: 14ft 9in
15ft 9in (Estate)
Width: 5ft 7in
Height: 4ft 9in
5ft 1in (Estate)
Wheelbase: 8ft 1in
9ft 8in (Estate)
Tyres: 175HR × 14
185SR × 14 (Estate)
Fuel tank: 12.3gal
13.2gal (Estate)
Max speed: 90mph — over 100mph depending on
model
Engine: 1,796cc four-cylinder ohv (Bore 84mm ×
Stroke 81mm) 73bhp (DIN). Compression ratio
7.5:1. Solex carburettor
1,871cc four-cylinder ohv (Bore 88mm × Stroke
81mm) 96bhp (DIN). Compression ratio 8.8:1. Twin
choke carburettor
Transmission: Four-speed manual gearbox,
automatic available for larger engine
Suspension: Independent by coil springs all round,
live axle on estates

Brakes: Servo-assisted, discs front and rear, drums
on estate (rear)

One of the older models, being introduced in the late
1960s, the 504 used to be the top of the Peugeot
range but was surpassed by the arrival of the 604
half a decade later. The 504 comes in two petrol
engine sizes (1.8 and 2litre) and a 2litre diesel
saloon. There are six estate versions including two
diesel versions. It says much for the clean lines of the
Pininfarina-designed body that it has not dated after
10 years of production. A number of European police
forces, and some further afield, use 504, including
the French Gendarmerie Nationale, the Belgian
police in Ghent, Brussels and Liège, the Norwegian
police in Oslo, the Dutch police in Rotterdam, the
German police in North Rhine-Westphalia, the
Jordan Police, the Nigerian and Gambian Police
forces in West Africa and the Jamaican Police in the
Caribbean.

604

Length: 15ft 6in
Width: 5ft 10in
Height: 5ft 10in
Wheelbase: 9ft 4in
T/circle: 11.3m
G/clearance: 6in
Tyres: 175HR × 14
Kerb weight: 1,455kg
Fuel tank: 15.5gal
Max speed: Over 100mph
Engine: 2,664cc V6 cylinder double ohc (Bore
88mm × Stroke 73mm) 136bhp (DIN). Compression
ratio 8.65:1. Single and compound carburettors
Transmission: Four-speed manual, all synchromesh
gearbox or optional automatic

Suspension: Independent coil springs all round
Brakes: Servo-assisted, dual circuit, discs all round

France's big prestige car, the Peugeot 604, has more
than a passing ressemblance to the Mercedes. It is
perhaps therefore not surprising that the only police
force known to use them is the West German one in
North Rhine-Westphalia.

The Pininfarina-styled body is propelled by a
2.7litre, light alloy, V6 engine from the Renault-
Peugeot-Volvo 'co-op' in northern France and the car
is impeccably trimmed in velour cloth and is
extensively equipped.

Plymouth   USA

The Plymouth Company is now part of the Chrysler
Corporation of Detroit, Michigan, making mainly
popular full-sized and compact cars. A number of
these have proved popular with police departments,
mainly in the USA and Canada.

Fury

Length: 18ft 2in (Saloon)
18ft 9in (Estate)
Width: 6ft 5.57in (Saloon)
6ft 6.75in (Estate)
Height: 4ft 6.25in (Saloon)
4ft 9in (Estate)
G/clearance: 5in (Saloon)
5.25in (Estate)
Cargo volume: 84.7cu ft (Estate)
Engines: (a) 3.7litre (225cu in) six-cylinder (Bore
86mm × Stroke 105mm) 110bhp at 3,600rpm.
Compression ratio 8.5:1. Single two-barrel
carburettor
(b) 5.2litre (318cu in) V8 cylinder (Bore 99m ×
Stroke 84mm) 140bhp at 4,00rpm. Compression
ratio 8.5:1. Single two-barrel carburettor. Alternate
5.2litre engine uses a four-barrel carburettor,
producing 160bhp
(c) 5.9litre (360cu in) V8 cylinder (Bore 102mm ×
Stroke 84mm) 140bhp at 4,000rpm. Compression
ratio 8.4:1. One two-barrel carburettor
(d) 6.6litre (400cu in) (Bore 110mm × Stroke
86mm) 145bhp at 3,600rpm. Compression ratio
8.2:1. One four-barrel carburettor
Transmission: (5.2litre) Three-speed manual or
Torqueflite three-speed automatic. 5.2/5.9/6.6 litre
engines automatic only

One of the most popular cars for police work in the
United States, the Fury is currently in use with the

New York Police Department, the New York State
Police, the Los Angeles PD, the Sacramento County
Sheriff, the Virginia State Police and the Washington
(DC) Metropolitan Police Department. Over the
border in Canada, users include the Royal Canadian
Mounted Police, the Quebec and Ontario Provincial
Police forces, and the city forces in Vancouver,
Calgary, Winnipeg, Toronto Metropolitan, etc.
Elsewhere the Fury is used by the Greek
Gendarmerie and the Puerto Rico Police. Five body
styles are offered: Fury, Fury Saloon, Fury Sport and
Fury Suburban/Fury Sport Suburban estate cars.
Police use is mainly confirmed to the four-door Fury
basic saloon and the Fury Suburban estate car.
Engine options comprise a 3.7litre, six-cylinder
unit and four V8 motors — two of 5.2litre capacity,
one 5.9litre and one 6.6litre. The Fury basic saloon
has the six-cylinder power unit as standard and all
the others as options; the Suburban estate car has
the 5.9litre as standard and the 6.6 as an option.
A special feature of the V8 Chrysler engines used
is the 'Lean Burn' characteristics which provide
smooth warm-up, improved engine performance,
acceleration, smoothness and consumption figures,
reduced exhaust emission and reduced maintenance.

Below: *Plymouth Fury, patrol car of the Los Angeles
County Sheriff's Dept.* Los Angeles County Sheriff

Gran Fury

Length: 18ft 6.5in
Width: 6ft 7.75in
Wheelbase: 10ft 1.5in
Engine: 7,212cc (440cu in) V8 cylinder
Transmission: Torqueflite automatic

Based on the Fury the Gran Fury is a larger, more
powerful car, using engines up to 7.2litre (440cu in)
which nevertheless finds favour with a number of
police departments for highway patrol. The Gran
Fury is used by the Texas Department of Public

Safety (State Police), the Florida Highway Patrol, the
Philadelphia City PD (blue and white patrol car), the
Puerto Rico Police and the City of Winnipeg Police.
Production ran from 1975 to 1977.

*Above: Plymouth Gran Fury of the Philadelphia
Police.*

Volaré

Length: 16ft 5.25in
Width: 6ft 1.25in
Wheelbase: 9ft 0.75in
Engine: See under Fury (3.7 and 5.2litre)

Another popular police car is the compact Volaré
which was introduced in 1976. Mainly favoured for
use by detective branches, users include the Los

Angeles PD, the Virginia State Police, the Dallas City
Police, the St Louis City Police, the Sacramento
County Sheriff, the Puerto Rico Police, the Royal
Canadian Mounted Police and the Edmonton City
Police.
  The principal power unit is the same 5.2litre
engine used in the Fury.

Pontiac   USA

Named after the city in Michigan, USA, where it has
its works. Pontiac is now part of the General Motors
Corporation, producing a limited range of full-sized

and compact cars. Some of these are offered with
special police packages.

Catalina Freeway Enforcer

Length: 17ft 9.75in
Width: 6ft 3.5in
Wheelbase: 9ft 8in
Tyres: GR70 × 15 Police Special
Engine: 6.6litre (400cu in) V8 cylinder. Two-barrel
carburettor
Transmission: Automatic
Suspension: Heavy duty springs front and rear and
specially calibrated shock absorbers
Brakes: Power assisted, HD semi-metallic discs
(front) 11in × 2in organic-lined HD drums (rear)

The Catalina was produced from 1974 and some
models are used as marked patrol vehicles by the
Sacramento County Sheriff as well as, no doubt,
several other forces, details of which are not
currently to hand. Two police packages are available
— a Police Patrol (light duty) and a Freeway Enforcer
(heavy duty) and details of the latter are given in the
specification details.
  Special features include a heavy duty frame and
heavy duty seats, calibrated speedometer and heavy
duty floor covering.

Laurentian

Produced in Pontiac's Canadian factory, the Laurentian was aimed specifically at the Canadian market and has been taken into use with the Royal Canadian Mounted Police (both saloons and estate cars) and the Quebec Provincial Police. The Laurentian is a full sized car (about 18ft in length, depending on model year) with a range of engine options from 4.1litre to 7.5litre.

Below: *Pontiac Laurentian of the Royal Canadian Mounted Police. RCMP*

Le Mans Enforcer

Length: 17ft 8in
Width: 6ft 5.5in
Height: 4ft 5.5in
Wheelbase: 9ft 8in
Tyres: GR70 × 15 radials
Fuel tank: 22 US gal
Engine: 6.5litre V8 cylinder 185bhp (SAE). Four-barrel carburettor
Suspension: High rate coil springs with front and rear stabilizer bars. Four link rear suspension; double acting shock absorbers
Brakes: Power assisted, ventilated discs (front) with semi-metallic pads, 11in x 2in drums (rear) with organic linings

Based on the popular Le Mans family saloon which has been a firm favourite with Americans for many years, the 'Enforcer' version is a limited-production specification, available for law enforcement use only. Current users include the Dallas City Police, the Sacramento County Sheriff and the Puerto Rico Police.

The Le Mans Enforcer is available in two or four-door hardtop saloon versions, with heavy duty bench seats and hard wearing rubber floor covering. The 6.5litre (400cu in) V8 engine has a four-barrel carburettor and three-speed Turbo-Hydramatic automatic transmission is standard equipment.

Below: *Pontiac Le Mans of the Dallas Police Dept.*

Porsche
West Germany

Ever since the immortal Ferdinand Porsche started his company in 1930 its high design skills have been famous in the European automobile industry. Today, looking at the high quality, limited production (and thus expensive) sports cars which bear the Porsche name, it is strange to recall that Porsche was responsible for the archetypal 'peoples' car', the ubiquitous Volkswagen.

911

Length: 14ft 5in
Width: 5ft 5in
Height: 4ft 5in
Wheelbase: 7ft 6.75in
T/circle: 10.7m
G/clearance: 5in
Tyres: Front — 185/79VR×15
Rear — 215/60VR×15
Kerb weight: 1,120kg
Fuel tank: 17.5gal
Max speed: 140mph approx
Engine: 2,993cc six-cylinder horizontally opposed, air cooled twin ohc (Bore 95mm×Stroke 70.4mm) 180bhp (DIN). Compression ratio 8.5:1
Transmission: Five-speed manual or three-speed Sportomatic
Suspension: Independent all round by torsion bars
Brakes: Servo-assisted, dual circuit, discs (front) and drums (rear)

This six-cylinder model, with variants of horse-power and cubic capacity has, since 1956, been the mainstay of the Company's business. It is still a steady seller, although overtaken in sales numbers by the newer 924. The most recent version of the 911 is the SC which is used by the police in Baden Württemberg for Autobahn patrol. Other police users of the 911 include the Belgian Gendarmerie, the Dutch Rijkspolitie and the police in North Rhine-Westphalia.

The horizontally opposed, air-cooled engine is mounted aft of the rear suspension where it contributes to impressive traction. Headlamp washers and an electric sun-roof are standard equipment.

924

Length: 13ft 8in
Width: 5ft 5in
Height: 4ft 3in
Wheelbase: 7ft 10in
T/circle: 10m
G/clearance: 5in
Tyres: 185/70+14
Kerb weight: 1,114kg
Fuel tank: 13.5gal
Max speed: 125mph approx
Engine: 1,984cc four-cylinder ohc (Bore 86.5mm×Stroke 84.4mm) 125bhp (DIN). Compression ratio 9.3:1. Bosch fuel injection
Transmission: Four or five-speed manual gearbox or automatic
Suspension: Independent all round by coil springs
Brakes: Servo-assisted, dual circuit, discs (front) and drums (rear)

Porsche's 'new generation' sports coupé, the front-engined 924 has been a tremendous success since it came on the market in 1976. Assembled at the Audi-NSU factory at Neckarsulm, the engine is derived from the Audi 100 power unit but has electronic fuel injection. The gearbox is rear-mounted to balance the weight of the engine.

The smaller capacity, four-cylinder, water-cooled engine, coupled with a considerably lower price have made the 924 attractive to a wider circle of customers and it will undoubtedly prove to be of interest to a number of European police forces. At present, however, only the North Rhine-Westphalia police are known to have taken 924s into service.

Renault
France

The Renault story began in 1898 when Louis Renault built a car in his garden shed near Paris. Friends begged him to build them replicas and so, in 1899, with his brothers Marcel and Fernand, he formed the company Renault Frères.

The company began entering races with immediate success but, in 1903, Marcel Renault was killed in an accident in the Paris-Madrid race. Fernand died in 1909 and Louis was left to carry on alone; by 1914 Renault vehicles almost monopolised the taxi-ranks of Paris, London, Berlin and New York.

Following the 1944 Liberation it was decided that the company should come under the control of the French Government but, although it is now State owned, the Régie Renault is run as a private company and has to be financially self-sufficient. The company is based at Régie Nationale des Usines Renault, 92109 Boulogne-Billancourt, France.

Renault 4F 7cwt Van

Length: 11ft 11.75in
Width: 4ft 11in
Height: 5ft 7.5in
Wheelbase: 7ft 10.5in
T/circle: 31ft 9in
Tyres: 145×13 radial ply
Kerb weight: 1,499lb
Fuel tank: 7.5gal
Payload: 937lb (inc driver)
Max speed: 62mph approx
Engine: 845cc four-cylinder (Bore 58mm×Stroke 80mm) 34bhp at 5,000rpm (DIN). Compression ratio 8:1. Zenith carburettor
Transmission: Four-speed manual gearbox
Suspension: Independent on all four wheels by torsion bars, longitudinal (front) and transverse (rear) with hydraulic shock absorbers
Brakes: Drums all round with pressure-limited valve in rear brake line. Drum diameter 9in (front) and 6.3in (rear)

Like the highly successful Renault 4 saloon from which it is derived, the 7cwt van (known in some countries as the 4F) is tough, versatile and has a tremendous capacity for voluminous or awkward shaped loads. The main rear door is wide opening and, at the top of the opening is a hinged flap which can be bolted shut or held open to take long articles. Headlight beams are adjustable for height according to the load at the flick of a switch.

The combination of low operating costs, all-round practicability and smooth-ride comfort endears it to Continental police forces and its users include the French Gendarmerie Nationale, the Liège City Police (Belgian) and the Garda Siochana in Eire.

Below: *Renault 4F.*

Renault 4

Length: 12ft 1in
Width: 4ft 10.5in
Height: 5ft 1in
Wheelbase: 7ft 10.5in
T/circle: 31ft 9in
Tyres: 135×13 radial ply
Kerb weight: 1,532lb
Fuel tank: 7.5gal
Max speed: 75mph approx
Engine: See Renault 4F van
Transmission: See Renault 4F van
Suspension: See Renault 4F van
Brakes: Drums all round with pressure-limited valve in rear brake line. Drum diameters 7.9in (front) and 6.3in (rear)

The Renault 4 is an economy car in every way but without sacrificing comfort. It has five doors and four soft, wide and comfortable seats which, in the front, are individually adjustable and, on the TL version, are reclining.

Police users include the French Gendarmerie Nationale and Police Nationale, the Belgian Gendarmerie, the Gambia Police, and the Brussels and Liège City Police in Belgium

For the French Police and Gendarmerie Renault provide and fit an extra external rear-view mirror, radio aerial and suppressor, two-tone horn mounting, 50A alternator and special regulator, heated rear window, 45A battery and map-reading lamp.

Renault 5

Length: 11ft 6in
Width: 5ft 0in
Height: 4ft 7in
Wheelbase: 7ft 10.5in
T/circle: 32ft
Tyres: (5/5TL) 135+13 (others) 145×13. Radial ply on all models
Kerb weight: 1,609lb to 1,764lb according to model
Fuel tank: 8.25gal
Max speed: (5) 76mph (5TL) 84mph (5GTL) 84mph (5 Auto) 87mph (5TS) 94mph
Engine: (5) 845cc four-cylinder (Bore 58mm×Stroke 80mm) 36bhp at 5,500rpm (DIN), belt driven fan. Compression ratio 8.1. Solex carburettor
(5TL) 956cc four-cylinder (Bore 65mm×Stroke 72mm) 44bhp at 5,500rpm (DIN), electric fan. Compression ratio 9.25:1. Solex carburettor
(5GTL/5 Auto/5TS) 1,298cc four-cylinder (Bore 73mm×Stroke 72mm) 42/55/64bhp (DIN), electric fan. Compression ratio 9.5:1. Solex carburettor (Weber 32 DIR on 5TS)
Suspension: Independent on all four wheels by torsion bars longitudinal (front) and transverse (rear)

with hydraulic shock absorbers, anti-rollbar at the front
Brakes: Dual circuit hydraulic with pressure limiting valve in rear. Servo-assisted on GTL/TS/Auto. 7.9in drums (front) and 6.2in drums (rear) on 5. All other models have 9in drums (front) and 7.1in drums (rear)

From the time it was introduced in 1972 the front wheel drive Renault 5 was acclaimed as a new breed of car to meet the changing demands of motoring well into the future. There is now a range of six models available — 5, 5TL, 5GTL, 5TS, 5 Auto and 5 Gordini (known as 'Alpine' in France). Each has performance and equipment levels designed to meet a different set of needs. All are easy to handle in town traffic, yet can cruise all day at motorway speeds. With the equipment and smooth ride of far bigger cars, they can park in incredibly small spaces. Bump-proof polyester shields give protection against minor knocks. Renault 5s are used by the French Police Nationale for traffic control work, and also by the Monaco Police for CID work.

Below: *Renault 5 of the French National Police.*

Renault 6

Length: 12ft 8in
Width: 4ft 11.25in
Height: 4ft 10in

Wheelbase: 7ft 10.5in
T/circle: 32ft 6in
Tyres: 145×13 radial ply

Kerb weight: 1,808lb
Fuel tank: 8.6gal
Engine: 1,108cc four-cylinder (Bore 70mm×Stroke 72mm) 48bhp at 5,300rpm (DIN). Compression ratio 9.5:1
Suspension: Independent on all four wheels by torsion bars, longitudinal (front) and transverse (rear), with hydraulic shock absorbers. Anti-rollbars front and rear
Brakes: Hydraulic with pressure limiting valve in rear brake line to prevent brakes locking. 9in discs (front) and 7in drums (rear)

The Renault 6 is basically a family car which offers estate car versatility with easy loading through a fifth door. A kind of refined and enlarged Renault 4, the Renault 6 is a real workhorse which offers a good level of passenger comfort.

The French Gendarmerie Nationale uses the Renault 6TL, adapted by the factory for police work by the provision of a passenger's exterior mirror, suppressors and radio aerial wiring, two-tone horns, heated rear window, 45Amp battery and four-wheel drive (normally front wheel drive only).

Renault 12

Length: 14ft 3in
Width: 5ft 3.5in
Height: 4ft 8.5in
Wheelbase: 8ft
T/circle: 32ft 9in
Tyres: 145×13 (Saloon)
155×13 radial ply (Estate)
Kerb weight: 1,984lb (Saloon)
2,116lb (Estate)
Fuel tank: 10.25gal
Max speed: (12) 84mph
(TL/Estate) 87mph
Engine: 1,289cc four-cylinder (Bore 73mm×Stroke 77mm) 54bhp at 4,250rpm (DIN) (TL and Estate). Compression ratio 8.5:1. 9.5:1 (TL and Estate). Zenith carburettor
Transmission: Four-speed gearbox, automatic available on Estate
Suspension: Front — Independent by wishbones and coil springs
Rear — Coil springs with pressed steel axle
Brakes: Hydraulic with 9in discs (front) and 7in

drums (rear) 9in on Estate. Dual circuit with pressure limiting valve in rear brake line. Servo-assisted except on basic saloon

The Renault 12 comes in both saloon and estate car versions which are used by both the Gendarmerie and the Police Nationale in France and also by the Monaco Police. The saloon version is also used by the Vaud Cantonal Police in Switzerland for telecommunications work. The vehicles supplied to the French Police and Gendarmerie are specially adapted by the factory, according to the use to which they are to be put. These adaptations include the provision of radio/aerial mountings, engine suppression, two-tone horn, flashing roof lamp, 'Police' signs, map reading lamps, heated rear window, 45Amp battery. In addition, some of the police estates are adapted to four wheel drive (instead of the usual front-wheel drive).

Below: *Renault 12 of the Monaco Police.*

Renault 14

Length: 13ft 2in
Width: 5ft 3.75in
Height: 4ft 7in

Wheelbase: 8ft 3.5in
T/circle: 32ft 10in
Tyres: 145SR×13

Kerb weight: 1,907lb
Fuel tank: 10.5gal
Max speed: 90mph approx
Engine: 1,218cc four-cylinder (Bore 75mm×Stroke 69mm) 57bhp at 6,000rpm (DIN). Compression ratio 9.3:1. Solex carburettor
Transmission: Four-speed manual gearbox
Suspension: Independent all round. MacPherson struts (front) and double transverse torsion bars (rear). Hydraulic telescopic dampers front and rear
Brakes: Hydraulic servo-assisted, dual circuit, with pressure limiting valve in rear. 9.5in discs (front) and 7in drums (rear)

The newest addition to the Renault family, the 14 appeared in 1976. It is an unusual looking, five door saloon with unusually large internal dimensions for a 1.2litre car. As with all Renaults it has front wheel drive, the engine being based on the smaller Peugeot 104, both companies (in alliance with Volvo of Sweden) receiving motors from their 'cooperative' factory at Douvrin in Northern France. The 14 is, in fact, built in an ultra modern factory at Douai, near Lille.

Mildly modified versions are currently supplied to the Police Nationale in France.

Renault 16

Length: 13ft 10.75in
Width: 5ft 4in
Height: 4ft 9in
Wheelbase: 8ft 8.75in
T/circle: 34ft 1.5in
Tyres: 145×14 or 155×14 radial ply
Kerb weight: 2,227lb-2,403lb
Fuel tank: 11gal
Max speed: (TL) 93mph and (TX) 106mph
Engine: 1,565cc (TL) or 1,647cc (TX) four-cylinder 66/90bhp (DIN). Compression ratio 8.6:1/9.25:1. Carburettor Solex 3 NIMAT/Weber DAR7
Transmission: Four or five-speed manual gearbox or automatic
Suspension: Independent torsion bars on all four wheels
Brakes: Hydraulic dual circuit, servo-assisted, with pressure limiter on rear brake line. 10in discs (front) and 9in drums (rear)

It was in 1965 that Renault pioneered the five door 'saloon-estate' type with the introduction of the 16 and the model remains as popular as ever. By a combination of comfort, performance and practicality, the 16 has earned itself a special place in motor car history.

Users of the Renault 16 include the Seychelles Police, the police in Monaco (a TX version being used by the Chief of Police as well as standard models for detectives) and both the Gendarmerie and Police Nationale in France. The Gendarmerie uses the TL version fitted with two-tone horns, heated rear window and special regulator. The Police also use similarly adapted TLs fitted with radio and map reading lamp, and also TX versions with two-tone horns, suppressors, radio/telephone, electric windows, laminated windscreen, heated rear window. The standard electro-magnetic door locks are removed from the TX for police work.

Renault 30TS

Length: 14ft 10in
Width: 5ft 8in
Height: 4ft 8.5in
Wheelbase: 8ft 9in
T/circle: 33ft (34ft 9in for automatic)
Tyres: 175 HR×14 radial ply
Kerb weight: 2,910lb (manual) 2,955lb (automatic)
Fuel tank: 14.75gal
Max speed: Over 100mph
Engine: 2,664cc V6 cylinder ohc (Bore 88mm×Stroke 73mm) 128bhp at 5,500rpm (DIN). Compression ratio 9.2:1. Weber 38 DGAR carburettor
Transmission: Front wheel drive via four-speed gearbox or optional automatic
Suspension: Independent on all four wheels with

telescopic hydraulic shock absorbers. Double wishbones (front) and three element system (rear). Anti-rollbars front and rear
Brakes: Servo-assisted, dual circuit, hydraulic. Ventilated 9.92in discs (front) and 10in discs (rear)

Only one version is made of this prestige model from one of France's biggest manufacturers. It has front wheel drive like all other Renaults and is powered by a 2.6litre V6 engine produced in the Peugeot/Renault/Volvo joint factory at Douvrin. A high standard of equipment is supplied including electrically operated windows, electro-magnetic door locks operated centrally, cigar lighters front and rear and thick carpeting throughout. One police user of this luxury model is the North Rhine-Westphalia force.

Renault Alpine A110/A310

Length: 13ft 11.25in
Width: 5ft 5.5in
Height: 3ft 10in
Wheelbase: 7ft 5.5in

T/circle: 4.9m
Tyres: Front — 185/70
Rear — 205/70 VR 13
Kerb weight: 980kg

Fuel tank: 63litre
Max speed: Over 135mph
Engine: 2,664cc V6 cylinders double ohc (Bore 88mm × Stroke 73mm) 150bhp at 6,000rpm (DIN). Compression ratio 10.1:1
Transmission: Four-speed gearbox
Suspension: Helicoidal springs with telescopic shock absorbers all round
Brakes: Discs all round, ventilated at front

The Alpine has a very distinguished sporting ancestry, stemming from the winner of the Le Mans 24 hour race and several other races and rallies. The earlier A110 model has now given way to the current A310 but both are in service with the French Gendarmerie for high speed auto-route patrol.

Described as a four-seater, the Alpine is essentially a two seater sports car with room at the back for perhaps, two children or, more commonly, additional baggage/equipment.

Below: *Renault Alpine A310 of the French Gendarmerie.*

Rover UK

The Rover Car Company built up an enviable reputation for itself as the manufacturer of reliable quality cars between the two wars. In common with many other firms, especially the smaller, specialist ones, the postwar years were difficult ones for Rover and a number of mergers ensued, first with the similar Triumph Company and eventually as part of the British Leyland combine.

Rover 3500 (1968/76)

Length: 15ft
Width: 5ft 6in
Height: 4ft 9.5in
Wheelbase: 8ft 7.25in
T/circle: 10.7m
Tyres: 185HR × 14
Kerb weight: 1,327kg
Fuel tank: 15gal
Max speed: Over 120mph
Engine: 3,528cc V8 cylinder ohv (Bore 88.9mm × Stroke 71.1mm) 152bhp (DIN). Compression ratio 9.25:1. Two SU carburettors
Transmission: Four-speed manual gearbox or automatic
Suspension: Front — Independent coil springs Rear — Coil springs with De Dion and Watts linkage
Brakes: Servo-assisted discs all round.

The 3500 V8 was introduced in 1968, using the same aerodynamic body as the 2000/2200 which first appeared five years earlier. In its eight years of production it amassed an international reputation for

smooth running and effortless fast cruising and became popular in the UK for police patrol work on motorways and other main roads. Users of the model, or its successor, the new 3500, include 29 forces in England, Wales, Scotland and Northern

Above: Rover 3500S of the Kent County Constabulary. Kent County Constabulary

Ireland. Two of these, Tayside and Lothian and Borders, also use the four-cylinder 2,200cc model.

Rover 3500 (1976 onwards)

Length: 15ft 5in
Width: 5ft 10in
Height: 4ft 6.25in
Wheelbase: 9ft 2.75in
T/circle: 9.5m
Tyres: 185HR × 14
Kerb weight: 1,356kg
Fuel tank: 14.5gal
Max speed: Over 120mph
Engine: See previous model except for electronic ignition, larger valves, porting and phased manifolds. 155bhp (DIN). Compression ratio 9.35:1
Suspension: As for previous model
Brakes: As for previous model

In 1976, the Rover 3500 took on a completely new body of revolutionary design, although retaining basically the same engine. The body is highly streamlined for performance and fuel economy and has five doors, room for five adults, self-levelling suspension, centralised door locking. With the rear seat folded there is a generous load space in the rear — an asset much appreciated by its police users (see under 1968/76 model). Not surprisingly, this car was voted 'Car of the Year' by leading motoring journalists shortly after its introduction.

Below: Rover 3500 (1976+) of the Kent Constabulary. Kent County Constabulary

Rover 2600

Dimensions: As for 3500
Max speed: 115mph approx
Engine: 2,597cc six-cylinder (Bore 81mm × Stroke 84mm) 136bhp (DIN). Compression ratio 9.25:1. Twin SU carburettor
Transmission: Five-speed manual gearbox
Suspension: Front — Independent coil springs Rear — Live axle with torque tube and Watts linkage
Brakes: Servo-assisted, dual circuit, discs (front) and drums (rear)

Following the success of the new 3500, smaller engined versions were introduced in 1977, using the same body but powered by an in-line ohc six-cylinder engine which features ingenious valve-gear. One of these, the 2,600 (the other being of 2,300cc) is used by the police in Northamptonshire, Sussex and Durham.

Land Rover

The success of the Jeep in World War II led to a number of four-wheel drive vehicles appearing on the public market in the immediate postwar years but none of these was more successful than the Land Rover. It has a non-rust, corrosion resistant body that shrugs off the worst of weather and terrain and comes in no less than 27 different body variations, based on either the short wheelbase or long wheelbase chassis.

The success of the Land Rover is reflected in its use for police work; probably no other vehicle is used as widely as the Land Rover and the list seems endless: Antwerp Police (Belgium), Bundesgrenzschutz (West German Federal Border Police), Belgian Gendarmerie, Bahamas Police, Belize Police, Botswana Police, Cyprus Police, French Gendarmerie (in overseas territories only). Fiji Police, Guyana Police, Greek Gendarmerie, Gibraltar Police, Gilbert Islands Police, Royal Hong Kong Police, Jamaica Constabulary, Jordon Police, Kenya Police, Royal Malaysia Police, Nigeria Police, Policia de Segurança Publica (Portugal), Punjab Police (India), Singapore Police, South Australia Police, Spain, Seychelles Police, Sierra Leone, and the Vaud Cantonal Police (Switzerland). And this is not to mention the 36 forces in the UK. The main type used is one of the personnel carrying versions for transporting policemen from one place to another but a number of variations exist, including a prison van version used by the South Australia Police. Both petrol and diesel engines are available.

Below: *Land Rover of the Royal Hong Kong Police.* Royal Hong Kong Police

73

Range Rover

Length: 14ft 8in
Width: 5ft 10in
Height: 5ft 10in
Wheelbase: 8ft 4in
T/circle: 37ft
G/clearance: 7.5in
Tyres: Michelin radials XM + S205 × 16 tubed or Firestone Town and Country radials 205 × 16
Kerb weight: 3,800lb
Payload: 1,720lb
Engine: As for Rover 3500 except 132bhp (DIN). Compression ratio 8.5:1. Twin Zenith/Stromberg carburettors
Transmission: Four-speed gearbox with two-speed transfer box (four-wheel drive)
Suspension: Independent by coil springs front and rear. Rear incorporates a 'Boge Hydromatic' self-energising, ride level unit
Brakes: Servo-assisted, dual-circuit, parking brake (drum type) operates on the transfer box rear output shaft. Discs front and rear.

Below: *Range Rover of the Utrecht City Police.* Gemeentepolitie Utrecht

Although the Land Rover was so successful, it became apparent that there was a latent demand for a vehicle combining the rugged, 'go anywhere' characteristics of the Land Rover with a greater measure of comfort than this strictly utilitarian vehicle could offer. And so it was, in 1970, that the Range Rover was born. A rugged, almost rustless vehicle, capable of battering its way through forests and climbing steep gradients on rough terrain, it has enormous carrying and towing capacity, and yet can be driven by a slightly built woman. The interior is well furnished with deep, comfortable seats and all the luxuries one expects from a good quality saloon.

Four-wheel drive is standard and power-assisted steering is available as an option. The engine is the same, powerful V8 3.5 litre unit which powers the 3500 saloon, although slightly detuned.

Almost every police force in the UK uses the Range Rover and, overseas, it is used by the Bahrain Police, the Tasmania Police, the Belgian Gendarmerie, the South Australia Police, the Oslo and Utrecht City forces, the Liechtenstein Police, the Cyprus Police, the Royal Malaysia Police and the Dutch Rijkspolitie (national police).

Range Rovers are also built in Australia by Leyland Australia, the specification of which differs slightly from the British built models.

Saab

Sweden

Built by the Saab-Scania Automotive Group, S-61101 Nyköping, Sweden, part of the same firm which builds Saab aircraft, Saab cars have become renowned for safety standards. They are extremely robust and have, in the past, had considerable success in rallies.

Saab 95/96

Data: 95
Length: 14ft 1.5in
Width: 5ft 2.5in
Height: 4ft 10.75in
Wheelbase: 8ft 2.5in
T/circle: 32ft 6in
G/clearance: 6.75in
Tyres: 155SR × 15
Kerb weight: 19.25cwt
Fuel tank: 9.5gal
Max speed: Over 90mph
Engine: 1,498cc V4 cylinder (Bore 90mm × Stroke 58.86mm) 65bhp (DIN). Compression ratio 9:1. Autolite down draught carburettor
Transmission: Four-speed manual gearbox

Suspension: Front — Independent coil springs
Rear — Trailing axle with coil springs
Brakes: Servo-assisted , diagonal circuit, discs (front) and drums (rear)

The Saab 96 was a two-door saloon, powered by the German Ford V4 engine, with front wheel drive, whereas the Saab 95 was an estate version of the same car. Both models were renowned for their longevity and continued in production from the early 1960s until 1976. Both versions are still in use with the Swedish police.

Below: *Saab 96GL.*

Saab 99

Length: 14ft 6in
Width: 5ft 7in
Height: 4ft 9.25in
Wheelbase: 8ft 1.5in
T/circle: 10.4m
Tyres: 165 × 15
Kerb weight: 1,154kg
Fuel tank: 12gal
Engine: 1,985cc four-cylinder ohc (Bore 90mm × Stroke 78mm) 100bhp (DIN). Compression ratio 9.2:1 Zenith/Stromberg carburettor
Transmission: Four-speed gearbox or automatic
Suspension: Front — Independent coil springs

Rear — dead axle coil springs
Brakes: Servo-assisted, dual circuit, discs (front) and drums (rear).

Big brother to the 95 and 96, the Saab 99 is the sole remaining example of the marque (apart from the new, very similar 900). First produced in 1969 with a 1.7litre engine, the 99 has been updated and modified over the years and now has a 2litre power unit.
Police in both Sweden and Norway use the Saab 99 for patrol work.

Simca

France

The French firm of Simca is yet another European motor manufacturer which has come under the umbrella of the American giant, Chrysler. It has its offices in the heart of Paris at Chrysler France, 136 Champs Elysées, 75 Paris 8.

Rancho

Above: *Simca Rancho.*

Length: 14ft 2in
Width: 5ft 5in
Height: 5ft 8in
Wheelbase: 8ft 3in
T/circle: 10.6m
Tyres: 185 × 14
Kerb weight: 2,490lb
Fuel tank: 13.5 gal
Payload: 1,103lb
Max speed: Over 90mph
Engine: 1,442cc four-cylinder (Bore 76.7mm ×
Stroke 80mm) 80bhp at 5,600rpm (DIN).
Compression ratio 9.5:1
Transmission: Four-speed manual gearbox driving
front wheels only
Suspension: Torsion bars front and rear, with anti-
rollbars and double acting shock absorbers
Brakes: Servo-assisted: dual circuit, discs (front)
and drums (rear)

The Rancho combines the versatility and carrying
capacity of an estate car with the traction and
ground clearance of a specialist vehicle and the
comfort, reliability and economy of a family saloon.
Developed by Matra in conjunction with Chrysler
France (Simca), the front-wheel drive Rancho is
designed as an answer for people who want a
capacious and rugged weekend 'get away' car but do
not wish to sacrifice the comfort and performance of
a conventional car. The body used the floorpan of a
Simca 1100, lengthened and strengthened with a
steel body front section, but the rear of the Rancho is
glass-fibre on a metal frame.

A number of police forces in Europe and
elsewhere have been carrying out trials with the
Rancho but, at the time of writing, none are known
to have taken it into regular service.

Simca 1100

Below: *Simca 1100 GLS.*

Length: 12ft 11.35in
Width: 5ft 2.25in
Height: 4ft 8.75in
Wheelbase: 8ft 3.25in
T/circle: 10.15m
Tyres: 145 SR × 13
Max speed: Over 80mph
Engine: 1,118cc four-cylinder ohv (Bore 74mm × Stroke 65mm) 50bhp at 5,800rpm (DIN). Compression ratio. 8.8:1. Bressel, Weber or Solex carburettor
Suspension: Front — Torsion bars, longitudinal

with transverse wishbones
Rear — Transversal torsion bars
Brakes: Servo-assisted, dual circuit, with pressure drop indicator, discs (front) and drums (rear)

French maid of all work, the Simca 1100 is a useful front wheel drive hatchback with a choice of three or five doors. There is also an estate car version, a van and pick-up. Both the Police Nationale and the Gendarmie Nationale in France use these useful little run-abouts for a variety of purposes, including investigations.

Skoda   Czechoslovakia

One of the few Eastern Bloc car manufacturers to export in any great numbers to the Western World, the old-established Czechoslovakian marque of Skoda produced two models for export between the

mid-1960s and 1977 — the 100 and 110 — both of which have been superseded by the 120 Estelle range.

Skoda 110

Length: 13ft 7.5in
Width: 5ft 3.75in
Height: 4ft 6.5in
Wheelbase: 7ft 10.5in
T/circle: 33ft 6in
G/clearance: 7in
Tyres: 155 SR × 14
Kerb weight: 16.5cwt
Fuel tank: 7gal
Max speed: 90mph approx
Engine: 1,107cc four-cylinder (Bore 72mm × Stroke 68mm) 52bhp (DIN)
Compression ratio 9.5:1 Double down draught carburettor

Transmission: Four-speed manual gearbox
Suspension: Front — Independent by coil springs
Rear — Swinging half axles
Brakes: Dual circuit: hydraulic discs (front) and drums (rear)

The 110 is a lively saloon of modest dimensions, low fuel consumption and a good standard of equipment characterise these low priced vehicles. Although most certainly used for police work behind the Iron Curtain, the only other force known to use the Skoda 110 is the Cyprus Police, which uses a very wide range of vehicles from all countries.

Toyota   Japan

One of the principal car manufacturers in Japan, Toyota pursue a vigorous export policy and their vehicles are to be found over almost the whole

world. Address: Toyota Motor Company Limited, Toyota-Shi, Aichi-ken, Japan.

Carina

Length: 13ft 8in
Width: 5ft 4in
Height: 4ft 8in
Wheelbase: 8ft 3in
T/circle: 10.9m
G/clearance: 6in
Tyres: 165×13
Kerb weight: 994kg
Fuel tank: 12.8gal
Max speed: Over 90mph
Engine: 1,588cc four-cylinder ohv (Bore 85mm×Stroke 70mm) 75bhp (DIN)
Compression ratio 9:1. Aisin down draught

carburettor
Transmission: Four-speed manual gearbox or optional three-speed automatic
Suspension: Front — Independent by coil springs
Rear — Live axle with coil springs
Brakes: Discs (front) and drums (rear)

The Carina is Toyota's mid-range car with a 1.6litre engine. Originally introduced in 1971, it received a major 'face-lift' in 1976, and two years later was fitted with an entirely new body which is larger and has more glass area than its predecessor. Modifications include increased interior dimensions, wider front seats, substantial sound insulation, galvanised sill panels, plastic liners in front wheel arches and a larger fuel tank. The Carina is in use with the Singapore Police for patrol work.

Celica

Data: 2000XT
Length: 14ft 3in
Width: 5ft 6in
Height: 4ft 5in
Wheelbase: 8ft 4in
Tyres: 156SR×14
Kerb weight: 1,051kg
Fuel tank: 13.5gal
Max speed: 105mph approx
Engine: 1,968cc four-cylinder ohc (Bore 88.5mm×Stroke 80mm) 85bhp (DIN) Compression ratio 8.5:1. Twin-choke Nikki down draught carburettor
Transmission: Five-speed gearbox or optional three-speed automatic
Suspension: Front — MacPherson strut
Rear — Live axle with coil springs
Brakes: Discs (front) and drums (rear)

The Celica first appeared in 1971 with a specification similar to the Carina but with an up-rated version of the 1,600cc engine. In 1975 a 2litre version was introduced to supplement the 1,600cc range and, in 1978, the whole range was revised, giving a 1600ST Coupe and four lift-back versions with the 2litre engine (ST/GT/XT/XT Auto). Celicas have been taken into use by the Botswana Police.

Corolla

Length: 13ft 1in
Width: 5ft 2in
Height: 4ft 8in
Wheelbase: 7ft 8.5in
G/clearance: 5.75in
T/circle: 9.24m
Tyres: 155SR×13
Kerb weight: 878kg
Fuel tank: 11gal
Max speed: 90mph approx
Engine: 1,166cc four-cylinder (Bore 75mm×Stroke 66mm) 56bhp (DIN) Compression ratio 9:1 Twin-choke down draught carburettor
Transmission: Four-speed manual or two-speed automatic gearbox
Suspension: Front — Independent by coil springs
Rear — Semi-elliptic leaf springs
Brakes: Servo-assisted, dual circuit, discs (front) and drums (rear)

Claimed to be the world's best selling car by a growing margin, the Corolla first appeared in 1967 as a two-door, four-seater saloon, powered by an 1,100cc engine. The engine was later increased to 1,200cc and remains the same today, although a 1,600cc lift-back version was introduced in 1976. Corollas are used by the Australian Capital Territory Police for their process servers, by the Punjabi Police in India, for CID work in Papua New Guinea, by the Royal Malaysia Police and the Jamaica Constabulary.

Corona 2000

Length: 14ft 1in
Width: 5ft 4in
Height: 4ft 8.5in
Wheelbase: 8ft 3.5in
G/clearance: 5.5in
T/circle: 9.8m
Tyres: 175SR×14
Kerb weight: 1,124kg
Fuel tank: 13.25gal
Max speed: Over 100mph
Engine: 1,968cc four-cylinder ohc (Bore 88.5mm×Stroke 80mm) 82bhp (SAE). Compression ratio 8.5:1. Twin-choke down draught carburettor
Transmission: Five-speed manual or automatic gearbox
Suspension: Front — Independent by coil springs
Rear — Asymmetric leaf springs
Brakes: Servo-assisted, dual circuit, discs (front) and drums (rear)

Although a 1.9litre version was available in the late 1960s, the 2litre version first appeared in 1972 with the same mechanical and body specification as its predecessor. A completely new version was introduced in 1975 but production ceased two years or so later with the introduction of the Cressida. Coronas are in use with the Royal Hong Kong Police (general purpose), the Royal Fiji Police, the Cyprus Police and the Jamaica Constabulary.

Cressida

Length: 14ft 10in
Width: 5ft 6in
Height: 4ft 9in
Wheelbase: 8ft 9.75in

G/clearance: 5.75in
T/circle: 10.2m
Tyres: 175SR×14
Kerb weight: 1,090kg
Fuel tank: 14.25gal
Max speed: Over 95mph
Engine: 1,968cc four-cylinder ohc (Bore 88.5mm×Stroke 80mm) 89bhp (DIN). Compression ratio 8.5:1. Twin-choke Nikki carburettor
Transmission: Four-speed manual or three-speed automatic gearbox
Suspension: Front — Independent by coil springs Rear — Live axle with coil springs
Brakes: Servo-assisted, dual circuit, discs (front) and drums (rear)

The Cressida replaced the Corona in 1977 and is mechanically very similar, although the cylinder head has been modified and a new carburettor fitted. The body is larger than the Corona and has all the refinements one has come to expect from a Japanese product, such as tinted windows, radio, four-speed heater booster, and two-speed wipers with intermittent wipe facility.

Toyota, the third largest manufacturers in the world, tries to capture both the European and the American markets with the same model which is why, to European eyes, the Cressida has too much chrome embellishment and yet mixes plastic with imitation wood in the interior trim — an unusual feature for a car on the 'Hollywood' style. The result is not unduly displeasing.

The Cressida would appear to have much to offer police users and it is perhaps surprising that, outside Japan, only the Cyprus Police are known to be using this model.

Crown

Above: *Toyota Crown Super.*

Length: 15ft 8in
Width: 5ft 7in
Height: 4ft 9.5 in
Wheelbase: 8ft 11in
G/clearance: 5.75in
T/circle: 10.8m
Tyres: 185SR×14
Kerb weight: 1,146kg
Fuel tank: 15.75gal
Max speed: 100mph approx
Engine: 2,563cc six-cylinder ohc (Bore 80mm×Stroke 85mm) 118bhp (DIN). Compression ratio 9.2:1. Aisin twin-choke carburettor
Transmission: Three-speed automatic gearbox
Suspension: Front — Independent by coil springs Rear — Live axle with four-link coil springs
Brakes: Servo-assisted discs (front) and drums (rear)

Toyota's prestige saloon first appeared in 1968 in both saloon and estate car versions. In 1975 the 2.3litre engine was up-rated to 2.6litre and the body given a face lift; in 1977 further improvements were made by increasing the engine output and compression ratio. The air-conditioning and automatic gearbox were revised and the car comes complete with rear passenger compartment lights, radio-cassette player, electric windows, central door locking system, timed rear window heater, clock with date, power steering and air-purification system. The Crown has been taken into use by the Royal Hong Kong Police, the Cyprus Police, the Jamaica Constabulary and the Korean National Police.

Land Cruiser

Length: 15ft 6.5in
Width: 5ft 9.5in
Height: 6ft 3in
Wheelbase: 9ft
G/clearance: 6.75in
T/circle: 12.4m
Kerb weight: 2,000kg
Seating capacity: 6
Engine: 4,230cc six-cylinder ohv (Bore 94mm×Stroke 101.6mm). Compression ratio 7.8:1
Transmission: Four-speed manual gearbox with two-speed helical gear, sliding type coupling transfer box
Suspension: Semi-elliptic leaf springs (front and rear) with double acting telescopic hydraulic shock absorbers and torsion bar rear stabiliser
Brakes: Hydraulic drums, 295mm diameter (front) and 290mm (rear)

Optional extras available including power-operated winch, external sun visor, air-conditioning, radio, tropical roof and Kangaroo guards.

The FJ55RV Land Cruiser is one of the latest of a line of four-wheel drive utility vehicles produced by Toyota. It provides estate car comfort and refinement with 'go-anywhere' capabilities much sought after by police forces responsible for patrolling difficult terrain. Current users of the Land Cruiser include the Tasmania Police, the South Australia Police, the Australian Capital Territory Police (water police, rural patrols, search and rescue), the Botswana Police and the Jamaica Constabulary. Users of other, similar 4×4 Toyota products (eg: FJ45, HJ45, BJ40, FJ40, FJ45RK) include the Northern Australia Police, the Tasmania Police, the Punjab Police, Papua New Guinea Police and the Queensland Police.

Hi-Ace

Length: 14ft 3in
Width: 5ft 6.5in
Height: 6ft 3.5in
Wheelbase: 7ft 8in
G/clearance: 7in
Kerb weight: 2,835lb
Payload: 2,455lb
Engine: 1,587cc four-cylinder ohv (Bore 80.5mm×Stroke 78mm) 68bhp (DIN). Compression ratio 8.5:1. Single twin-choke down draught carburettor
Transmission: Four-speed manual gearbox
Suspension: Front — Independent double

wishbone with coil springs
Rear — Live axle, semi-elliptic leaf springs
Telescopic shock absorbers all round
Brakes: Servo-assisted 10in diameter drums all round

The Hi-Ace is Toyota's version of the popular one-ton van and personnel carrier. Although only 14ft long it has a surprising 190cu ft of load space, access to which is via a sliding side door and a lift-up tail-gate. Police users of the Hi-Ace include the Jamaica Constabulary and the Royal Fiji Police.

Triumph

UK

The Triumph Car Company was renowned in the prewar years for its high quality, fast, sports saloons of which the original Dolomite was a superb example and is now a collector's car. After the war Triumph continued, mainly in the same pattern but, like so many other, smaller companies, found it necessary

to effect mergers, firstly with the Standard Company, then Rovers and, eventually, it became part of the British Leyland combine. The cars which bear the Triumph badge are still quality vehicles, such as the TR range of sports cars, the current Dolomite saloon, and the now defunct 2000/2500 saloons.

Dolomite

Length: 13ft 5in
13ft 6in (Sprint)
Width: 5ft 3in
Height: 4ft 7in
Wheelbase: 8ft 6in
T/circle: 9.1m
9.8m (Sprint)
Tyres: 155 × 13
175/70HR × 13 (Sprint)
Kerb weight: 945kg
1.043kg (Sprint)
Fuel tank: 12.5gal
Max speed: 85mph (1,300cc)

Over 110mph (Sprint)
Engine: 1,300cc — 1,296cc four-cylinder ohc (Bore 74mm × Stroke 76mm) 58bhp (DIN). Compression ratio 8.5:1. SU carburettor
Sprint — 1,998cc four-cylinder ohc (Bore 90mm × Stroke 78mm) 127bhp (DIN). Compression ratio 9.5:1. Twin SU carburettors
Transmission: 1,300cc — Four-speed manual gearbox
Sprint — Four-speed manual with overdrive or automatic gearbox
Suspension: Front — Independent by coil springs
Rear — Four-link coil springs (1,300cc/1,500cc) or

live axle with coil springs (Sprint)
Brakes: Servo-assisted, dual circuit, discs (front) and drums (rear)

The Dolomite is a shortened, lower powered version of the Triumph 2000 with similar interior appointments, including the walnut wood fascia and door cappings. It first appeared in 1972 with an 1,850cc engine and was complemented by a 1,300cc and a 1,500cc version in 1976. All three engine variations are currently available, as well as a two-litre 'Sprint' model. Externally, the 1,300cc and 1,500cc models may be distinguished by their rectangular headlamps, as opposed to the four round units on the 1850 and Sprint models.

The Dolomite's compact dimensions and lively performance made it a useful car for police work and versions are currently in use with the Avon and Somerset Police, West Yorkshire Police, Nottinghamshire Police (all using 'Sprint' versions), the Derbyshire Police, the Staffordshire Police and the Royal Ulster Constabulary.

Triumph 2500

Length: 15ft 3in
Width: 5ft 8in
Height: 4ft 8.5in
Wheelbase: 8ft 11.5in
G/clearance: 4.75in
T/circle: 10.4m
Tyres: 185SR × 13
Kerb weight: 1,225kg
Fuel tank: 12.75gal
Max speed: 105mph approx
Engine: 2,498cc six-cylinder (Bore 74.7mm × Stroke 95mm) 106bhp (DIN). Compression ratio 8.5:1. Two SU carburettors
Transmission: Four-speed manual with overdrive or three-speed automatic gearbox
Suspension: Independent all round by coil springs
Brakes: Servo-assisted, discs (front) and drums (rear)

Developed from the Triumph 2000 and using the same body and an up-rated version of the same engine, the 2500 first appeared in 1968 with petrol injection only. This system was not an unqualified success however, and, in 1974 the 2500 was fitted with twin SU carburettors. The body of the 2500 bears a close family resemblance to the Dolomite but is longer and wider than its younger brother. The interior is extremely well equipped in traditional British fashion with walnut fascia and door cappings, deep seats of simulated leather and a feeling of solid dependancy. This is matched, however, by a crisp, sparkling performance.

The Triumph 2500 makes a good patrol car and has been adopted by about 20 police forces in the United Kingdom, some of whom also use the PI (petrol injection version) and the 2000. Outside the United Kingdom, Triumph 2500s are also used by the Dutch Rijkspolitie. Production of both the 2000 and the 2500 ceased in 1977.

Vauxhall

Vauxhall perhaps had its heyday soon after World War I when its cars had considerable success on the racing scene. As time progressed it concentrated more on family saloons and, after World War II, was taken over by the giant American General Motors Corporation. Today its products bear a close similarity to those of its West German cousin, Opel, although it retains its address at Vauxhall Motors Limited, Luton, Bedfordshire, England.

Cavalier

Length: 14ft 7in
Width: 5ft 5in
Height: 4ft 2.5in
Wheelbase: 8ft 3in
T/circle: 31.1ft
Tyres: 165SR × 13
Kerb weight: 2205lb (1973)
Fuel tank: 11gal
Max speed: 90-over 100mph depending on model
Engine: 1300 — 1,256cc four-cylinder ohv 57.7bhp (DIN)
1600 — 1,584cc ohc four-cylinder 75bhp (DIN)
2000 — 1,979cc ohc four-cylinder 100bhp (DIN)
Transmission: Four-speed manual gearbox or automatic optional (1600/2000 only)
Suspension: Front — Independent coil springs

Rear — Live axle with coil springs
Anti-roll bars front and rear
Brakes: Servo-assisted, dual circuit, with 9.7in discs (front) and 9.1in diameter drums (rear). Pressure conscious valve

One of Vauxhall's latest products, the Cavalier is available in two or four-door saloons or sporty coupé versions. Engine sizes range from 1.3 to 2litre (coupés 2litre only). The smaller-engined versions are powered by the well-tried 'Viva' engine and are assembled at the Luton works but the larger engined cars are assembled in Belgium from Opel (Ascona and Manta) parts. The finished product bears a close resemblance to the Opel Ascona.

Cavaliers are used by the English police forces in

South Yorkshire, Merseyside and Hampshire and, over the border, in Lothian and Borders and Central Scotland.

Above: *Vauxhall Cavalier GL.*

Chevette

Length: 13ft 8.75in
Width: 5ft 1.75in
Height: 4ft 3.5in
Wheelbase: 7ft 10.25in
T/circle: 30.2ft
Tyres: 155SR × 13
175SR × 13 (GLS Saloon)
Kerb weight: 1,821-1,929lb
Fuel tank: 10gal
Max speed: Over 85mph
Engine: 1,256cc four-cylinder ohv (Bore 81mm × Stroke 61mm) 58bhp (DIN). Compression ratio 9.2:1. Zenith carburettor
Transmission: Four-speed manual gearbox
Suspension: Front — Independent by coil springs
Rear — Live axle and coil springs
Anti-roll bars front and rear
Brakes: Servo-assisted, dual circuit, with 9.4in diameter discs (front) and 7.9in self-adjusting drums (rear). Pressure conscious valve

A 'Panda' car specification is available on demand incorporating a choice of laminated windscreen, heated rear window, passenger's exterior mirror, HD battery, HD rear suspension, HD alternator, hazard warning flashers, 16in zip in headlining, 'Police' in reflective tape on doors, front doors painted white.

The Chevette is the British version of the Opel Kadett, coming in saloon, hatchback, estate and van versions, each of which has up to four levels of trim. All versions share the 1.25litre engine which powers the Viva and smaller Cavalier models.

A nippy, manoeuvrable little car, the Chevette is well suited for urban police work as a 'Panda' car or for CID use. As such it is used by the South Yorkshire Police, the Merseyside Police, the Bedfordshire Police and the Northern Constabulary (Scotland). The latter also use the van version.

Magnum

The Magnum, fitted with either an 1,800 or a 2,300cc engine and using a 'Viva' bodyshell, was in production from 1973 to 1977. Although roomy and well-sprung, the Magnum had more than a touch of the sports model in its make-up and standard specification included a tachometer, four headlamps, well-shaped, cloth-covered seats, etc. The 1,800cc Magnum has now been replaced by the Viva

1800GLS, while the larger engine is only found today in the VX series.

Police users of the Magnum are the South Yorkshire Police, the Hampshire Constabulary and the Tayside Police.

Data: As for the Viva 1800GLS (For 2300 engine see Victor/VX)

Ventora/Victor/VX Range

Length: 15ft
Width: 5ft 7in
Height: 4ft 4.25in
Wheelbase: 8ft 8.75in
T/circle: 37.1ft
Tyres: 175SR × 13 radials (Michelin radial XV5 185/70HR × 14 tyres available for police work)
Kerb weight: 2,604lb

Max speed: over 100mph
Engine: 2,279cc four-cylinder ohc 108bhp (DIN) at 5,000rpm. Viscous fan, automatic choke
Transmission: Four-speed manual or automatic gearbox
Suspension: Front — Independent by coil springs
Rear — Live axle and coil springs
Anti-roll bars front and rear

Brakes: Servo-assisted, dual circuit, with 9.4in diameter discs (front) and 9in diameter self-adjusting drums (rear). Load conscious valve

The 'Victor' range of 1.8litre, 2.3litre and 3.3litre saloons and estates and the Ventora 3.3litre range were in production until 1976 when they were supplanted by the VX series. With roomy bodywork and powerful engines the VX series is a good proposition for the motorist, civilian and police, who needs plenty of space and good pulling power. If the saloon is not big enough the estate car version is almost bound to be! The live rear axles are well located for good handling and there is a choice of manual or automatic transmissions.

Apart from the basic 1800 and 2300 four-door saloons and five-door estates there is the VX490 sports saloon and the luxury VX2300 GLS saloon. The latter is so well equipped that the only option is the GM automatic transmission.

Police users of either the Victor or the VX range include the Durham Police, the Devon and Cornwall Constabulary, the North Wales Police, the Sussex Police, the Bedfordshire Police, the Dumfries and Galloway Police, the Strathclyde Police and the Northern Constabulary. The Royal Ulster Constabulary use them, as do the Punjab police, the Garda Siochana in Eire, the Greek Gendarmerie and the Cyprus Police.

Special police equipment is available on the VX2300 such as passenger's exterior mirror, HD suspension, HD battery, brighter interior lamp, GLS instrumentation, HD axles, larger front disc brakes, zipped headlining, improved performance engine, calibrated speedometer, switch panel (for air-horn,

Above: Vauxhall Victor estate motorway patrol car.

beacon and police sign) and charging socket. At additional cost, laminated windscreens and a front-end spoiler with halogen fog lamps are available.

Viva

Below: Vauxhall Viva 'Panda' car.

Length: 13ft 7in
Width: 5ft 4.75in
Height: 4ft 5.25in
Wheelbase: 8ft 1in
T/circle: 32.2ft
Tyres: 155SR × 13/175SR × 13 (Michelin radial XV5 185/70HR × 14 tyres available for police work)
Kerb weight: 1,927-2,273lb
Fuel tank: 8-12gal
Max speed: 85mph (1300cc)
100mph approx (1,800cc saloon)
Engine: 1,800cc (for 1,300cc see 'Chevette') — 1,759cc four-cylinder ohc 88bhp (DIN) at 5,800rpm. Viscous drive fan, automatic choke.
Transmission: Four-speed manual or automatic (1800 only) gearbox
Suspension: Front — Independent by coil springs
Rear — Live axle and coil springs
Front anti-roll bar on 1800 only
Brakes: Servo-assisted, dual circuit, with 8.5in diameter discs (front) and 8in diameter self-adjusting drums (rear)

The first Viva appeared in 1963 and it has progressed from the HA version, through the HB (1966/70) to the HC1100 model in 1970. In the following year the engine capacity was increased to 1,256cc and, in 1976 the range was redesignated to the Viva 1300 series. At the same time a 1,600cc version, which first came on the market in 1968, followed a similar progression, being up-rated to the 1,800cc in 1972. In the same year a 2,300 version was also introduced but this only lasted until the following year.

The current Viva range uses the 1,300 and the 1,800cc engines to power a range of two and four-door saloons and three door estates, all of which are used by one police force or another. Current users include the Gloucestershire Constabulary, the North Wales Police, the West Yorkshire Metropolitan Police, the Lancashire Constabulary, the Royal Ulster Constabulary, the Central Scotland Police, the Lothian and Borders Police and the Strathclyde Police. For police work the 1,300cc basic models may be fitted with special options including laminated windscreen, passenger's exterior mirror, HD front suspension, HD alternator, reversing lamps, heated rear window, hazard warning flashers, roof bow to accommodate roof beacon, zipped headlining, doors painted white, reinforced cross-member, 'Police' in reflective tape on doors.

Volkswagen

West Germany

Ferdinand Porsche evolved the idea of a 'Volkswagen' or peoples' car in the early 1930s and it became a reality just before World War II when production was diverted to military use.

After the war production of civilian vehicles resumed, concentrating at first on the ubiquitous 'Beetle', based on the original 'Volkswagen' but gradually extending into other private and commercial vehicles. The current range is an impressive one and some models have come a long way from the original, very basic and somewhat spartan 'peoples' car'.

Beetle

Data: 1200L
Length: 13ft 4.5in
Width: 5ft 1in
Height: 4ft 4in

Below: *Volkswagen Beetle of the Bavarian Police.*
The Bavarian Minister of the Interior

Wheelbase: 8ft
T/circle: 11m
Tyres: 5.60×15
Kerb weight: 820kg
Fuel tank: 8.8gal
Engine: 1,192cc four-cylinder ohv (Bore 77mm×Stroke 64mm) 34bhp (DIN). Compression ratio 7:1. Solex carburettor. Air-cooled engine at rear
Transmission: Four-speed manual gearbox
Suspension: Independent all round by torsion bars
Brakes: Drums all round

The original beetle-shaped Volkswagen is known variously as the Beetle (GB), Coccinelle (France), Käfer (Germany), Kever (Holland), Bug (USA) and other local variations on the same theme. One of the great motoring phenomena of our time, the Beetle continued in production from about 1938 to 1977 — nearly 40 years — and its origins were still clearly recognisable after all this time.

Early Beetles used a 1,200cc engine (air-cooled) which was later complemented by a 1,300cc version and, in 1966, by a 1,500cc model. The latter was uprated to 1,600cc in 1970.

The list of police users seems endless — the municipal forces in Ghent, Antwerp and Liège in Belgium (control of traffic), the Bavaria and Schelswig-Holstein Police in West Germany, the Austrian Police, the Monaco Police, Oslo City Police in Norway, the Swedish State Police, the city of Zurich and the cantons of Geneva and Vaud in Switzerland, the City of Hague Police in Holland, the Jordan Police, the Royal Oman Police, the Punjab Police in India, the Singapore Police and the Bahamas Police. The Beetle is mainly used to sort out traffic problems in the larger cities but other uses include CID (Bavaria, Zurich, Geneva), officers' use (Jordan) and harbour patrol section (Monaco).

Golf

Length: 12ft 2in
Width: 5ft 4in
Height: 4ft 7.5in
Wheelbase: 7ft 10.5in
T/circle: 34ft 4in
Tyres: 145×13
Fuel tank: 10gal
Max speed: 90mph approx
Engine: 1,093cc four-cylinder ohc (Bore 69.5mm×Stroke 72mm) 50bhp (DIN). Compression ratio 8:1. Down draught carburettor
Transmission: Four-speed manual gearbox
Suspension: Independent all round by coil springs
Brakes: Servo-assisted discs (front) and drums (rear)

Below: *Volkswagen Golf in the green/white colours of the German police.*

The Golf came on the scene in 1974 as a front-wheel drive saloon with a water-cooled, front-mounted engine and a choice of three or five doors. The rear seats fold to convert the car into a near estate. Original specification gave a choice of 1.1 or 1.5 litre engines which have been supplemented by a 1,600cc fuel-injection version. The name, in fact, is German for 'Gulf' and refers to a type of wind.

Since its introduction the Golf has been taken into use by the West German forces in Schleswig-Holstein, West Berlin and North Rhine-Westphalia and by the Austrian Police. In Belgium, the municipal force in Liège use them for traffic control whilst in Holland the Rijkspolitie use the diesel version. The city forces in the Hague and in Oslo use Golfs and in Switzerland the Vaud Cantonal Police, the Geneva police and the Valais Cantonal Police also use them. Another user is the Rikspolisstyrelsen or National Swedish Police Board.

Kombi

Length: 15ft 2in
Width: 5ft 8.5in
Height: 6ft 6.5in
Wheelbase: 8ft
Kerb weight: 1,305kg (1.6litre)
1,325kg (2litre)
Payload: 995kg (1.6litre)
975kg (2litre)

Max speed: 66mph (1.6litre)
76mph (2 litre)
Engine: 1.6litre — 1,584cc four-cylinder air cooled
50bhp (DIN) at 3,800rpm
2litre — 1,970cc four-cylinder air cooled 70bhp
(DIN) at 4,200rpm
Suspension: Independent by torsion bars
Brakes: Discs (front) and drums (rear)

Below: *Volkswagen Kombi accident investigation vehicle of the Bavarian Police.*
The Bavarian Minister of the Interior

Bottom: *Volkswagen Kombi of the Utrecht City Police.* Gemeentepolitie Utrecht

Vehicles of around one ton capacity, both vans and personnel carriers, are extremely popular with police forces as they combine reasonable carrying capacity (about 10 men in mini-bus versions) with speed and manoeuvrability. The VW Kombi is one such vehicle which has been taken into use by police forces all

over the world as patrol vehicle, accident investigation, CID, dog section and general transport for men and materials. It is a very practical vehicle with a sliding door in the side and a large door at the rear affording easy access. In its personnel-carrier guise it will seat up to nine persons in comfort and the seats can be removed by simply unscrewing two butterfly nuts to transform the vehicle into a practical load carrier. Two engine options are available — 1.6litre or 2litre air-cooled units.

VW Kombis are used by just about every police force in West Germany including the Bundesgrenzschutz (Federal Border Police). In Belgium they are used by the Gendarmerie Belge and by many of the municipal forces (eg Ghent, Liège), whilst in Holland they are used by the Rijkspolitie and by many city forces (eg Utrecht, The Hague). In Switzerland the cantonal forces in the Valais and Vaud and the Zurich City Police use Kombis, as do the Liechtenstein Police. The Rikspolis in Sweden and several forces in Norway use them, as do the Austrian Police. Further afield Kombis may be found in use with the Cyprus Police, the Royal Malaysian Police, the Jamaica Constabulary, the Australian Capital Territory Police and also the Sierra Leone Police.

Passat

Length: 14ft 4in
Width: 5ft 4.5in
Height: 4ft 6in (Estate slightly shorter and higher)
Kerb weight: 860kg (two-door)
885kg (four-door)
920kg (Estate)
Max speed: 90mph (1.3litre)
100mph approx (1.6litre)
Engine: 1.3litre — 1,297cc four-cylinder water cooled ohc 55bhp (DIN) at 5,500rpm
1.6litre — 1,588cc four-cylinder water cooled ohc 75bhp (DIN) at 5,600rpm
Transmission: Four-speed manual or automatic gearbox
Suspension: Front — Independent by coil springs
Rear — Beam axle and coil springs
Brakes: Servo-assisted, dual circuit, discs (front) and drums (rear)

Another VW named after a wind, the Passat is a five-door hatchback saloon or even more commodious estate. The smooth but lively engine runs on 91 octane fuel and the front bumper is made of deformable plastic which will absorb light traffic contacts. The Passat seats up to five persons and can be supplied in the German police colours of green and white, fitted with radio-mountings, roof unit containing loud-hailers and flashing lamp and two-tone horns. Drive is by a front-mounted, water-cooled engine driving the front wheels.

In West Germany, the Passat is used by the police in the 'Länder' of Baden-Württemberg, Schleswig-Holstein, Hamburg, North Rhine-Westphalia, and also by the Bundesgrenzschutz. Passats are also used in Austria, Sweden, Portugal, Switzerland (Geneva, Vaud and Valais cantons) and by the city forces in Antwerp and The Hague.

Below: *Volkswagen Passat.*

Polo/Derby

Length: 11ft 6in
12ft 8in (Derby)
Width: 5ft 1in
Height: 4ft 5in
Wheelbase: 7ft 9.5in
T/circle: 10m
Tyres: 145SR×13
Kerb weight: 712kg
Fuel tank: 8gal
Max speed: 85mph approx
Engine: 895cc — Four-cylinder water cooled ohc 40bhp (DIN). Compression ratio 8.2:1. Solex down draught carburettor
1,093cc — Four-cylinder water cooled ohc 50bhp (DIN). Compression ratio 8:1. Solex carburettor
Suspension: Coil springs all round, independent at front

The Polo is a three-door hatchback which needs major servicing at only 10,000-mile intervals and runs on 91 octane fuel. Two engine sizes are available, both mounted transversely at the front where they drive the front wheels through four-speed manual gearboxes. Weight has been minimised by the use of light alloy radiators and magnesium sumps and the finish is to VWs exacting standards. The rear seat folds to provide almost estate car advantages through the tailgate. The rear suspension uses a novel system of torsional cross-shaft with trailing arms. Since its introduction in 1975, the Polo has proved itself to be a useful little car and has been taken into use by the police for urban patrols. Current users include the Austrian Police and the city forces in Oslo and the Hague. The Liège city police in Belgium use the Derby, which is essentially a Polo with a boot added to the body to make it into a three-box car instead of a hatchback.

Dune Buggy

Based on the original 'Beetle', Dune Buggies are constructed by specialist firms for sporting and leisure activities. The Los Angeles County Sheriff was not slow in recognising the value of these vehicles for carrying out beach patrols which, in a State where much of the population practically lives on, or occupies houses fronting on to the extensive, sandy beaches, form a major occupation.

Details of these vehicles vary according to the firm carrying out the adaptations but the basic specification is the same as for the Beetle.

Below: *Volkswagen Dune Buggy of the Los Angeles County Sheriff's Dept on beach patrol.*
Los Angeles County Sheriff

Volvo

Sweden

The first Volvo car was produced in 1927 and was designed specifically for the Scandinavian market. However, it was Volvo's trucks which made their name outside Scandinavia and the export of cars did not really get under way until the 1950s. The model then in production was the PV444 which remained the mainstay of the company from 1944 to 1958. In the latter year the PV544, a thoroughly revised version of the PV444 made its appearance and sales continued for another seven years, until the arrival of the 121/122S or, as it was known in Scandinavia, the Amazon.

All Volvos have earned a reputation for durability and economy, despite the bad roads which exist in the northern region. The 121/122S also represented a new systematic and advanced line of safety thinking in car manufacture which has been continued ever since. Volvos are probably the safest cars on the road today. In the early 1970s, Volvo bought shares in the Dutch DAF firm which is now, Volvo Car BV, a subsidiary of the Volvo Group of Companies.

140/240 Series

Length: 16ft 0in
Width: 5ft 7.75in
Height: 4ft 8.25in
Wheelbase: 8ft 8in
G/clearance: 7in
T/circle: 32ft 2in
Tyres: 185/70SR×14
Kerb weight: 2,830lb
Fuel tank: 13.25gal
Max speed: 100mph approx
Engine: 2,127cc four-cylinder ohc 100bhp (DIN) at 5,250rpm. Compression ratio 8.5:1
Transmission: Four-speed manual gearbox with overdrive
Suspension: Front — Independent by MacPherson

struts, coil springs, shock absorbers and anti-roll bars
Rear — Live axle with coil springs, longitudinal control arms and torque rods, shock absorbers and roll bar
(HD estate car springing used on police versions)
Brakes: Vacuum servo-assisted, dual circuit, hydraulic
Front — 10.25in diameter ventilated discs
Rear — 11in diameter discs
The handbrake operates drum brakes fitted to the rear wheels through mechanical linkage

Below: *Volvo 144 of the Iceland Police.*
Iceland Police

The 144 saloon replaced the 121/122S range in 1966 and with it came the now famous triangle-split braking system which retains up to 80% of full braking power, even if only one circuit is in operation. Other safety features included the energy-absorbing front and rear body sections, the split safety columns and the burst-proof door locks which stay closed even in a serious collision. The 144 was closely followed by the 145 estate car version and both remained in production until 1974 when they were replaced by the 240 series (244 saloon/245 estate). The 240 series made full use of the success of the 140 series but added refinements of its own, such as a lengthened front end and built-in front and rear crumple zones which prevent the engine from entering the passenger compartment in the event of a collision. The fuel tank is moved close to the rear axle to protect it from damage in the event of a tail crash.

With such an accent on safety, coupled with excellent road-holding and powerful engines, it is not surprising that Volvos have proved the choice of many police forces, especially for main road and motorway patrols. The estate version, in particular,

89

can carry an enormous amount of police equipment for use at the scene of accidents and catastrophies. To cater for this demand Volvo offer specially adapted police versions of their cars in which all embellishments are removed and the carpeting replaced by rubber matting. The seats are the heavy duty Volvo taxi seats and the driver's is thermostatically heated. An anti-spin differential gives a better grip on slippery surfaces. Police versions use the Bosch continuous fuel injection system which was specially conceived for Volvo and Porsche and has no electronic parts, relying on a

Above: *Volvo 244GL.*

vacuum principle which makes for simple design, quiet running and reliability.

Police forces using either the 140 or 240 Series include all those in the Scandinavian countries, several British forces, the Indonesian National Police, the Kenya Police, the Peruvian Civil Guard, some of the Swiss forces, the Greek Genarmerie, the Liechtenstein Security Corps, the Royal Malaysia Police, the Singapore Police and the Icelandic Police.

160/260 Series

Dimensions: As for 240 series
Tyres: 175SR × 14
Kerb weight: 1,390kg
Max speed: Over 100mph
Engine: 2,664cc V6 ohc (Bore 88mm × Stroke 73mm) 125bhp (DIN). Compression ratio 8.7:1.
Transmission: Four-speed manual with overdrive or optional automatic gearbox
Suspension: As for 240 series
Brakes: As for 240 series

The 160 Series (164 saloon, 165 estate) was introduced in 1968, offering a bigger, more powerful alternative to the 140 Series, but with all the safety

features which had made Volvo's name. In 1975 it was replaced by the 260 series (264 and 265) using a 2.7litre V6 engine.

Like the 240 Series, the 260 Series cars are fitted with daytime 'running lights' which are automatically turned on with the ignition. The interior is luxuriously trimmed with wide, comfortable seats. The six-cylinder engine is a product of the Renault-Peugeot-Volvo 'cooperative' which makes the 2.7litre, light-alloy units in Northern France for all three firms.

Police users of the 260 series include the Durham Constabulary and the Vaud Cantonal Police in Switzerland.

343

Length: 14ft 9.25in
Width: 5ft 4.5in
Height: 4ft 9.5in
Wheelbase: 7ft 10.25in
T/circle: 9.2m
Tyres: 155SR × 13
Kerb weight: 979kg
Fuel tank: 10gal
Engine: Renault — 1,397cc four-cylinder ohv (Bore 76mm × Stroke 77mm) 70bhp (DIN).
Compression ratio 9.5:1. Down draught carburettor
Transmission: Four-speed manual or automatic gearbox

Suspension: Front — Independent by coil springs
Rear — de Dion axle with single leaf spring
Brakes: Servo-assisted, dual circuit, discs (front) and drums (rear)

When the Volvo 343 was unveiled in the spring of 1976, it was the first completely new car to result from the cooperation between the technicians at Volvo Car BV in Eindhoven (formerly DAF) and Volvo in Gothenburg.

The 343 has many excellent features. In spite of its compact exterior dimensions, there is plenty of room inside. The large hatchback and the folding rear seats mean that space can be used effectively for both passengers and luggage.

The 343 originally only used the continuously variable automatic transmission which is unique to cars from the former DAF factory but a four-speed manual box is now also available, fitted directly over the rear axle to maintain an ideal weight distribution. Volvo 343s are used by some of the Dutch Municipal Police forces, including, not surprisingly, that in Eindhoven.

C303 Cross Country

Length: 14ft 0in
Width: 6ft 3in
Height: 7ft 8in
Wheelbase: 7ft 5in
G/clearance: 15in
T/circle: 11.46m
Tyres: 280/85 × 16 4PR
Kerb weight: 2,250kg
Payload: 1,200kg
Climbing ability: 45deg
Fording depth: 27.5in
Max speed: 72mph
Engine: 2,980cc six-cylinder in-line ohv (Bore 88.9mm × Stroke 88mm) 125hp (DIN) at 4,250rpm. Two carburettors
Transmission: Four-speed manual all-synchromesh gearbox with two-speed transfer box
Suspension: Front — Underslung semi-elliptical leaf springs. Hollow rubber springs
Rear — Overslung semi-elliptical leaf springs. Hollow rubber springs
Double acting shock absorbers front and rear
Brakes: Vacuum-hydraulic drums front and rear. Triangle split dual circuit system, one vacuum cylinder per circuit. Anti-skid by engaging four-wheel drive when braking. Mechanical handbrake acting on propeller shaft

The Volvo C303 is a vehicle that has been specifically designed for advanced military and civilian cross-country transportation purposes and is used by Scandinavian forces and also the Royal Malaysian Police. It gives excellent riding comfort when running on ordinary road surfaces but its four-wheel drive makes it a true cross-country vehicle. The engine is located centrally and the passengers/cargo are placed directly above and between the axles, giving an ideal weight distribution both empty and loaded.

The C303 can be built and equipped to suit various types of jobs but there are two basic versions — Hardtop and Canvas top. Both have the same all-steel driving cab with opening windscreen. The rear of the hardtop can seat five persons on two folding seats and a bench transversely behind them.

Below: *Volvo C303.*

Volvo 66

Length: 12ft 9.75in
Width: 5ft 0.5in
Height: 4ft 6.5in
Wheelbase: 7ft 4.5in
G/clearance: 6.75in
T/circle: 9.4m
Tyres: 155SR × 13
Kerb weight: 835kg
Fuel tank: 9.25gal
Max speed: 85mph approx
Engine: 1,289cc four-cylinder ohv (Bore 73mm × Stroke 77mm) 57bhp (DIN). Compression ratio 8.5:1. Solex carburettor
Transmission: Variomatic gearbox
Suspension: Front — Independent torsion bars

Rear — de Dion axle, single leaf spring
Brakes: Servo-assisted, dual circuit, discs (front) and drums (rear)

Originally the DAF 66, this lively little automatic became the Volvo 66 after the Volvo take-over of the Dutch firm. It used the Renault 1.3litre engine and the 'Variomatic' continuously variable automatic transmission. Typically Volvo, the 66 bristled with aids to safety, including energy-absorbing bumpers but production ceased in 1978.

No doubt-because of its local connections, a number of municipal police forces in Holland use the 66 for patrol and CID work, including Rotterdam and Eindhoven.

Yue Loong Motor Company   Taiwan

The Yue Loong Motor Company is a small manufacturer of cars, somewhat on the Japanese lines. The registered office of the company is at 150

Nanking E. Road, Section 2, Taipeh, Taiwan, Republic of China.

YLN 803/803SD

Length: 15ft 8.25in
Width: 5ft 6.5in
Height: 4ft 8.75in
Wheelbase: 8ft 10in
G/clearance: 7in
T/circle: 11m
Tyres: 175SR × 14
Kerb weight: 1,395kg
Fuel tank: 67litre
Max speed: over 100mph
Engine: 2,393cc six-cylinder ohc (Bore 83mm × Stroke 73.7mm) 130bhp at 5,600rpm (SAE). Compression ratio 8.6:1. Two-barrel carburettor
Transmission: Four-speed manual gearbox
Suspension: Front — Independent double-action coil springs

Rear — Semi-elliptic leaf springs, double action telescopic shock absorbers and torsion bar stabilisers front and rear
Brakes: Servo-assisted, dual circuit, discs (front) and drums (rear)

The 803SD was introduced in October 1977 to replace the 803 which was a 2litre saloon. The mechanical specifications of the two are similar except the 803SD now has a 2.4litre engine and is fitted with power steering. Both models are used by the Taipeh Municipal Police.

Below: *YLN 803 SD of the Taipeh Municipal Police, Taiwan.* Taipeh Municipal Police

BMW

West Germany

Over 50 years of well tried tradition with constant modernisation and design development result in BMW producing powerful and comfortable machines which are outstanding examples of motorcycling engineering. The basic design of a horizontally-opposed, twin-cylinder engine with shaft drive has not changed since the R32 model was displayed at the 1923 Paris Motor Show.

The company originally made aircraft engines and did not go into motorcycle production until the 1920s. Since then they have pioneered a number of innovations including shaft drive, hydraulically damped forks, perforated disc brakes and electric starters.

Head Office — Bayerische Motoren Werke, Motorrad GmbH, 8 München 40, Völckerstrasse 9, West Germany.

R45

Length: 6ft 11.1in
Width: 2ft 3.1in
Seat height: 2ft 6.3in
Wheelbase: 4ft 6.7in
Weight: 452lb (dry)
Fuel tank: 4.84gal
Max speed: Over 90mph
Engine: 473.4cc horizontally opposed 180deg twin Compression ratio 9.2:1. Wet sump. Two Bing V64/11 carburettors. 35bhp (DIN) at 7,250rpm.
Transmission: Single plate clutch and five-speed gearbox driving rear wheels
Suspension: Telescopic two-way damped front forks. Pivoted rear forks with three position spring pre-load adjustment
Brakes: Front — Single 10.25in perforated disc Rear — 8in drum

The latest and smallest addition to the BMW range, the R45 only appeared in 1978 but has already been taken into use by a number of police forces in West Germany. Based on the more sophisticated, larger models, the quality, reliability and finish are in accordance with BMW's high standards. Retaining the flat-twin cylinder engine which has proved so successful, new styling and new frame geometry with very low seats have been developed for the R45/R65. Coupled with the narrower engine, this ensures above average handling. The aluminium wheels give optimum safety thanks to their CP safety profile which, in the event of a puncture, prevents the tyre from slipping into the wheel rim well.

R50/60/65

Details: As for R45
Max speed: Over 100mph
Engine: 649cc four-stroke ohv flat twin, 45bhp (DIN) at 7,250rpm. Compression ratio 9.2:1. Wet sump. Two Bing 32mm V64/11 carburettors.

The R60 specification was similar except the engine was 599cc, producing 40bhp and drum brakes were used front and rear.

The R50 (500cc) model was one of BMW's most popular machines until 1973 when it was replaced by the R60/5 with 600cc engine. Both of these are widely used by police forces throughout the world including most, if not all the West German forces, the French and Greek Gendarmeries, the French Police Nationale, several of the Swiss cantonal and city forces, the Monaco Sûreté Publique, the Danish Police, the Argentine Policia Federal, the Austria Police, the Cyprus Police, the Liechtenstein Security Corps, the Malta Police, the Central Scotland Police, the Eindhoven and Antwerp City Police (solos and combinations) and the City of London Police. The

Right: *BMW R50 of the Danish Police.*

R60 has now been superseded by the R65 which first appeared in 1978 with the redesigned frame as used on the R45 and a 650cc engine. It is anticipated that users of the R50 and R60 will, in future, go for either the R45 or the R65, depending

Above: *BMW R60 of the Monaco Police.*
Sûreté Publique de Monaco

on whether they need the lighter 475cc model or the more powerful 650cc R65.

R75/R80

Length: 7ft 3in
Width: 2ft 5.4in
Seat height: 2ft 7.9in
Wheelbase: 4ft 9.7in
Weight: 480lb
Fuel tank: 5.25gal

Max speed: 107mph approx
Engine: 797.5cc, four-stroke, horizontally opposed twin-cylinder. ohv (Bore 84.8mm x Stroke 70.6mm)

Below: *BMW R75 of the Kent County Constabulary.*
Kent County Constabulary

55bhp. Compression ratio 9.2:1. Two 32mm Bing carburettors
Transmission: Five gears, shaft drive
Suspension: Front — Telescopic forks
Rear — Twin sprung dampers
Brakes: Front — Discs (double discs from 1979)
Rear — Drum

The 750cc R75 was in production from 1970 until 1978 when the R80/7, powered by an 800cc engine, replaced it. It is generally considered that the R80/7 represents the ideal medium size machine. Its special power and performance features make it ideal for touring and for main road patrol work. The massive torque available provides extremely good acceleration at all road speeds. From 1979 the R80/7 has been fitted with cast aluminium wheels and double disc brakes on the front wheel.

The list of police users is impressive, including as it does the West German Police in Bavaria, Baden-Würrtemberg, North Rhine-Westphalia and the Bundesgrenzschutz (Federal Border Police), the Dutch Rijkspolitie, the Swiss Police in the Cantons of Vaud, Geneva and Basle, the Carabineros de Chile, the Policia de Sergurança Publica of Portugal, the Utrecht, Rotterdam, Ghent and Oslo Municipal forces, the Rikspolis in Sweden, the Nigeria Police, the Directorate of Public Security in Jordan, the City of Winnipeg Police Department in Canada and 34 forces in the United Kingdom, including the London Metropolitan Police where some are ridden by policewomen.

R90/R100

Length: 7ft 3in
Width: 2ft 5.4in
Seat height: 2ft 8.3in
Wheelbase: 4ft 9.7in
Kerb weight: 485lb
Fuel tank: 5.25gal
Max speed: Over 120mph
Engine: 980cc four-stroke, horizontally opposed flat twin ohv (Bore 94mm × Stroke 70.6mm) 70bhp at 7,250rpm. Compression ratio 9.5:1. Two Bing V94 carburettors (40mm)

Transmission: Five-speed gearbox, shaft drive to rear wheel
Suspension: Front — Telescopic forks with double-action hydraulic dampers
Rear — Twin sprung dampers
Brakes: Front — Perforated double disc 10.2in diameter
Rear — Perforated single disc 10.2in diameter

Top of the BMW range, the 900cc R90 was in production until 1977 but has now been superseded by the R100 range. There are, in fact, four versions of the R100; the R100T (formerly R100/7) standard machine with a 65bhp engine, the R100S with a 70bhp power unit, R100RT developed specifically for the touring rider with an all-round fairing, R100RS the pinnacle of motor cycling luxury with integral

Below: *BMW R90 of the Bavarian Police, fitted with 'Traffipax' and folding 'Polizie' sign.*

Below right: *BMW R100S.*

fairing and dashboard, finished in either gold or silver/blue metallic paintwork. Users of the R90 include the Belgian Gendarmerie, the Vaud Cantonal Police (Switzerland), the Humberside Police (UK) and the Baden-Württemberg and Bavarian Police in West Germany. The Bavarian Police have already started to replace their R90s with the R100S and it is anticipated that this version will be the most popular

for police work. The R100 features a special torsion damper integrated into the drive shaft power transmission and cast-alloy wheels (in common with the R45 and R65). The R100S is fitted with a quartz clock, luggage support, high rise handlebars and cylinder protection bars. Next to the R100RS, it is the sportiest machine in the BMW range.

BSA   UK

The BSA (Birmingham Small Arms) Motor Cycle Company, which derived from a group of gun-makers, was formed in 1861, continuing to make only weapons until about 1880 when it branched out into the manufacture of bicycles. The first BSA motorcycle appeared in 1910 and the company became one of the foremost motorcycle manufacturers in England and throughout the world. In 1951, BSA took over the Triumph motorcycle company and, in 1971 the BSA plant at Small Heath, Birmingham, transferred production to the Triumph

factory at Meriden. Both Triumph and BSA machines were produced here until later the same year when production of BSA motorcycles ceased. In 1973 the BSA interests were taken over by Norton Villiers Triumph Limited.

BSA motorcycles were popular with police forces in Great Britain and elsewhere and a number remain in use throughout the world, although the number is gradually diminishing as the older machines are replaced — often by Japanese products.

BSA 250 Star

Engine: 247cc, single-cylinder four-stroke
Transmission: Four-speed, chain drive
Suspension: Telescopic forks.
Brakes: Drums front and rear.

This lightweight 250cc machine has always been popular with police forces for patrolling both urban and rural areas where speed is not essential. Although not produced for a number of years, a number of BSA 250s are still in service in the UK — a tribute to their longevity and reliability.

BSA A50 Royal Star

T/circle: 12ft 6in
Weight: 385lb
Fuel tank: 4gal
Engine: 499cc four-stroke vertical twin-cylinder 28.5bhp
Transmission: Four-speed, constant mesh gearbox. Wet clutch. Chain drive

This 500cc twin is an honest, rather unspectacular performer, whose merit lies in reliability and safety. Designed as a comfortable touring machine, the A50 was adopted by a number of police forces which sought reliability rather than high performance (although with a top speed around 95mph it is no sluggard.) Examples remain in use in Greece, Cyprus and the Gambia.

BSA A65/A65T Range

Below: *BSA A65 of the Luxembourg Police.* Corps de la Police Luxembourgoise

Length: 7ft 1.25in
Wheelbase: 4ft 7.5in
Tyres: 3.25 × 19 (front) 4.00 × 18 (rear)
G/clearance: 8.5in
Weight: 391lb
Fuel tank: 3.5gal
Engine: 654cc four stroke twin cylinder (Bore 75mm × Stroke 74mm). Compression ratio 9:1. Single Amal monobloc carburettor
Transmission: Four-speed foot change constant mesh gearbox. Wet multiplate clutch. Chain drive to rearwheel

Brakes: Front — 8in single leading shoe.
Rear — 7in single leading shoe.

The A65 range, fitted with the powerful 650 twin-cylinder engine, was the most powerful and luxurious of the whole BSA fleet before its sadly lamented demise. The range included the Rocket, Lightning, Star as well as the Thunderbolt.

This latter machine, finished in all black paintwork, was a well made touring machine favoured by a number of police forces and remaining in use in Cyprus and in Luxembourg.

Ducati

Italy

A comparative newcomer to the field of motorcycle manufacture, Ducati only began in 1954, concentrating on lightweight machines and scooters. The firm has since established themselves as experts with single and vee-twin racers which have given birth to similar road machines. Latest developments have been with parallel twin machines.

Ducati was nationalised in 1969 and most of its products are sold on the home market, although some are exported, notably to France, UK and North America.

Head Office — Ducati Meccanica SpA, Casella Postale 313, 40100 Bologna, Italy.

Ducati 450/500cc

Length: 6ft 9.9in
Seat height: 2ft 4.6in
Wheelbase: 4ft 7.1in
G/clearance: 6.7in
Weight: 374lb (dry)

Above: *Ducati 500cc twin of the Vigili Urbani, Bologna.*

Fuel tank: 2.5gal
Max speed: Over 100mph

Engine: 496cc four-stroke, twin-cylinder ohc, (Bore 78mm × Stroke 52mm). 39.5bhp. Compression ratio 10:1. Two 30mm Dell 'Orto carburettors.
Transmission: Five-speed gearbox
Suspension: Front Telescopic forks.Twin sprung dampers
Brakes: Front — Disc
Rear — Drum

Still in use with the Vigili Urbani (City Police) in a number of Italian towns, the 450cc, single-cylinder

machine dates from about 1970 and is no longer in production, being replaced by the 500cc twin. A special version of the Ducati 500 known as the 500 'Vigil Urbani' is available for police work. It uses the standard parallel twin-cylinder engine with over head camshaft and is fitted with a siren (electrically operated), drum brakes on rear wheel, and is fitted with a single seat behind which is a platform for radio mounting. Two capacious pannier boxes provide storage for the essential bits and pieces required by police riders.

Ducati 750/900cc

Length: 7ft 2.6in
Seat height: 2ft 7.4in
Wheelbase: 4ft 11.8in
G/clearance: 7in
Weight: 450lb (dry)
Max speed: Over 115mph
Engine: 864cc four-stroke, vee-twin ohc (Bore 86mm × Stroke 74.4mm) 74bhp. Compression ratio 9.5:1. Two 32mm Dell 'Orto carburettors
Transmission: Five-speed gearbox
Suspension: Front — Telescopic forks
Rear — Twin sprung dampers
Brakes: Disc brakes front and rear (twin front discs on 900 models)

The 750cc vee-twin was introduced in 1974 and was soon taken into use with the Vigili Urbani of several Italian towns. The 750cc has now been replaced by the 860 and 900 models, both of which use the same 864cc engine but have slightly different degrees of tuning, etc. The police versions are fitted out in a similar manner to the 500cc range.

Below: *Ducati 750cc of the Vigili Urbani, Bologna.*

Enfield
India

Enfield India was founded in 1955 when, in collaboration with the Enfield Cycle Company of Redditch, England (makers of the Royal Enfield motorcycles) it was set up to assemble the 350cc Bullet and 150cc Royal Enfield machines. The 350cc Bullet is now manufactured in its entirety in the

factory near Madras and is used on the home market as well as being exported to several Third World countries.

Head Office — The Enfield India Limited, 3B Eldams Road, Madras 600-018.

350cc Bullet

Length: 6ft 11in
Width: 2ft 3in
Height: 3ft 6in
Wheelbase: 4ft 6in
G/clearance: 5.5in
Weight: 163kg
Engine: 346cc four-stroke single-cylinder ohv (Bore 70mm x Stroke 90mm) 18bhp at 5,625rpm. Compression ratio 6.5:1
Transmission: Four-speed gearbox, chain drive to rear wheel
Suspension: Front — Telescopic hydraulic forks
Rear — Swinging arm suspension with telescopic, oil damped units
Brakes: Drums front and rear

The 350cc Bullet has been made the exclusive, standard machine for the Indian Defence forces, the police and the Border Security Force. They are also used by the armies of Nepal, Bangladesh and Nigeria. The original Royal Enfield Bullet was first developed in the 1930s and was used extensively for military purposes during World War II. After the war both 350cc and 500cc versions were available featuring the then novel swinging arm rear suspension. Production of all Royal Enfield bikes finally ceased in 1970 and the products of Enfield India are the sole survivors. They have changed very little over the years and the present day Bullet bears a very close resemblance to the early postwar models. A 'Casquelle' fork head houses head and parking lamps, speedo, ammeter and switch.

Harley Davidson
USA

The Harley-Davidson Company was formed in 1907 by William Harley and his friends, the Davidson brothers. The cessation of motorcycle production in Europe between 1914/18 gave the American firm a big boost and, by 1918, 18,000 bikes were leaving the factory in Milwaukee each year.

During the 1930s Harley-Davidson became known for their huge, long-stroke vee-twins and the

WL 1,100cc side-valve became the first choice of the US forces in World War II. The postwar model featured hydraulic valve lifters and aluminium heads previously used only on aircraft engines.

Head Office — Harley-Davidson Motor Company Inc, 3700 W. Junean Avenue, PO Box 653, Milwaukee, W153201.

Model 45 Servi-car

Wheelbase: 5ft 1in
G/clearance: 5in
Weight: 925lb
Engine: 750cc four-stroke, vee-twin, side valve, air cooled
Transmission: Three-speed plus reverse. Dual rear wheel drive through a differential by chain
Suspension: Front — Hydra-Glide forks utilising long helical springs contained in main tubes, oil damped
Rear — Two helical leaf springs with two hydraulic shock absorbers
Brakes: Front — Hydraulically operated 10in disc, operated by handlebar lever
Rear — Bendix 9in hydraulic, right foot operated
Parking brake acts on right rear wheel

The Servi-car is a three-wheel machine using a motorcycle front end with a large container behind the saddle, supported by a wheel on each side. This configuration gives the Servi-car a small turning circle and stability coupled with extreme manoeurvrability. Optional equipment includes a hand or foot controlled siren, police calibrated speedo, flashing red or blue lights and radio speaker mounting. The storage compartment is made of fibreglass. The Ottawa Police in Canada and Hawaii County Police Department, amongst many others, use the Servi-car, mainly for parking control. Production ceased in 1973.

Electraglide Police Special

Wheelbase: 5ft 1.5in
G/clearance: 5in
Tyres: 5.10 × 16 (on safety rims)
Weight: 660lb
Fuel tank: 5gal
Max speed: 105mph approx

Below: *Harley-Davidson 'Electraglide' of the City of Philadelphia PD.*

Bottom: *Harley-Davidson 'Electraglide' of the Quebec Police.* Sûreté Provinciale de Quebec

Engine: 1,200cc four-stroke air-cooled vee-twin ohv
Transmission: Four-speed, foot change gearbox. Chain drive to rear wheel
Suspension: Front — Hydraulically damped forks Rear — Swing-arm type suspension with helical coil springs controlled by car-type shock absorbers
Brakes: Front — 10in diameter disc, hydraulically operated by right handlebar lever
Rear — 10in diameter disc, hydraulically operated by right foot pedal

The quintessential American police bike, familiar to all cinema-goers from the 1930s onwards, the 'Electraglide' Police Special is basically the 1,200cc civilian motorcycle with extras for police work includ-

ing sirens, pursuit lights (red and/or blue) 'police' signs, heavy duty suspension, radio-mounting and solo saddle (with extra heavy seat post to order).

Some US police forces no longer use motorcycles but the vast majority of those which do, use the 'Electraglide'. Similarly in Canada, nearly every force, from the RCMP to most city forces (Edmonton, Regina, Calgary, Vancouver, etc) use this machine. Elsewhere on the American continent, 'Electraglides' may be found in Puerto Rico and in El Salvador whilst, in Europe, they are used by the Greek Gendarmerie, the Swiss Police in the Vaud canton, the Cyprus police and the Icelandic Police. They can even be found in Africa where they are used by the Sierra Leone Police.

Hercules
West Germany

The Hercules factory was founded in 1905 and, in 1966, it merged with DKW, to create the biggest manufacturer of motorcycles in West Germany.

Exports are marketed under the DKW name.
Head Office — Zweirad Union AE, 85 Nürnberg 1, Nopitschstrasse 70.

K125BW

Max speed: 60mph approx
Engine: 122cc Sachs two-stroke, single-cylinder (Bore 54mm × Stroke 54mm). 198bhp at 8,800rpm. Compression ratio 11.8:1. Single 24mm Bing carburettor
Suspension: Front — Telescopic hydraulic forks with swinging arm
Rear — Swinging arm rear suspension with hydraulically damped coil springs
Transmission: Five-speed gearbox, chain drive to rear wheel
Brake: Drum brakes front and rear (5.5in diameter)

The K125BW is the principal machine used by the German Federal Forces and, as such, is used by the Bundesgrenzschutz (Federal Border Police) in their para-military role. It is a starkly functional cross-country machine, based on the very successful civilian trials bike.

Below: *Hercules K125 BW.*

Honda   Japan

Honda, which is now the world's largest manufacturer of motorcycles, only began in 1948, using war-surplus parts. By 1959 it had grown enormously and a subsidiary was established in the United States. Honda became involved in racing and, in 1966, won all five solo world championships.

Honda now produce over two million machines each year and almost half the total Japanese motorcycle exports are Hondas.

Head Office — Honda Motor Company Limited, 5 Yaesu 5-Chome, Chuo-Ku, Tokyo.

Honda C90

Length: 6ft
Seat height: 2ft 5in
Wheelbase: 3ft 11in
G/clearance: 5.25in
Tyres: 2.50×17
Weight: 74kg (dry)
Max speed: 50mph approx
Engine: 89.5cc four-stroke, single cylinder ohc (Bore 50mm×Stroke 45.6mm) 7.5bhp. Compression ratio 8.2:1. Single Keihen carburettor
Transmission: Three-speed gearbox, automatic clutch, chain drive to rear wheel
Suspension: Front — Leading link forks

Rear — Swinging arm suspension
Brakes: 4.5in drums front and rear

A lightweight machine, little bigger than one of Honda's famous mopeds, the C90 is a useful runabout and represents a step up for the policeman who previously used a pedal cycle to patrol his area and serve summonses etc.

Present police users are widely scattered, from Strathclyde in Scotland to Papua, New Guinea, from Washington DC to the Seychelles and back to Jamaica. A 50cc version is used in Antwerp and also in Cyprus.

Honda 175/185

Length: 6ft 5.25in
Width: 2ft 3.25in
Height: 3ft 4.25in
Tyres: 3.00×17
Kerb weight: 311lb
Fuel tank: 10litre
Max speed: Over 70mph
Engine: 180cc four-stroke twin-cylinder ohc 17bhp (DIN) at 9,500rpm. Compression ratio 9:1. One 22mm Keihen carburettor
Transmission: Four-speed gearbox, wet multi-plate clutch, chain drive
Suspension: Front — Telescopic forks

Rear — Swinging arm suspension
Brakes: 6in drums front and rear

A genuine lightweight motorcycle, the CD175 road machine was a popular choice until its replacement by the CD185 in 1978. A rapid economical means of transport, especially in urban areas, the CD175 or its successor have been taken into use by the Ottawa Police Force, the Punjab Police, the Devon and Cornwall Constabulary and Norfolk Constabulary in England and the Tayside and Strathclyde Police Forces in Scotland.

CB200

Length: 6ft 5in
Seat height: 2ft 6in
Wheelbase: 4ft 3.5in
G/clearance: 6in
Tyres: 2.75×18 (front) 3.00×18 (rear)
Weight: 132kg (dry)
Fuel tank: 9litre
Max speed: 75mph approx
Engine: 198cc four-stroke twin-cylinder ohc (Bore 55.5mm×Stroke 41mm) 17bhp at 9,000rpm. Compression ratio 9:1. Two 20mm Keihin carburettors. Electric starter
Transmission: Five-speed gearbox, wet multiplate clutch, chain drive
Suspension: Front — Telescopic forks
Rear — Swinging arm
Brakes: Front — 9.5in diameter disc
Rear — 6in diameter drum

The now obsolete CB200 was a delightful lightweight machine which offered just that little bit extra than the CD175. However, the up-rating of the latter to 180cc made the gap too narrow and the CB200 was dropped, leaving the 250cc models to represent the next step up.

Used by the police in Avon and Somerset, Gloucestershire, Hampshire, Kent and South Wales, it is also employed by the Grampian Police and the Northern Constabulary in Scotland and the Ottawa Police in Canada.

Above: *Honda CB200 of the Kent County Constabulary.* Kent County Constabulary

CB250

Length: 6ft 11.3in
Seat height: 2ft 8in
Wheelbase: 4ft 7.5in
Tyres: 3.60×19 (front) 4.10×18 (rear)
Kerb weight: 375lb
Max speed: Over 80mph
Engine: 249cc four-stroke twin-cylinder air-cooled ohc (Bore 64mm×Stroke 41.4mm) 27bhp (DIN) at 10,000rpm. Compression ratio 9.4:1. Two 28mm Keihin carburettors
Transmission: Six-speed gearbox, wet multiplate clutch, chain drive
Suspension: Front — Telescopic forks
Rear — Pivoted forks with two-stage FVQ damping system

Brakes: Front — Single hydraulically-operated 10.9in diameter disc
Rear — 6in diameter drum

Unlike most of its competitors, the Honda 250cc twin uses a four-stroke system which has been tried and tested over more than a decade. The six-valve, twin-cylinder configuration is unique to Honda and has proved very reliable in service.

Honda 250s are used by the Australian Capital Territory Police, the French Gendarmerie, the Geneva Police, the Seychelles Police, and Sussex Police, the Devon and Cornwall Constabulary and the Strathclyde Police.

Honda 350/360cc

Data: CB360
Engine: 365cc four-stroke twin-cylinder air-cooled
Transmission: Five-speed gearbox, wet multiplate clutch, chain drive to rear wheel
Suspension: Front — Telescopic forks
Rear — Swinging arm
Brakes: Drums front and rear

The Honda 350cc twin was in production during the early 1970s, being replaced by the 360cc model in 1976. Production has now ceased but a number of examples remain in use with police forces throughout the world, including the Guyana Police, the Bermuda Police, the Seychelles Police, the Austrian Police, the Botswana Police, the Western Samoa Police, the Dorset Police and the Antwerp Police.

Below: *Honda 350 of the Guyana Police.* Guyana Police

Honda 400/450/500cc Twins

Length: 7ft 10.5in
Seat height: 2ft 8in
Wheelbase: 4ft 7.5in
G/clearance: 5.5in
Tyres: 3.25×19 (front) 3.75×19 (rear)
Weight: 193kg (dry)
Fuel tank: 16litres
Max speed: 100mph approx
Engine: 498cc four-stroke air-cooled double ohc twin-cylinder (Bore 70mm×Stroke 64.8mm) 42bhp at 8,000rpm. Compression ratio 8.5:1. Two 32mm Keihen carburettors. Electric starter
Transmission: Five-speed gearbox, wet multiplate clutch, chain drive to rear wheel
Suspension: Front — Telescopic forks
Rear — Swinging arm

Brakes: Front — 230mm disc
Rear — 180mm drum

The Honda mid-range of motorcycles features both twin and four-cylinder machines. The first of these more powerful twins appeared in the 1960s as the CB450 which remained in production until 1972, when it gave way to the new range of four-cylinder models. It became apparent, however, that a number of motorcyclists still preferred the twin and so, in 1975, it was reintroduced as the CB500T with the engine increased from 450cc to 500cc. This model was dropped in 1977 and the CB400T Dream was introduced, developing into the CB400N Super Dream the following year.

These twin-cylinder machines made useful police bikes and one or other of these models is used in Basle, Switzerland (400cc), Bahrain, Guyana (450cc), Tasmania, Fiji, Singapore (450cc and 500cc), Bermuda, Liège and Eire (500cc).

Below: *Honda CB500 twin in Western Samoa.*

Honda 500/550cc Four-Cylinder

Data: CB550-K3
Length: 6ft 11.75in
Height: 3ft 5.5in
Tyres: 3.25×19 (front) 3.75×18 (rear)
Kerb weight: 463lb
Fuel tank: 3.5gal
Max speed: 110mph approx
Engine: 544cc four-stroke, four-cylinder air-cooled ohc (Bore 58.8mm×Stroke 50.6mm) 50bhp at 8,500rpm. Compression ratio 9:1. Four 22mm Keihin carburettors. Electric starter
Transmission: Five-speed gearbox, wet multiplate clutch, chain drive to rear wheel
Suspension: Front — Telescopic forks
Rear — Swinging arm with twin dampers
Brakes: Disc (front) and drum (rear)

Honda was one of the pioneers of four-cylinder machines of medium capacity, the CB500T being introduced in the early 1970s as a replacement for the twin-cylinder machines of like capacity. Variations on this theme have been played ever since, current models being the CB550-F2 and CB550K3. The four-cylinders give ample reserves of smooth cruising power, coupled with good economy. A police version has been available, similar to the bigger patrol machines, and users of the mid-range 'fours' include the Belize Police, New South Wales Police (Australia), the Cleveland Police (UK), Eindhoven Muncipal Police (Holland), the Cyprus Police, the Royal Malaysia Police and the Singapore Police.

Honda 750cc

Length: 7ft 5.5in
Seat height: 2ft 8in
Wheelbase: 4ft 10in
G/clearance: 5.5in
Tyres: 3.25×19 (front) 4.00×18 (rear)
Weight: 550lb
Fuel tank: 17litre
Max speed: Over 110mph
Engine: 736cc four-stroke four-cylinder air-cooled ohc (Bore 61mm×Stroke 63mm) 67bhp at 8,500rpm. Compression ratio 9.2:1. Four 28mm Keihin carburettors. Electric starter
Transmission: Five-speed gearbox, wet multiple clutch, chain final drive
Suspension: Front — Telescopic forks
Rear — Swinging arm
Brakes: Front — 12in diameter disc
Rear — 7in diameter drum

The Honda 750cc four-cylinder machines appeared in 1969 and represented the top of the Honda range until the introduction of the 1,000cc models in the mid-1970s. The current models are the CB750-K7 and CB750-F2. A 'Police Special' (CB750P-K7) is available.

The extra power of these motorcycles makes them well suited for main road patrols and it is noticeable that, where police departments in the States have deserted the traditional Harley-Davidson, it is for this type of machine. For example, Honda 750s are now used by the Los Angeles Police Department and the Puerto Rico Police and also by the Royal Canadian Mounted Police and the Winnipeg and Montreal municipal forces in Canada. In South America they are used by the Policia Federal of Argentina whilst in Australia they are in service with the Northern Territories Police, the Australian Capital Territories Police, the Western Australia Police and the Queensland Police. Other users include the Jordanian Police, the Ghent City Police (Belgium), the Gibraltar Police and the Garda Siochana in Eire. In England they are used by the police forces in Sussex, Greater Manchester, Bedfordshire, Cleveland and Durham. Last but by no means least, they are one of the mainstays of the Japanese Police.

Below: Honda 750-Four of the South Australia Police. South Australia Police.

Honda 1,000cc Gold Wing

Length: 7ft 7.5in
Height: 3ft 9in
Seat Height: 2ft 7in

Wheelbase: 5ft 1in
G/clearance: 6in
Tyres: 3.50×19 (front) 4.50×17 (rear)

Kerb weight: 635lb
Fuel tank: 19litre
Max speed: Over 125mph
Engine: 999cc four-stroke flat four-cylinder water cooled ohc (Bore 72mm×61.4mm) 80bhp at 7,500rpm (DIN). Compression ratio 9.2:1. Four 32mm Keihin carburettors. Electric starter
Transmission: Five-speed gearbox, semi-wet multiplate clutch, shaft drive
Suspension: Front — Telescopic forks
Rear — Swinging arm with twin sprung dampers
Brakes: Front — Twin, hydraulically operated discs, 10.5in diameter
Rear — Single hydraulically operated 11.5in disc

Pride of the Honda fleet is the huge, flat-four, water-cooled GL1000 'Gold Wing' which took the motorcycle world by storm when it first appeared in 1974. Since that time it has been taken into use by the Puerto Rico Police and the Dutch Rijkspolitie have been carrying out trials with some examples. In Houston, Texas, the police motorcycle patrols purchase their own machines for which they are paid an allowance; some have plumped for one of these 'Hyper-bikes'.

Honda/DLB

Below: *Honda/DLB emergency rescue bike.*

An interesting development is the road rescue motorcycle, based on the Honda 1,000cc Gold Wing, which has been developed by DLB, 61 Grande Rue, 59145 Berlaimont, France. The machine is fitted with a two-way radio, sirens, warning lights and a floodlight for night work. It also carries a Hurst power rescue tool for cutting metal work, an auxiliary engine with hydraulic pump, chains, hooks, power shears, flexible hose, two fire extinguishers (dry chemical type) and a full first-aid kit.

The manufacturers have chosen to base this specialist vehicle on the Honda 'Gold Wing' because of its compact layout, good power output and flexibility, capacity for stationary running (water/fan cooled) and the minimal maintenance required. A special frame is employed made of steel tubing with

brazed joints. A heavy duty parking stand is operated by a lever which incorporates the existing Honda kickstart pedal.

The realisation of a rescue motorcycle which conformed to vital specifications without resulting in monstrous proportions was a technological breakthrough. Only by taking a completely fresh approach, breaking away from tradition and making better use of space and materials has it been possible to obtain a solution to the problems such a project presented.

The constructors of this novel machine are now seeking to interest police and other emergency services in their project. A second, similar project will equip a motorcycle with full medical and resuscitation equipment.

Jawa-CZ

Czechoslovakia

Jawa motorcycles were first produced in 1929 and, in the early days, they used Villiers engines. After the war the Jawa factory was nationalised and concentrated on economy machines and some trial bikes.

The CZ factory has been making two-stroke engines since 1932 although in 1955 it started producing fast 125cc, 250cc and 350cc double overhead camshaft racing machines. Some 30,000 CZ motorcycles are produced each year and the factory at Strakonice makes the engines for all Jawa machines.

Factory — Jawa NP, Tynec n. Sazavou, Czechoslovakia.

Jawa CZ250

Length: 6ft 7.5in
Width: 2ft 2in
Height: 3ft 3.25in
Wheelbase: 4ft 4in
G/clearance: 8in
Tyres; 3.00 × 18 (front) 3.25 × 18 (rear)
Weight: 313lb (net)
Fuel tank: 3gal
Max speed: 75mph approx
Engine: 246cc two-stroke, twin-cylinder, (Bore 52mm × Stroke 58mm) 17bhp at 5,250rpm. Compression ratio 9.3:1
Transmission: Four-speed gearbox, chain drive to rear wheel
Suspension: Front — Telescopic forks

Rear — Swinging arm suspension
Brakes: 160mm diameter drums front and rear

The excellent handling and roadholding offered by the semi-duplex frame and race-proved geometry of the 250cc two-stroke twin has prompted the police in Nottinghamshire, Staffordshire and Lothian and Borders, as well as the Cyprus Police, to adopt these machines for police work. They are also used by the police in their native Czechoslovakia and certain other East European countries, but details of such use is more difficult to come by.

Below: *Jawa-CZ250 de luxe.*

Jawa CZ350

Length: 6ft 10in
Width: 2ft 4in
Height: 4ft 6in

Wheelbase: 4ft 5in
G/clearance: 8in
Tyres: 3.25 × 18 (front) 3.50 × 18 (rear)

Weight: 346lb (net)
Fuel tank: 3.5gal
Max speed: Over 80mph
Engine: 349cc two-stroke, twin-cylinder air cooled (Bore 58mm × Stroke 65mm) 28bhp at 5,250rpm. Compression ratio 9.3:1
Transmission: Four-speed gearbox, chain drive to rear wheel
Suspension: Front — Telescopic forks

Rear — Swinging arm suspension
Brakes: 6.25in diameter discs front and rear

The Jawa 350cc twin incorporates a full duplex frame, trafficators and a fully enclosed chain. It is also available as a combination known in Britain as the 350 Javelin. Police users of the 350 (outside the Eastern bloc) include the Cyprus Police and the Greek Gendarmerie.

Kawasaki   Japan

A newcomer to the motorcycle manufacture field, Kawasaki produced their first machine in 1968 but have now made such great strides that they are counted among the 'Big Four' Japanese motorcycle constructors.

Originally shipbuilders and railway rolling stock builders, the Kawasaki company now has interests in aircraft and commercial vehicles as well as general engineering and their motorcycles are assembled in a former aircraft factory at Akashi. A subsidiary factory has been opened in the United States and there are plans to open others in various parts of the world.

Head Office — Kawasaki Heavy Industries, Nissei Kawasaki Building, 16-1 Nakamachi-dori, 2-Chome, Ikuta-ku, Kobe-shi, Hyogo-Ken, Japan.

Kawasaki 200cc

Tyres: 2.75 × 18 (front) 3.25 × 17 (rear)
Weight: 278lb (dry)
Fuel tank: 2gal
Max speed: 70mph approx
Engine: 198cc four-stroke single-cylinder air-cooled ohc (Bore 65mm × Stroke 58mm) 18bhp. Compression ratio 9:1. One 28mm Mikuni carburettor
Transmission: Five gears, chain drive to rear wheel
Suspension: Front — Telescopic forks
Rear — Swinging arm suspension with twin sprung dampers

Brakes: Front — Mechanical single disc
Rear — Drum

Intended as a lightweight commuter machine, the 200 is in fact a lively all round performer with many of the refinements of its larger relations, such as electric starter and disc front brake.

A useful general purpose machine for the police, it is used as such by the Monaco Sûreté Publique and the Royal Hong Kong Police.

Kawasaki 250/350cc

Length: 6ft 10in
Height: 3ft 5in
Wheelbase: 4ft 6in
G/clearance: 6in
Tyres: 3.25 × S18 4PR (front) 3.50 × S18 4PR (rear)
Weight: 353lb (dry)
Fuel tank: 14litre
Max speed: 87mph approx
Engine: 249cc two-stroke, three-cylinder, air-cooled (Bore 45mm × Stroke 52.3mm) 28bhp. Compression ratio 7.5:1. Three 22mm Mikuni carburettors. Kick start
Transmission: Five-speed gearbox, multiplate clutch, chain drive
Suspension: Front — Telescopic forks

Rear — Swinging arm suspension with twin sprung dampers
Brakes: Front — Single disc 8.9in diameter
Rear — Drum 7in diameter

In 1972 Kawasaki produced their unusual three-cylinder 250cc two-stroke — the only one in the world. At the same time a similar machine with a larger, 350cc engine was launched but this only lasted for two years before it was replaced by a 400cc version. The 250cc model has, however, continued from the date of its first appearance up to the present day with only minor modificiations.

The Guyana Police use both the 250 and the 350cc models, the latter being gradually replaced by the 400cc version.

Kawasaki KH400

Tyres: 3.25 × S18 4PR (front) 3.50 × S18 4PR (rear)
Weight: 364lb (dry)

Fuel tank: 3gal
Max speed: Over 100mph
Engine: 400cc three-cylinder, two-stroke, air-cooled

(Bore 57mm × Stroke 52.3mm) 36bhp. Compression ratio 6.5:1. Three 26mm Mikuni carburettors
Transmission: Five-speed gearbox, wet multiplate clutch, chain drive
Suspension: Telescopic front forks, swinging arm rear suspension with twin sprung dampers
Brakes: Front — single disc, 9in diameter Rear — 6.3in drum

Developed out of the 350cc three-cylinder machine of 1972/3 the 400cc version retains many similarities to this, and to its smaller brother, the 250cc triple. First appearing in 1974, the 400 has established a firm footing in the mid-power range of motorcycles. Like the smaller versions, the Guyana Police make use of these interesting three-cylinder machines.

Kawasaki Z400

Length: 6ft 10in
Seat height: 2ft 8in
Wheelbase: 4ft 6in
G/clearance: 5in
Tyres: 3.00 × S18 4PR (front) 3.50 × S18 4PR (rear)
Weight: 168kg (dry)
Fuel tank: 14litre
Max speed: 100mph approx
Engine: 398cc twin-cylinder, four-stroke, air-cooled ohc (Bore 64mm × Stroke 62mm) 36bhp at 8,500rpm. Compression ratio 9.5:1. Electric starter
Transmission: Six-speed gearbox, wet multiplate clutch, chain drive to rear wheel
Suspension: Telescopic front forks, swinging arm rear suspension

Brakes: Front — Single 9in disc
Rear — 6.25in drum

Concurrently with the 400 triple, Kawasaki launched a twin-cylinder machine of the same capacity. Originally designed as a mild-mannered commuter machine, the Z400 has been improved over the recent years and now represents an excellent all-rounder, unperturbed by adverse road and climatic conditions and forgiving rider error.

Such qualities are always attractive to the police rider who has to use his machine in all weathers and conditions and the Guyana Police and the Singapore Police have not been slow in making use of them.

Below: *Kawasaki Z400.*

Kawasaki Z900/Z1000

Length: 7ft 4.5in
Seat height: 2ft 7.5in
Wheelbase: 4ft 11in
G/clearance: 6.5in
Tyres: 3.25 × H19 4PR (front) 4.00 × H18 4PR (rear)
Police version Goodyear Eagle tyres MN90-18 front and rear on cast alloy wheels
Weight: 529lb (dry)
Police version some 50lb extra
Fuel tank: 3.75gal
Max speed: Over 125mph in civilian trim
Engine: 1,015cc four-stroke four in-line cylinders double ohc (Bore 70mm × Stroke 66mm) 83bhp at 8,000rpm. Compression ratio 8.7:1. Four 26mm Mikuni carburettors. Electric starter
Transmission: Five-speed gearbox, wet multiplate clutch, chain final drive
Suspension: Telescopic front forks (heavyweight racing type on Police special), pivoted rear forks with twin sprung dampers
Brakes: Front — Twin discs
Rear — Single disc

In 1973 Kawasaki produced the first of their 'super bikes' with a four-cylinder, four-stroke engine of 900cc, producing 82bhp. In 1977 this was bored out by 4mm to give 1,000cc and further refinements

added. It is now one of the most popular of the super bikes and has been adopted by a number of police forces for highway patrol, notably in North America where users include the Los Angeles Police Department, the California Highway Patrol, the Houston and Dallas City Police Departments, the Vancouver Police (Canada) and the New South Wales Police (Australia). For the American market a 'Police 1000' is available, featuring a number of modifications to suit US riders such as footboards (folding), heel and toe gearchange and a monster rubber pedal for the rear brake. The single saddle is mounted on two long spring damper units and handlebars have an American sweep back shape. The 'four-into-two' exhausts terminate into silencers which are set lower than on the civilian version to permit the installation of capacious pannier boxes. Fat tyres (with extra strong sidewalls to make them controllable when flat) add to the American look of this Japanese machine. Even with the extra weight of police fitments, the Z1000 will still top 115mph. An option on the police bike is a pair of 120mph speedometers, one of which is connected to the blue pursuit lights and, when switched on, records the maximum speed attained during the chase or speed check.

Below: *Kawasaki Police 1000.*

Kreidler

The Kreidler Company was set up in 1950 and concentrates on mopeds and ligthweight machines, holding the world speed record for 50cc engines of 225km/h. Its limited range features some exceptionally well-designed and engineered little machines.

Head Office — Kreidler Werke Gmbh, Fahrzengwerke, 7014 Kornwestheim.

Florett

Length: 6ft 3.5in
Seat height: 2ft 7.25in
Wheelbase: 3ft 11.75in
Tyres: 2.75 × 17
Weight: 81kg
Fuel tank: 15litre
Max speed: 40mph approx
Engine: 49cc horizontal single cylinder, two-stroke, fan-cooled (Bore 40mm × Stroke 39.7mm). 3.6bhp at 6,500rpm. One Bing carburettor
Transmission: Three-speed gearbox, foot change.

Wet multiplate clutch, chain drive to rear wheel
Suspension: Front — Telescopic fork, long swinging arm
Rear — Hydraulically damped shock absorbers
Brakes: Light alloy drum brakes (solid hub) 4.75in diameter

The little Florett is a typical example of Kreidler's excellent workmanship and provides cheap, reliable transport. Police users include some of the Dutch forces and Geneva in Switzerland.

Moto-Guzzi

The Guzzi factory was started in 1921 by Carlo Guzzi and quickly made its name in racing and for good quality road machines. After the war Guzzi returned to production with their 'Gambalunga' (or 'long-leg') 500cc single designed for racing and the postwar years tended to be dedicated to smaller production machines, mainly between 50 and 250cc. Today the name of Moto-Guzzi is mainly associated with mighty 750 and 850cc transverse V-twins with shaft drive.

Since 1967 Moto-Guzzi has been run by SEIMM as a result of financial difficulties experienced during the mid-1960s motorcycle depression. Head Office — SEIMM Moto-Guzzi SpA 22054 Mandello del Lario, Como, Italy.

V35/V50

Data: V50
Length: 7ft 5in
Seat height: 2ft 8in
Wheelbase: 4ft 10in
G/clearance: 7.5in
Tyres: 3.25 × 18 (front) 3.50 × 18 (rear)
Weight: 335lb (dry)
Fuel tank: 3.5gal
Max speed: Over 100mph
Engine: 490cc twin-cylinder, four-stroke, air-cooled ohv (Bore 74mm × Stroke 57mm).
Compression ratio 10.8:1. 45bhp. Twin 24mm Dell'Orto carburettors. Electric starter
Transmission: Five-speed gearbox, shaft drive
Suspension: Telescopic front forks, swinging arm rear suspension
Brakes: Front — Twin discs
Rear — Single disc
Integral brake system

One of the principal mounts of the Italian Carabinieri, these mid-range V-twins are typical of the sort of bike one normally associates with the name of Moto-Guzzi.

Right: *Moto-Guzzi V50 of the Italian Carabinieri.*

V7-750/850-T3

Data: 850-T3
Length: 7ft 5in
Seat height: 2ft 8in
Wheelbase: 4ft 10in
G/clearance: 7.5in
Tyres: 3.50 × 18 (front) 4.10 × 18 (rear)
Weight: 535lb (dry)
Fuel tank: 24litre
Max speed: 120mph approx
Engine: 844cc parallel V-twin cylinder, air-cooled, four-stroke, (Bore 83mm × Stroke 78mm). Compression ratio 9.5:1. 68bhp at 7,000rpm. Twin 30mm Del 'Orto carburettors. Electric starter
Transmission: Five gears, shaft drive
Suspension: Telescopic front forks, swinging arm rear suspension
Brakes: Front — Twin discs
Rear — single disc

For a time both the 750cc and 850cc parallel V-twins were produced but the 750cc model was dropped in 1976 and production concentrated on the bigger machine. Some of the 750s are still in service with the police in Holland and by the Policia Stradale in Italy but it is the later and bigger 850 models which have the lion's share of the police market with users in the Greek Gendarmerie, the Italian Carabinieri, the Rome Vigili Urbani, the Vaud Canton Police in Switzerland, the Los Angeles PD, the Arizona Department of Public Safety (Highway Patrol) and the Norfolk and Sussex forces in England, the latter sporting bright yellow fairings.

The 'California' version of the 850-T3 is a cruising bike on typical American lines complete with wide handlebars and footboards.

Below: *Moto-Guzzi V7 Special of the Greek Gendarmerie.* Greek Gendarmerie

Moto-Guzzi 1000

Length: 7ft 5in
Seat height: 2ft 8in
Wheelbase: 4ft 10in
G/clearance: 7.5in
Tyres: 3.50 × 18 (front) 4.10 × 18 (rear)
Weight: 462-560lb (dry) depending on model
Fuel tank: 5.25gal

Max speed: 110-128mph depending on model
Engine: 948.8cc four-stroke, V-twin cylinder, ohv (Bore 88mm × Stroke 78mm). Compression ratio 9.2:1. 71bhp. Two 30mm Del 'Orto carburettors. Electric starter
Transmission: Five gears (an automatic version is available). Shaft drive

Suspension: Telescopic front forks, swinging arm rear suspension with sprung dampers
Brakes: Front — Twin discs
Rear — Single disc
Integrated braking system

The Italian answer to the Japanese 'super bikes', the Moto-Guzzi V-twin is the fastest and most sophisticated Guzzi yet produced. It handles extremely well at all speeds and holds the road well in the wet. Progress is smooth, thanks to the shaft drive and the integrated braking system ensures safe braking as application of the footbrake pedal operates both the rear brake and one disc on the front wheel. The second front disc is brought into operation by the handlebar lever.

Users of the V-1000 include the Los Angeles Police Department, the Valais and Vaud Cantonal Police in Switzerland and the Sussex Police in England. The specification laid down by the latter force includes a Comaco Pantera full fairing in Coventry Fire Engine Yellow (BS6698) with extended panels for foot protection, quartz halogen headlamp, front indicators and flashing blue quartz halogen lamps incorporated in the fairing, two-tone horn, calibrated speedometer, Craven rear panniers, single seat, radio mounted on rear carrier, rear illuminated Police/Stop sign, heightened windscreen panel, and Avon Road Runner tyres 410-H-18/425/85-H18.

Right: Moto-Guzzi 1000 of the Sussex Police.
Sussex Police

NVT (Norton)

UK

The initials NVT stand for Norton-Villiers-Triumph and represent an attempt to salvage the declining fortunes of the British motorcycle industry in the 1960s by an amalgamation of two of the principal motorcycle manufacturers and an important manufacturer of engines.

The Norton Company made its first motorcycle in 1902 and, from the early days, the name of Norton became synonymous with racing and was advertised as 'the unapproachable Norton'. In 1950 the firm produced a new, pivoted rear fork duplex frame which was so much more comfortable than its predecessors it was instantly nicknamed the 'Featherbed' Norton.

In 1962 Norton was taken over by AMC (the makers of AJS and Matchless machines) which ceased to exist in its turn and became Norton-Villiers Limited. A move to amalgamate Norton-Villiers with Triumph in 1973 was opposed by the workforce at the latter company's Meriden factory which set up its own, independent cooperative. NVT now mainly make lightweight motorcycles and mopeds and a project to make a Police Special based on the Yamaha XS750 folded in 1978 due to pressure of work on the small workforce (see under Yamaha).

Head Office — NVT Motorcyles Limited, North Way, Walworth Industrial Estate, Andover, Hampshire, England.

Commando 750/850cc and Interpol

Length: 7ft 4in
Seat height: 2ft 8in
Wheelbase: 4ft 9in
G/clearance: 6in
Tyres: 4.10 × 19
Weight: 446lb (dry)
Fuel tank: 5.25gal
Max speed: 105mph approx
Engine: 828cc air-cooled, vertical twin-cylinder

four-stroke, ohv (Bore 77mm × Stroke 89mm). Compression ratio 8.5:1. 58bhp at 5,900rpm. Two Amal concentric carburettors. Electric starter
Transmission: Four-speed gearbox, multi-disc clutch, chain drive to rear wheel
Suspension: Telescopic front forks with two-way damping. Swinging arm rear suspension with Girling sprung units. Patented 'Isolastic' anti-vibration system isolates engine, transmission and rear wheel

Above: *Norton Commando Interpol of the Kent County Constabulary.* Kent County Constabulary

assembly from frame and rider
Brakes: Front — 10.7in disc
Rear — disc

Trident/Cardinal

Length: 7ft 4in
Seat height: 2ft 7in
Wheelbase: 4ft 10in
G/clearance: 6.5in
Tyres: 4.10 × 19
Weight: 50.3lb
Fuel tank: 4.75gal
Max speed: Over 110mph
Engine: 740cc air-cooled, transverse three-cylinder, four-stroke, ohv. Compression ratio 9.5:1. 58bhp at 7,250rpm. Three Amal carburettors. Electric starter. Four pipe exhaust to central collector pipe and two silencers.
Transmission: Five-speed gearbox. Single dry-plate clutch. Chain drive

The Commando was originally powered by a 750cc engine but this was increased to 850cc and a police version known as 'Interpol' was made available. A large number of the 'Interpol' versions are in use with police forces, both in the UK and abroad. At the present time more than half the forces in the United Kingdom are using 'Interpols' and they are also used by the Greek Gendarmerie, States of Jersey (CI) Police, the Jamaica Constabulary, the Gambia Police and the Kenya Police.

Suspension and brakes: As for Commando but disc brakes 10in diameter

Marketed under the 'Triumph' brand name, the Trident was made by the NVT firm and not by the breakaway Triumph (Meriden) cooperative. A police version, known as the Cardinal was also available during the time the Triumph three-cylinder was in production, up until 1977, but both have now been discontinued.

Police users in the UK include the Devon and Cornwall Constabulary and the Fife Police. Abroad, the Saudi Arabian Police also use modified Cardinals.

Rickman

UK

Rickmans are a small, specialist firm of motorcycle constructors who use mainly existing parts from production models to produce unique models. Much

of their output has been aimed at the police market.

Head Office — Rickman, Stem Lane, New Milton, Hampshire.

Rickman 125

Engine: 123cc two-stroke, single-cylinder, air-cooled, (Bore 54mm × Stroke 54mm). 17bhp at 7,600rpm.
Compression ratio 12.4:1. One 27mm Bing carburettor

The demise of the water-cooled LE Velocette left a large gap in the motorcycle fleets of many British police forces and Rickman endeavoured to step into the breach with a specially designed 125cc police lightweight. This was fitted with the German

Zundapp engine, housed in a modified version of the 125 Six-Day Enduro frame. Production started around 1972 and ceased in 1975.

The 125 was an ideal lightweight motorcycle and came equipped with full weather and luggage equipment. Its performance would have done credit to a machine of 350cc. Output was limited to some 300 units, all of which were sold to police forces, mainly in the South of England, eg Avon and Somerset, Bedfordshire, Hampshire, Humberside, West Midlands and Norfolk.

Below: *Rickman 125.*

Rickman 650

Data: See Triumph 650

Rickman's big bike was based on their successful road racer, using a standard Triumph TRGP engine and was a purpose-built police machine and not a converted road machine. Some 300 of these machines were sold between 1970 and 1975 when production ceased due to the inability to get the engines from the strife-torn Triumph factory, and examples remain in use in Avon and Somerset and on Humberside.

The 650 was greatly appreciated for its superb handling, light weight and excellent braking capabilities. The Mark I version had disc brakes front and rear but a number of riders thought the rear brake was too fierce and so, on the Mk II version, the Triumph conical rear hub was fitted. Special features were the plug-on wiring to the fairing to facilitate easy removal, a special petrol tank with built-in radio mounting and a built-in storage box for charge sheets, logbook, etc.

Left: *Rickman 650.*

Sanglas

Spain

Since the early 1950s, Sanglas have produced a series of mid-sized machines, featuring the best of contemporary technological innovations. These have been taken into use by the Spanish Police forces, in particular the 400cc range.

Head Office — Talleres Sanglas SA, Rambla Justo Oliveras 472-476, Hospitalet (Barcelona), Spain.

Sanglas 400F

Seat height: 2ft 7.5in
Wheelbase: 4ft 7in
G/clearance: 6.25in
Tyres: 3.25×18 (front) 3.50×18 (rear)
Weight: 173kg (dry)
Fuel tank: 15.5litre
Max speed: 87mph approx
Engine: 423cc four-stroke, single-cylinder (Bore 82.5mm×Stroke 79mm) 25bhp at 5,800rpm. Compression ratio 7.5:1. One Amal 27mm carburettor
Transmission: Four-speed gearbox, wet multiplate clutch, chain drive
Suspension: Telescopic front forks, swinging arm rear suspension

Brakes: Front — Double central discs protected from dust and water
Rear — Drum

The Sanglas 400 is a medium powered machine with excellent handling characteristics for town traffic and sufficient power for rapid motoring on all types of roads. It is basically a robust touring machine where the rider's comfort has been given prime consideration. For police work the machine is finished in blue and fitted with a screen and a siren, and has been the mainstay of the Civil Guard Traffic Group (Agrupación de Tráfico de la Guardia Civil) and several municipal police forces for some 14 years.

Suzuki

Japan

An old-established textile firm, Suzuki only went into motorcycle manufacture in 1952 but its two-stroke products were an immediate and lasting success. Starting with a simple 60cc lightweight, the company now produce a range from 50cc to 1,000cc — all two-strokes until recent years when the big, multi-cylinder models were introduced.

Head Office — Suzuki Motor Company Limited, 300 Takatsuka, Near Hamamatsu, Shizuoka-Pref, Japan.

Suzuki FR70/FR80

Data: FR80
Length: 6ft
Height: 3ft 5.25in
G/clearance: 5in
Tyres: 2.25×17 4PR
Weight: 73kg (dry)
Fuel tank: 4litre
Max speed: 45mph approx
Engine: 79cc two-stroke, air-cooled, single-cylinder 6.8bhp at 6,500rpm (SAE). One 15mm Mikuni carburettor
Transmission: Three-speed gearbox, automatic clutch, chain drive to rear wheel
Suspension: Bottom link front fork with hydraulic damper. Swinging arm rear suspension with hydraulic damper
Brakes: Drum brakes front and rear

The Royal Malaysia Police have taken these little run-abouts into use for their patrol officers. The original 70cc engine has been bored out to 80cc to provide a little more power and the FR80 will take two persons without undue difficulty. And yet these machines are virtually as simple to ride as a bicycle.

Suzuki A100

Length: 6ft
Height: 3ft 3.75in
Seat height: 2ft 9.5in
Wheelbase: 3ft 11.25in
Tyres: 2.50×18 4PR
Weight: 183lb (dry)
Fuel tank: 7.5litre
Max speed: 65mph approx
Engine: 98cc two-stroke, single-cylinder (Bore 50mm×Stroke 50mm). 9.3bhp at 7,500rpm

Transmission: Four-speed gearbox
Suspension: Telescopic front fork, swinging arm rear suspension with twin sprung dampers
Brakes: 5.5in drums front and rear

Unlike the FR80, the A100 is a true motorcycle although it has only 20cc more. The manufacturers describe it somewhat extravagantly as a 'sports cycle to make sprinting around town more exhilarating' but there is no doubt that this is a lively and economical lightweight. The primary kick starting allows the machine to be started in any gear and a rotary disc valve ensures a better delivery of power to the single cylinder. Thick seat padding and front/rear suspension provide large bike comfort and good lights, plus flashing direction indicators are useful safety factors. For police work the A100 is used by the Cyprus Police and by the Jamaica Constabulary.

Suzuki GT185

Length: 6ft 6in
Height: 3ft 3.75in
Wheelbase: 4ft 3in
G/clearance: 6.5in
Tyres: 2.75+18 (front) 3.00×18 (rear)
Weight: 253lb (dry)
Fuel tank: 10litre
Max speed: 80mph approx
Engine: 184cc two-stroke, twin-cylinder, Ram-Air cooled (Bore 52mm×Stroke 43mm). 20bhp (SAE) at 7,500rpm. Electric starter. Two Mikuni carburettors
Transmission: Five-speed gearbox, chain drive to rear wheel

Suspension: Telescopic front forks, two oil damped units to rear
Brakes: Front — Single disc
Rear — Drum

The 185 is a useful machine, both for around town and for touring, having sufficient power to cope with most eventualities. It offers many of the refinements of larger bikes including electric starting, disc brake and Ram-Air cooling. The Jamaica Constabulary used GT185s extensively.

Suzuki GT250

Length: 6ft 8.5in
Height: 3ft 8.5in
Wheelbase: 4ft 4in
G/clearance: 6.25in
Tyres: 3.00×S18 (front) 3.25×S18 (rear)
Weight: 322lb (dry)
Fuel tank: 15litre
Max speed: 95-100mph
Engine: 247cc two-stroke, two-cylinder (Bore 54mm×54mm). 32bhp (SAE at 7,500rpm. Two 28mm Mikuni carburettors
Transmission: Six-speed gearbox, chain drive to rear wheel
Suspension: Telescopic front forks, swinging arm

rear suspension with twin sprung dampers
Brakes: Front — Disc
Rear — Drum

Quick response, fast acceleration and good handling are the claimed features of this popular lightweight two-stroke twin, all features which appeal to police forces who want a general run-about. The GT250s are to be found in service with the Royal Papua New Guinea Police, the Royal Malaysia Police and the Fife Police in Scotland, where they are used for urban patrols and traffic supervision or as a means of transport for rural officers.

Suzuki GS550

Below: *Suzuki GS550P Police Special.*

Length: 7ft 4.25in
Height: 3ft 9in
G/clearance: 5.75in
Tyres: 3.25×H19 4PR (front) 3.75×H18 4PR (rear)
Weight: 478lb (dry)
Fuel tank: 17litre
Max speed: 100mph approx
Engine: 549cc four-stroke, air-cooled, four-cylinder, double ohc (Bore 56mm×Stroke 55.8mm). 51bhp at 9,000rpm. Four 22mm Mikuni carburettors. Electric starter
Transmission: Six-speed gearbox, chain drive
Suspension: Telescopic fork with hydraulic damper at front, swinging arm with hydraulic dampers
Brakes: Front — Twin discs
Rear — Drum

A successful middleweight touring machine, the GS550 was made more attractive to police buyers by the introduction of a 'Patroller Series GS550P'. This particular model replaced the GT550 three-cylinder version and is in use in a number of forces, including the Royal Malaysia Police and the Jamaica Constabulary as well as in Japan. The GS550P is a highly manoeuvrable, high performance patrol bike giving quiet cruising as well as outstanding speed and acceleration. Its special equipment includes a windscreen, speedometers with a 'pointer-stop' indicator to record speed of other vehicles, electric siren, extra large patrol lamps, waterproof document box and pannier boxes.

Suzuki GS750

Length: 7ft 5.75in
Height: 3ft 9.75in
Wheelbase: 4ft 10.75in
G/clearance: 6in
Tyres: 3.25×H19 4PR (front) 4.00×H18 4PR (rear)
Weight: 540lb (dry)
Max speed: Over 115mph
Engine: 748cc four-cylinder, four-stroke, air-cooled, double ohc (Bore 65mm×Stroke 56.4mm) 68bhp at 8,500rpm. Compression ratio 8.7:1. Four 26mm Mikunis. Electric starter
Transmission: Five-speed gearbox, chain drive to rear wheel
Suspension: Telescopic front forks, swinging arm rear suspension with hydraulic damper
Brakes: Front — Twin disc brakes
Rear — Single disc

Like the GS550, the GS750 is also offered in 'Patroller' guise with the same special equipment. The additional power gives the GS750P tremendous acceleration and it has a stable high speed performance, coupled with tractability and manoeuvrability in traffic. At low speeds it handles well and quietly, making it suitable for leading parades and for escort duties, as well as for high speed highway chases.

Users of the GS750 include the Bahamas Police, the Vaud Cantonal Police (Switzerland), the California Highway Patrol ('Chips') and the Jamaica Constabulary. The Indonesian Police use the earlier GT750 which had a three-cylinder, water-cooled engine.

Below: *Suzuki GS750P Police Special.*

Triumph

Founded as a pedal cycle manufacturer in 1885, Triumph produced their first motorcycle in 1902. Between the two world wars Triumph carved out a formidable name for themselves in the racing world as well as producing excellent touring machines. In 1938 a 500cc twin-cylinder machine called the 'Speed Twin' was introduced and which altered the whole trend of motorcycle engine design throughout the world. In a modified form, this model continued in production for around 30 years — a record probably only equalled by Volkswagen.

In 1951 the company was taken over by BSA but continued to produce motorcycles under its own marque. An official move to amalgamate Triumph with Norton Villiers in 1973 was resisted by the work force at the Meriden factory which set up its own cooperative company to continue to produce Triumphs. There are thus two Triumph motorcycle manufacturers — the 'official' Norton-Villiers-Triumph (NVT) concern and the Triumph (Meriden) Company. The latter continues to produce the 650cc 'Bonneville' models at Meriden Motorcycles Limited, Meriden Works, Allesley, Coventry, Warwickshire.

Triumph machines were always very popular with police forces in both Great Britain and abroad. In particular, the maroon-painted 'Speed Twin' with its distinctive headlamp nacelle was probably the most widely used road patrol machine in the 1950s and 1960s. This was eventually supplanted by the 650cc and, later, 750cc machines, both of which remain in everyday use with a number of police forces.

Triumph T100/5T

Max speed: 100mph approx
Engine: 490cc two-cylinder, four-stroke, ohv, air-cooled. Two Amal carburettors
Transmission: Four-speed gearbox, wet multiplate clutch, chain drive to rear wheel
Suspension: Telescopic front forks, swinging arm rear suspension
Brakes: Drums front and rear

The original 'Speed Twin' or 5T, and the increased performance 'Tiger 100' or T100 continued in production in one form or another until the mid-1970s and a number remain in use with police forces throughout the world. Current, or recent, users of the 500cc Triumph include the Bermuda Police, the Cyprus Police, the Devon and Cornwall Constabulary, the Royal Fiji Police, the Lothian and Borders Police (Scotland) and the Thames Valley Police. A special military/police 350cc model was available for some time and is in use in Bermuda, the Bahamas, Gwent (Wales) and Devon and Cornwall.

Right: *Triumph T100 of the Fiji Police.*

Triumph 650

Max speed: Over 100mph
Engine: 649cc vertical twin-cylinder, four-stroke, 46bhp at 6,500rpm. Compression ratio 8.5:1
Transmission: Four gears, wet multiplate clutch, chain drive

Two principal versions of the 650cc Triumph were produced — the Tiger 650 (TR6) and the Bonneville. In addition, specially adapted TR6s were made available to police forces under the name of 'Saint'.

None of these machines is now produced, production being confined to the 750cc models. However, a number of 650s remain in use with police forces throughout the world — not surprising when one considers that, at one time, over 250 forces were using 'Saints'. Current users include the Gloucestershire Constabulary, Devon and Cornwall Constabulary, Strathclyde Police, Metropolitan Police (London), Staffordshire Police, the South Wales Police and the Jamaican Constabulary.

119

Triumph 750

Data: Bonneville
Seat height: 2ft 7in
Wheelbase: 4ft 9in
G/clearance: 5in
T/circle: 16ft
Weight: 395lb (dry)
Fuel tank: 4gal
Max speed: 110mph
Engine: 744cc ohv twin cylinder (Bore 76mm ×
Stroke 82mm). 54bhp at 6,200 rpm. Compression
ratio 7.9:1. Two Amal concentric carburettors
Transmission: Five-speed gearbox, wet multiplate
clutch, chain drive
Brakes: Hydraulically operated 10in discs, front and
rear

The first machines fitted with 750cc engines were
produced around 1973 and were known as the Tiger
750 and Bonneville 750. A police version of the
Tiger 750, the 'Saint' was also produced and used
widely for road patrol, as were standard machines.
Only the Bonneville is now produced, the sole
remaining product of the Meriden Workers'
Cooperative. Police users include the Gambia Police,
the Strathclyde Police, the Sussex Police and the
Devon and Cornwall Constabulary.

Above: *Triumph 750 Tiger.*

Vespa

Italy

Vespa is the name of a range of scooters and
mopeds manufactured by Piaggio of Genoa (name
'Vespa' being Italian for 'Wasp'). The Piaggio firm
was formed as a ship's outfitters in 1884 and
diversified over the years into the manufacture of
railway carriages and aircraft. Following destruction
of the Pontedera factory in 1943 Piaggio hit upon
the idea of making scooters. The Vespa scooter was
an immediate success from the date of its

introduction in 1946 and has continued to be in
production in largely the same form ever since.

Piaggio branched out into mopeds in 1967 and
later took over the firm of Gilera, one of the oldest
motorcycle manufacturers in Italy. Vespas are also
produced under licence in Malaysia, Indonesia,
Nigeria, Taiwan and Pakistan and there are assembly
plants in a number of African countries and South
America.

Vespa Ciao

Length: 5ft 4.5in
Seat height: 2ft 6.25in
Wheelbase: 3ft 3.5in
G/clearance: 7in
Tyres: 2.00 × 17
Weight: 90lb (dry)
Fuel tank: 2.8litre
Max speed: 25mph approx
Engine: 49.77cc two-stroke, rotary-valve, single-
cylinder (Bore 38.4mm × Stroke 43mm) 1.25bhp.
Compression ratio 8:1. One 12mm Dell 'Orto
carburettor
Transmission: Single gear, automatic clutch

Suspension: Leading link front suspension, rigid
rear frame
Brakes: Front — 89mm drum
Rear — 133mm drum

A simple, traditional and reliable moped, the Ciao
provides transport one step up from a pedal cycle.
Not to be compared with the high powered, highway
patrol machines, or even with the lightweight
motorcycles, the moped does find a place in police
work and the Ciao is no exception, being used by the
Zurich Stadtpolizei, for both uniformed and criminal
police, as well as by some African forces.

Vespa Scooters

Data: 90cc Standard
Length: 5ft 5.5in

Seat height: 2ft 7in
Wheelbase: 3ft 10.5in

G/clearance: 9in
Tyres: 3.10 × 10
Weight: 73kg (dry)
Fuel tank: 5litre
Max speed: 40mph approx
Engine: 88.5cc two-stroke, rotary-valve, single-cylinder, (Bore 47mm × Stroke 51mm). Compression ratio 7.2:1. 3.1bhp at 5,200rpm. One 16mm Dell 'Orto carburettor. Kick start
Transmission: Three gears, direct drive
Suspension: Trailing link front forks, damped swinging arm rear suspension

Brakes: Front — 5in drum
Rear — 5.5in drum)

The Vespa range of scooters are basically similar but the engines range from 50cc to 200cc. The 90cc version is used by the Bermuda Police, whilst the Strathclyde Police, the Cambridgeshire Constabulary, the Zurich Stadtpolizei, the Puerto Rico Police and the Singapore Police use either 125cc or 145cc versions.

Yamaha

Japan

Yamaha is another Japanese company which has acquired a world-wide reputation in a comparatively short time. Originally manufacturers of organs and pianos, the firm entered the motorcycling scene in 1954 with the 125cc YA2. Other bikes followed and it was not long before Yamahas were winning races.

Over half the Yamaha output is exported and there are a number of overseas assembly plants.

Head office — Yamaha Motor Company Limited, 2500 Shinghai, Iwatsa-Shi, Shizuoka-Pref, Japan.

Yamaha V70/V75

Length: 6ft 0.5in
Seat height: 2ft 4.75in
Wheelbase: 3ft 10in
Tyres: 2.25 × 17
Weight: 75kg
Fuel tank: 5.3litre
Engine: 72cc two-stroke, reed valve, single-cylinder, (Bore 47mm × Stroke 42mm). 6.2bhp. Compression ratio 6.8:1. One VM 15SC carburettor. Kick start
Transmission: Two-speed gearbox, centrifugal automatic clutch, chain drive to rear wheel
Suspension: Leading link front forks, swinging arm rear suspension

Brakes: Drum brakes front and rear (4.5in) with labyrinth, double ridge design to prevent ingress of dust and water.

One of Yamahas smallest machines the V75, which replaced the V70, is a manoeuvrable and economical machine. The two-stroke engine has a special reed-valve mechanism for positive intake/exhaust and the two-speed transmission is clutchless. The frame is of the 'step-thro' design which makes it easy to mount and dismount. The Royal Malaysia Police use these machines for general police work.

Yamaha YB100

Length: 6ft 1in
Seat height: 2ft 7in
Wheelbase: 3ft 10.5in
Tyres: 2.50 × 18
Fuel tank: 8.6litre
Max speed: 70mph approx
Engine: 97cc two-stroke, rotary-valve, single-cylinder (Bore 52mm × Stroke 45.6mm). 9.8bhp at 8,000rpm. Compression ratio 6.5:1. One VM20SC carburettor, kick start.
Transmission: Four-speed gearbox, multiplate wet clutch, chain drive to rear wheel

Suspension: Front — Telescopic forks
Rear — swinging arm suspension
Brakes: Drum brakes front and rear

The YB100 is a lightweight machine which combines speed, economy and all-round performance and is ideally suited to urban motoring. Handling almost as easily as a bicycle and the Autolube oil injection system obviates the need to mix oil and petrol for the two-stroke engine. Like the V75, the YB100 is in use with the Royal Malaysian Police.

Yamaha RD125

Tyres: 2.75 × 18 (front) 3.00 × 18 (rear)
Weight: 244lb (dry)
Fuel tank: 2.5gal
Max speed: 75mph approx
Engine: 124cc twin-cylinder, two-stroke, air-cooled (Bore 43mm × Stroke 43mm). 16bhp. Compression

ratio 6:8:1. Two 18mm Mikuni carburettors
Transmission: Five gears, foot change
Suspension: Telescopic front forks, swinging arm rear suspension
Brakes: Front — Single disc
Rear — drum

Another of the machines used by the Royal Malaysian Police is the RD125, a small capacity bike which has many of the advantages of a large machine, including cast wheels and disc brakes

Yamaha RD200/RD250

Length: 6ft 6.5in
Height: 3ft 5.5in
Seat height: 2ft 7in
Wheelbase: 4ft 4in
Tyres: 3.00 × S18 (front) 3.25 × S18 (rear)
Weight: 154.5kg (net)
Fuel tank: 16.5litre
Max speed: 100mph approx
Engine: 247cc twin-cylinder, two-stroke (Bore 54mm × Stroke 54mm) 32bhp at 8,000rpm. Compression ratio 5.8:1. Kick start.
Transmission: Six-speed gearbox
Chain drive to rear wheel, wet multiplate clutch
Suspension: Front — telescopic forks
Rear — swinging arm suspension
Brakes: 10.5in discs front and rear

Below: *Yamaha RD200 of the Bermuda Police.* Bermuda Police

One of the very first sports machines ever introduced by Yamaha was a 250cc two-stroke twin which earned a reputation as one of the toughest and fastest bikes in its class. Some 15 years later Yamaha are still making a 250cc sports machine and also a smaller brother, the 200cc. The two machines are very similar with twin cylinder, air-cooled engines with more than just a passing resemblance to the racing power units of the same size. They have the same seven-port transfer system which revolutionised two-stroke performance and also feature the reed valve Torque Induction that controls the carburation. The engines also have the Yamaha Autolube system of throttle controlled automatic oiling in which a cable links the oil pump to the throttle twistgrip.

These features make these power units among the cleanest running, efficient and most economical two-strokes on the road today. Police users of either the RD200 or the RD250 include the Bahamas Police, the Bermuda Police, the Punjab Police (India) and the Cumbria Constabulary in England.

Yamaha RD350

Length: 6ft 9in
Seat height: 2ft 7in
Wheelbase: 4ft 5in
G/clearance: 7.5in
Tyres: 3.00 × 18 (front) 3.50 × 18 (rear)
Weight: 151kg (dry)
Fuel tank: 15litre
Max speed: Over 95mph
Engine: 347cc twin-cylinder, two-stroke (Bore 64mm × Stroke 54mm). 39bhp at 7,500rpm. Compression ratio 6.6:1. Two 28mm Mikuni carburettors. Kick start
Transmission: Six-speed gearbox, multiplate wet clutch, chain drive to rear wheel
Suspension: Front — Telescopic forks

Rear — swinging arm suspension
Brakes: Front — 10.5in disc
Rear — 7in drum

Yamaha made a 350cc twin for some seven years but the last of the line, the RD350, ceased production in 1976 when the 350 was replaced by a 400cc model. The 350 was, however, a popular machine and examples remain in use in the Bermuda Police, the Bahamas Police, the Punjab Police, the Royal Malaysia Police and the British South Africa Police (Rhodesia).

Below: *Yamaha RD350 of the Bermuda Police.*
Bermuda Police

Yamaha RD400 Police Bike

Length: 6ft 7.75in
Wheelbase: 4ft 3.75in
G/clearance: 5.75in
Tyres: 3.25 × S18 (front) 3.50 × S18 (rear)
Weight: 180kg (net)
Fuel tank: 16.5litre
Max speed: 100mph approx
Engine: 398cc two-stroke, parallel twin. Torque induction with reed-valve intake assembly. (Bore

65mm × Stroke 62mm). 38bhp at 7,000rpm. Compression ratio 6.2:1. Autolube lubrication. Kick start.
Transmission: Six-speed gearbox, chain drive
Suspension: Front — Telescopic forks
Rear — swinging arm suspension
Brakes: Disc brakes front and rear

Worthy successor to the 350cc machine, the RD400 Police Bike is a fine example of quality craftmanship. Powered by a parallel twin, two-stroke engine, the RD400 is responsive and highly manoeuvrable — two important characteristics for police work, both in town and on the open road.

Fundamentally the same as the RD400 commercial machine, the Police Bike is supplied with a number of special features including a windshield, emergency warning lamps mounted on the front crashbar, front and rear crashbars in durable chrome, siren operated by a drive rotor which is turned by the sidewall of the rear tyre, single saddle with document case behind, plastic saddle bags etc. The whole machine is finished in white and black.

These special machines are used by the Belize Police, the Royal Malaysia Police and the Singapore Police, as well as in Japan.

Yamaha XS500

Length: 6ft 10.75in
Height: 3ft 8in
Seat height: 2ft 7.5in
Wheelbase: 4ft 7in
Tyres: 3.25 × H19 (front) 4.00 × H18 (rear)
Weight: 193kg (net)
Fuel tank: 15litre
Max speed: 110mph approx
Engine: 498cc four-stroke, twin-cylinder, dohc (Bore 73mm × Stroke 59.6mm) 48bhp at 8,500rpm. Compression ratio 8.5:1. Electric start. Two BS38 SU type carburettors
Transmission: Five-speed gearbox, wet multiplate clutch, chain drive
Suspension: Front — Telescopic forks

Rear — swinging arm suspension
Brakes: Front — 11.75in disc
Rear — 10.5in disc
Hydraulically operated

The XS500 is a handsome, middleweight twin with smooth, vibration free performance which has been selected by several Indian forces for road patrol work. The double ohc, eight valve engine has the patent omniphase balancing mechanism which cancels out any vibration inherent in the vertical twin design.

Below: *Yamaha XS500.*

Yamaha XS650 Police bike

Length: 7ft 1.75in
Height: 3ft 9.5in
Seat height: 2ft 7.5in
Wheelbase: 4ft 8.25in
G/clearance: 5.5in
Tyres: 3.50 × H19 (front) 4.00 × H19 (rear)
Weight: 212kg
Fuel tank: 15litre
Max speed: Over 100mph
Engine: 653cc Four stroke, ohc, parallel twin, air-cooled, forward inclined (Bore 75mm × Stroke 74mm) 53bhp at 7,500rpm. Compression ratio 8.4:1. Two 38mm Mikuni carburettors. Electric starter.
Transmission: Five-speed gearbox, constant mesh, wide ratio
Suspension: Front — Telescopic forks
Rear — Swinging arm suspension

Brakes: Front — 11.75in disc
Rear — drum

The XS650 Police Bike was introduced in 1976 since when it has proved a popular choice for police work throughout the world. Current users include the Royal Hong Kong Police, the Kenya Police, the Sierra Leone Police and the Singapore Police.

The XS650 possesses the necessary qualities for police duties with its large engine that is very smooth from walking pace to high-speed highway patrol work, good disc/drum brakes and excellent frame configuration.

The XS650 Police Bike, based on the civilian XS650 road machine offers the same level of additional equipment as the XS400.

Below: *Yamaha XS650 Police Bike.*

Norton-Yamaha Police Special

Length: 7ft 1in
Seat height: 2ft 8in
Wheelbase: 4ft 9.75in
Tyres: 3.25 × 19 (front) 4.00 × 18 (rear)
Weight: 232kg
Fuel tank: 17litre
Max speed: 115mph approx
Engine: 747cc four-stroke, three-cylinder, dohc. (Bore 68mm × Stroke 68.6mm) 64bhp at 7,500rpm. Compression ratio 8.5:1. Three 34mm Mikuni carburettors
Transmission: Five-speed gearbox, wet multiplate

clutch, shaft drive to rear wheel
Suspension: Front — Telescopic oil damped forks
Rear — Swinging arm suspension with adjustable dampers
Brakes: Front — Twin hydraulic 10.5in discs
Rear — single 10.5in disc.

In 1977/78, the NVT Motorcycle Company in England produced a modified Yamaha 750cc, adapted for police work. It featured a Polaris fairing, designed specifically for the purpose, with a blue flashing lamp mounted on it. A rear mounted radio

carrier was located behind the single saddle. Electrical equipment included a rear mounted Police/Stop sign, four-way hazard warning flashers, two-tone Maserati air horns and electric starter. CDM panniers were fitted to either side of the rear wheel and a certified speedometer fitted.

Only a limited number of these machines were produced and production ceased in 1978. However,

Above: *Yamaha Norton Police Special.*

a small works in Stevenage, Hertfordshire has taken up where NVT left off, although, in this case, the fairing is an Avon Arrow. Otherwise these later bikes are closely similar to their experimental predecessors.

Yamaha XS1100

Length: 7ft 5in
Height: 3ft 9in
Seat height: 2ft 8in
Wheelbase: 5ft 0.75in
Tyres: 3.50 × V19 (front) 4.50 × V17 (rear)
Weight: 256kg

Fuel tank: 24litre
Engine: 1101cc four-stroke, four-cylinder, air-cooled, dohc (Bore 71,5mm × Stroke 68.6mm)

Below: *Yamaha XS1100.*

95bhp at 8,000rpm. Compression ratio 9.2:1. Four 34mm Mikuni carburettors. Electric starter
Transmission: Five-speed gearbox, wet multiplate clutch, shaft drive to rear wheel
Suspension: Front — Telescopic forks
Rear — swinging arm suspension with two sprung dampers
Brakes: Front — Two 11.75in discs
Rear — single 11.75in disc

The biggest bike from Japan, the XS1100 is a big tough, fast machine, well suited to high speed, main highway patrol work and is used for such by the Singapore Police as well as in Japan. Everything about the XS1100 is big — the engine, brakes, frame and performance. An interconnected, vacuum-operated ignition control unit retards the ignition for easy starting and then automatically advances. Fully-transistorised ignition aids easy starting by the electric starter (a separate kick start is regarded as being for emergencies only and is not even connected to the engine).

All main controls are located on the handlebars within easy reach of the rider at all times. Speedometer and tachometer are located in neat, rectangular housings, either side of the warning lights (turn, high beam, oil, neutral) panel. The turn indicators are self-cancelling. The headlamp is of the halogen type and this, too, is rectangular. Cast alloy wheels are standard.

Zündapp   West Germany

The Zünder-und-Apparatebau Company was formed in 1917 as part of the munitions industry for World War I. After the Armistice it switched to motorcycles, its first product appearing in 1921, and also produced light commercial vehicles, aero engines and light cars. After World War II the 600cc flat twin motorcycle with shaft drive appeared and, later, Bella scooters. Nowadays Zündapp concentrates on the lighter motorcycles and mopeds and is Germany's largest motor cycle manufacturer.

Head Office — Zündapp-Werke GmBH, Anzinger Strasse-3, 8000 Munchen 80.

ZD40

Fuel tank: 6.5 litres
Weight: 64kg (net)
Max speed: 25mph
Engine: 49.9cc, two-stroke with non-induced air-cooling, 2.9bhp. Kick starter.
Transmission: Three-speed, pedal gear shift, wet multiplate clutch chain drive
Suspension: Front — Telescopic forks
Rear — Swinging Arm suspension
Brakes: 4.75in drum brakes front and rear

The little ZD40 moped typifies Zündapp's insistence on functional, modern design. It must be one of the smallest machines to employ die-cast aluminium wheels. Primarily intended as a very lightweight run-about for one person, the ZD40 is equipped to take a pillion passenger and can do so without too much difficulty.

Police users in West Germany include the force in North Rhine-Westphalia

RS50

Below: *Zündapp RS 50.*

Length: 5ft 10in
Seat height: 2ft 6in
Wheelbase: 4ft 0.5in
Weight: 84kg
Fuel tank: 7.5litre
Max speed: 41mph approx
Engine: 49.9cc fan-cooled, two-stroke, 4.6bhp. Kick start
Transmission: Four-speed gearbox with pedal gearshift, wet multiplate clutch
Suspension: Front — Swinging fork
Rear — hydraulically damped suspension units
Brakes: 4.75in drum brakes front and rear

Direct descendant of the Bella scooters of the 1950s, the RS50 is of classic scooter design, incorporating Zündapp's excellent technical know-how. It has an 'unburstable' 50cc engine, a finely tuned suspension, good brakes, excellent steering and road holding.

The North Rhine-Westphalia police in West Germany use these machines for a number of police tasks in the urban areas.

KS175

Length: 6ft 10.25in
Seat height: 2ft 6.5in
Wheelbase: 4ft 4in
Weight: 123kg (net)
Fuel tank: 14.25litre
Max speed: 70mph approx
Engine: 163cc water-cooled, two-stroke. 17bhp at 7,400rpm. Kick start. Electronic ignition.
Transmission: Five-speed gearbox, wet multiplate clutch, chain drive to rear wheel
Suspension: Front — Telescopic forks
Rear — Swinging arm suspension with sprung units
Brakes: Front — 10.25in disc brake
Rear — 6.25in drum

These water-cooled lightweights are Zündapp's newest model and represent the latest trends. Thanks to the water-cooled, twin-jacketed cylinder, the engine runs very quietly. These machines have outstanding riding properties even at full throttle. A tough frame, functional springing, die-cast aluminium wheels and front disc brakes, plus aerodynamic styling, all add up to excellent little machines.

Below: *Zündapp KS 175.*

Aerospatiale

France

France's great, nationalised aerospace company Aerospatiale was formed out of the amalgamation of a number of small and medium sized aircraft manufacturers into a national conglomerate. Its principal products include the Airbus (with Britain and Germany) Concorde (with Britain) and the Caravelle.

Such exotic aircraft are not, however for police work and it is in the helicopter field that Aerospatiale has most to offer law enforcement agencies.

Head Office — Societé Nationale Industrielle Aerospatiale, Division Helicoptères, Etablissement de la Courneuve 2-20 Avenue Marcel-Cachin 93126 La Courneuve Cedex.

Alouette 2 (SA318C)

Rotor diameter: 33ft 5.5in
Fuselage length: 31ft 11.75in
Gross weight: 3,630lb
Speed: 112mph (cruising)
Range: 186/447 miles

Aptly named after the skylark, the Alouette 2 was originally produced by Aviation Sud-Est before its incorporation into the Aerospatiale Company. Original versions were powered by the Artouste engine but later models used a 530shp Turbomeca Astazon IIA.

The SA315B Lama is similar but has the dynamic components of the Alouette 3.

The French Gendarmerie Nationale has a number

Above: Aerospatiale Alouette 2 of the New Caledonian Gendarmerie.
Gendarmerie Nationale Francaise

of airborne sections, each comprising between two and six helicopters or aircraft, and the Alouette 2 and Alouette 2 Lama form the backbone of these sections. Other police users include the New Caledonian Gendarmerie, the Belgian Gendarmerie, the Danish State Police and the West German forces in Baden-Württemberg, Hamburg, North Rhine-Westphalia and the Bundesgrenzschutz (Federal Border Police). The latter uses both Atouste and Astazon powered versions.

Alouette 3 (SA316B/SA319B)

Data: SA316B
Accommodation: Pilot and up to 6 passengers
Rotor diameter: 36ft 1.75in
Fuselage length: 32ft 10.75in

Gross weight: 4,850lb
Speed: 115mph (cruising)
Range: 298/335 miles

The Alouette 3 first flew in 1959 as an improved and enlarged version of the Alouette 2, the original models being produced by the Sud-Est Company (SE3160). the Aerospatiale version was powered by a derated Artouste IIIB engine giving 570shp and known as the SA316B is a development of this machine, using an Astazon XIV engine derated to give 600shp.

Above: *Aerospatiale Alouette 3 of the French Gendarmerie.*

The French Gendarmerie use both the SE3160 and the SA319B to complete their helicopter fleet and the police in North Rhine-Westphalia also use Alouette 3s.

Gazelle (SA341G)

Rotor diameter: 34ft 5.5in
Fuselage length: 39ft 3.25in
Gross weight: 3,970lb
Speed: 164mph (cruising)
Range: 223/416 miles

Produced in both civil and military versions, the Gazelle is of French origin but now forms part of a joint venture with the Westland Helicopter Company in England. The principal civil version is known as the SA341G, which uses a 590shp Turbomeca Astazon IIIA engine.

Production of French versions began in 1967 and deliveries from the British production lines started in 1973.

The Gazelle is used for police work in the North Rhine-Westphalia region of West Germany.

Below: *Aerospatiale Gazelle of the North Rhine-Westphalia Police.*

Puma SA330

Accommodation: Crew of two plus 16-20 passengers
Engines: Two 1,320shp Turbomeca Turmo IIIC4 turbo shafts
Rotor diameter: 49ft 2.5in
Fuselage length: 48ft 1.5in
Gross weight: 14,110lb
Speed: 174mph (max)
Range: 390 miles

The Puma is essentially a military machine and is used by the para-military Bundesgrenzschutz (Federal Border Police) in West Germany.

Like the Gazelle, the Puma was first produced as an entirely French aircraft to meet French Army requirements and originally flew in 1965. In 1968 an agreement was entered into with Westland Helicopters in the UK for them to produce certain components and assemble some of the models destined for use by the RAF.

Below: *Aerospatiale Puma of the Belgian Gendarmerie.*

Beechcraft   USA

Beech Aircraft Corporation has been building fine general aviation aircraft for more than 40 years. The Beech Staggerwing 17 set world records in the early 1930s and the Beechcraft name has been in the forefront of aviation constructors ever since.

Head Office — Beech Aircraft Corporation, Wichita, Kansas 67201, USA.

Beechcraft 18

Accommodation: 2 pilots and 5-7 passengers
Engines: Two 450hp Pratt & Whitney piston engines
Wingspan: 49ft 8in
Length: 35ft 2.5in
Gross weight: 9,900lb
Speed: 220mph at 10,000ft (max cruising)
Range: 1,530 miles

Over 9,000 Beechcraft 18s were built during its long production life which spanned from 1937 to 1969 — almost certainly a record of longevity for any aircraft. During its lifetime many changes were introduced and modifications made but the basic design remained the same for nearly 33 years.

The Indonesian Police currently use Beechcraft 18s for Search and Rescue work and also as a means of transport across the vast territory under its jurisdiction.

King Air E90

Accommodation: 2 pilots and 6 passengers
Engines: Two Pratt & Whitney PT6A-28 turboprops, 680shp
Wingspan: 50ft 3in
Length: 35ft 6in
Gross weight: 9,650lb
Speed: 287mph at 12,000ft (max cruising)

Below: *Beechcraft King Air of the Royal Canadian Mounted Police.* RCMP

Range: 1,870 miles
Service ceiling: 27,620ft

The King Air began life in 1964 as an extension of the piston-engined Queen Air, incorporating turboprop engines and a pressurised cabin. In 1972 a version known as the E90 appeared, using uprated engines and it is this model which is at present in service with the Royal Canadian Mounted Police, based at Ottawa.

Super King Air 200

Accommodation: 2 pilots and 8 passengers
Engines: Two 850shp Pratt & Whitney turboprops
Wingspan: 54ft 6in
Length: 43ft 9in
Gross weight: 12,500lb
Speed: 333mph (max)
320mph at 25,000ft (max cruising)

Below: *Beechcraft Super King Air of the Royal Canadian Mounted Police.* RCMP

Range: 2,172 miles
Service ceiling: Over 31,000ft

Introduced in 1974 as an addition to the King Air range, the Super King Air has more powerful engines, moved out along the wings away from the fuselage to reduce cabin noise and a T tail. The fuselage is longer and the span greater than the King Air.

The Royal Canadian Mounted Police have a Super King Air based at Victoria BC.

Queen Air A80

Accommodation: 1 or 2 pilots and 4-9 passengers
Engines: Two 380hp Lycoming piston engines
Length: 35ft 6in
Speed: 183/224mph (cruising)
Range: 1,550 miles

The first Queen Air flew in 1958 and a number of variations followed, the prototype 80 taking to the air in June, 1961. Production models were designated A80 and B80, the latter having an increased wingspan. Production of the Queen Air has now ceased. The Texas Department of Public Safety (State Police) use a Queen Air A80 for police work.

Bell   USA

It is the proud boast of Bell Helicopter that there are more Bell helicopters at work in the world than all other makes combined and this claim is clearly reflected in the use made by the police of Bell products. At the Bell factory at Fort Worth/Dallas are to be found the world's largest and most comprehensive facilities devoted exclusively to the manufacture of rotary wing aircraft.

Head Office — Bell Helicopter, Post Office Box ⸱ 82, Forth Worth, Texas 76101, USA.

Bell 47

Accommodation: 3 seats
Engine: Lycoming 220 or 265bhp according to model
Rotor diameter: 37ft 1.5in
Fuselage length: 31ft 7in
Gross weight: 2,850lb/2,950lb
Speed: 84/98mph (cruising)
Range: 236/277 miles
Service ceiling: Up to 20,000ft

Below: *Bell 47 of the El Salvador Police.*
El Salvador National Police

The popular little 47 was in production from 1946 until 1974, both at the parent company's factory and also by Augusta in Italy. A version was also manufactured by Kawasaki in Japan. The list of police users of the Bell 47 is impressive — the Los Angeles Police Department, the New York PD, the Dallas City Police, the Washington (DC) Metropolitan PD, the San Francisco PD, the Chicago City Police, the Italian Carabinieri, the Swedish Police, the Kenya Police, the Austrian Police, the West German Federal Border Police (Bundesgrenzschutz), the Metropolitan Police in London and the Surrey Police.

Bell UH-1B/UH-1D/205

Accommodation: 2 crew and 12-14 passengers
Engine: One 1,400shp Lycoming turboshaft
Rotor diameter; 48ft
Fuselage length: 41ft 10.75in
Gross weight: 9,500lb
Speed; 127mph (max)
Range: 318 miles at 127mph
Service ceiling: 12,600ft

The UH-1B (then known as the HU-1B) first flew in 1960 and was produced in large numbers for the US Army and for the armed forces in many other countries. It was also manufactured by Fuji in Japan. A great many UH-1Bs were used in the war in Vietnam and the New York State Police purchased an army surplus model for police work.

The UH-1D was an enlarged version of the UH-1B and was also produced in civilian guise as the 205. Both military and civilian versions are used by police forces throughout the world, notably the West German Bundesgrenzschutz (Federal Border Police), the Italian Carabinieri, the Peruvian Gardia Civil, the Dubai Police and the Bahrain Police. These models are built by Augusta in Italy, Fuji in Japan and by the Chinese Nationalist state-owned factory in Taiwan.

The UH-1D has been supplanted by the UH-1H and the 205 by the 205A-1 but at the time of writing, these have not found their way into any police helicopter units.

Below: *Bell 205.*

Bell 206A/206B Jet Ranger

Accommodation: 5 seats
Engine: One Allison 250-C20 (400shp)
Rotor diameter: 33ft 4in
Fuselage length: 31ft 2in
Gross weight: 3,200lb
Speed: 138mph (cruising)
Range: 345/388 miles
Service ceiling: 13,500ft

The Jet Ranger is claimed, not without justification, to be the world's most popular, most widely used five-place turbine helicopter. Certainly there are

probably more Jet Rangers in use for police work than any other single model.

The 317shp 206A has now been replaced by the more powerful 206B but examples of both may be found on active police service with the New York State Police, the Texas Department of Public Safety, Los Angeles PD, New York PD, Dallas City PD, Virginia State Police, Arizona Department of Public Safety, Maryland State Police, Delaware State Police, Palm Beach Sheriff's Department, Pennsylvania State Police, Ontario Provincial Police, Quebec Provincial Police, the Royal Canadian

Mounted Police (at Victoria BC, Comox BC and Fort McMurray, Alberta), Caracas Metropolitan Police (Venezuela), the Korean National Police, The Victoria Police (Australia), the Swedish National Police, the Austrian Police and the Italian Carabinieri.

Top: *Bell 206B of the Arizona Dept of Public Safety.*

Above: *Bell 206B of the Royal Canadian Mounted Police.* RCMP

Bell 206L Long Ranger

Accommodation: 7 seats
Engine: Allison 250-C20B (420hp)
Speed: 150mph (max)
Range: 350 miles
Service ceiling: 15/20,000ft

The seven-place, 140mph turbine powered Long Ranger is a larger version of the highly popular Jet Ranger and is also used by the police, although to a lesser extent as the extra carrying capacity and other refinements are often unnecessary for their purposes. The Ontario Provincial Police use a Long Ranger for search and rescue work and they are also

used by the Royal Canadian Mounted Police (in Newfoundland) and the Texas Department of Public Safety.

Above: *Bell 206L*.

Bell 212

Accommodation: 15 seats
Engine: Pratt & Whitney Twin-pac coupled turboshaft 1,800shp
Rotor diameter: 48ft 2.25in
Fuselage length: 42ft 4.75in
Gross weight: 11,200lb
Speed: 126mph
Range: 273 miles
Service ceiling: 13,200/20,000 plus

Below: *Bell 212 of the Royal Canadian Mounted Police.* RCMP

The 212 is a development of the 205, the principal difference lying in the engine — a twin-pac coupled turboshaft. The 212 was designed with this twin power plant, twin hydraulic and electrical systems, twin fuel systems, even twin fire detectors and extinguishing systems. It is IFR certified for night and adverse weather flying. The Royal Canadian Mounted Police have a 212 at St John's, Newfoundland and examples are also in use in West Germany with the Baden-Württemberg police and the Bundesgrenzschutz.

Cessna

If Bell are the principal suppliers of helicopters for police work, Cessna must be the equivalent for light, fixed wing aircraft. The company's claim to be No 1 in the sky is certainly true so far as the police are concerned.

Head Office — Cessna Aircraft Company, Wichita, Kansas 67201, USA.

Cessna 150/152

Data: 150
Accommodation: 2 seats side by side
Engine: Continental piston engine 100hp
Wingspan: 32ft 8.5in
Length: 23ft 9in
Gross weight: 1,600lb
Speed: 93/117mph (cruising)
Range: 475/725 miles

The 150 is a small two-seater of which around 24,000 were built before the model 152 was substituted in its place in 1977, thus ending nearly 20 years continuous production. Versions of these aircraft are built in France by Reims Aviation and also in Argentina.

The 150 is used by the Carabineros de Chile for patrolling their extensive, sparsely populated rural zones and is also used by the Surrey Police (hired).

Cessna 172/Skyhawk and 182/Skylane

Data: Skyhawk
Accommodation: 4 seats
Engine: One Lycoming 160hp piston engine
Wingspan: 35ft 10in
Length: 28ft 2in
Gross weight: 2,300lb
Speed: 150mph (cruising)
Range: 864 miles
Service ceiling: 14,200ft

The 172 and its deluxe version, the Skyhawk, represent Cessna's middle range of four-seater, all-metal aircraft. Its light weight is easily propelled by the powerful 160hp engine and a new 28 volt electrical system aids cold weather starting. Police users of the 172 or Skyhawk include the New York State Police, the Florida Highway Patrol, the Dutch Rijkspolitie and the Sussex Police (hired). The Ontario Provincial Police used the Skyhawk until recently. The 182 and its deluxe version the Skylane are similar models, fitted with a 230hp Continental engine. These are used by the Florida Highway Patrol, Los Angeles County Sheriff, Arkansas State Police, Virginia State Police, the Victoria (Australia) Police and the Austrian Police.

Cessna 180/185 Skywagon

Accommodation: 6 seats
Engines: (180) Continental 230hp piston engine (185) Continental 300hp piston engine
Wingspan: 35ft 10in
Length: 25ft 9in
Gross weight: 2,800/3,360lb
Speed: 175/180mph (cruising)
Range: 829/1,025 miles
Service ceiling: 17,700ft

The two versions of the Skywagon are basically the same apart from the power plant and come with land, snow and water landing equipment. Coupled with short landing and take-off capabilities and seating for up to six people, this adds up to a very useful light aircraft.

The Queensland Police in Australia use two 180s for police personnel and prisoner transportation, traffic surveillance, drug trafficking detection and search and rescue tasks. The 185 is also used in Western Australia and the City of Winnipeg hire a 180 as required.

Cessna 206 Stationair

Engine: Continental 300hp piston engine
Accommodation: 6 seats (grouped in pairs)
Wingspan: 35ft 10in
Length: 28ft
Gross weight: 3,600lb
Speed: 180mph (cruising)
Range: 870 miles
Service ceiling: 14,800ft

As the name implies, the Stationair is Cessna's 'Stationwagon' of the air — a combined six-seater passenger craft and a useful cargo-carrying workhorse. The quiet running engine is fitted with a three-bladed propeller and gives good high altitude and hot weather performance. Principal police users are the Gendarmerie Nationale in France and the Kenya Police.

Cessna 210 Centurion

Accommodation: 6 seats
Engine: One 300hp Continental piston engine
Wingspan: 36ft 9in
Length: 28ft 3in
Gross weight: 3,800lb
Speed: 210mph (cruising)
Range: 1,227 miles
Service ceiling: 17,300ft

The 210, which first flew in 1957, was the first high-wing monoplane with a retractable undercarriage manufactured by Cessna. In 1967 the wing struts were dispensed with to give a full cantilever wing. In 1977 a pressurised version was announced, the world's first single-engine aircraft so equipped.

The Los Angeles Police Department have taken the Centurion into use for Police work.

Below: *Cessna 210 Centurion.*

Cessna 310

Accommodation: 6 seats
Engine: Two Continental 285hp engines, fuel injected
Wingspan: 36ft 11in
Length: 31ft 11.5in
Weight: 5,500lb (max)
Speed: 255mph (max)
Service ceiling: 19,750ft

The 310 is one of the American classic aircraft, its sleek lines matched by its handling and speed. It is the world's best selling light twin, capable of cruising for 570 miles at 238mph on standard fuel tanks. Optional fuel tanks increase the range to over 1,000 miles. The 310 is presently in service with the Kenya Police.

Cessna 337 Skymaster

Accommodation: 6 seats
Engines: Two Teledyne Continental fuel injection piston engines, 210bhp
Wingspan: 38ft 2in
Length: 29ft 9in
Weight: 4,648lb (Max)
Speed: 220mph
208mph (cruising)
Range: 770 miles (standard tanks)
Service ceiling: 18,000ft

The first flight of this revolutionary 'push/pull' aircraft took place in 1961 and it went into production in

1963. The Skymaster combines all the advantages of a conventional twin-engined light aircraft but with simpler handling characteristics, especially in the event of one engine failing. Early Skymasters had a fixed undercarriage but the version with retractable undercarriage replaced it in 1965.

Variations of the Standard 337 include pressurised versions and the 'Turbo' model with turbo-charged engines. Standard versions are also assembled by Reims Aviation in France and it is these which have been taken into use by the Dutch Rijkspolitie.

Cessna 401/402/402B

Accommodation: 8-10
Engines: Two Continental 300hp piston engines
Wingspan: 39ft 11in
Length: 36ft 1in
Speed: 282mph (max)
259mph (cruising)
Range: 1,420 miles
Service ceiling: 26,180ft

These additions to the Cessna range were announced in 1966. The 401 seated 6/8 persons and was designed for the executive market whilst the

402, which had similar dimensions and performance, had 9/10 seats in rather less sumptuous surroundings. The 402B, which was introduced in 1971, has a longer nose than the early 401/402 which it replaced and is available in two versions, the 402B Businessliner with seating for up to eight, and the 402B Utililiner with up to 10 seats. All dimensions and performance data are the same for both versions.

The Texas Department of Public Safety (State Police) use one Model 401 and two Model 402Bs. The Kenya Police are currently using the Model 402.

Cessna 404 Titan

Accommodation: Up to 11 seats
Engines: Two Continental 375hp piston engines, turbocharged and fuel injected
Wingspan: 46ft 4in
Length: 39ft 6.5in
Weight: 8,400lb (max)
Speed: 286mph (max)
245mph (cruising)
Range: 700 miles (standard tanks)
Service ceiling: 26,000ft

Cessna's big workhorse, the Titan, is made in three versions — the Courier, a quickly convertible cargo/passenger hauler, the Ambassador, a big, luxury executive aircraft and the Freighter, specifically designed to carry bulk cargo.

In all three versions, an optional digital fuel flow gauge and computer provides highly accurate readouts on the amount of fuel remaining and facilitates the choice of optimum fuel flow rates.

The Titan is another of the Cessna products which the Kenya Police use in their Air Branch.

De Havilland
Canada

In 1928 de Havilland of Canada Limited started as a small sales and service outlet for British built aeroplanes; from this, the company has grown to be the world leader in design and construction of STOL (short take-off and landing) transport aircraft.

De Havilland of Canada's first real impression on the world's aviation market made its debut in 1947, the DHC-2 Beaver, the forerunner of the company's successful range of STOL aircraft — the DHC-2 Mk III Turbo-Beaver, DHC 3 Otter, DHC-4 Caribou,

DHC-5 Buffalo and the DHC-6 Twin Otter.

The Company's latest design, the DASH 7 'Quiet STOL Airliner' was introduced into airline service in 1977.

With a reputation for engineering excellence de Havilland Canada is also actively involved in aerodynamic and hydrodynamic research.

Head Office — The de Havilland Aircraft of Canada Limited, Downsview, Ontario, Canada.

DHC-2 Beaver

Below: *De Havilland Beaver.*

Accommodation: 1 crew and up to 7 passengers
Engine: One Pratt & Whitney 578hp piston engine (radial)
Wingspan: 48ft
Length: 35ft 3in
Gross weight: 5,370lb
Speed: 140/157mph (cruising)
Range: 260 miles (677 with reserve tanks)

The highly successful Beaver bushplane first flew in 1947 and was the forerunner of the de Havilland range of STOL utility aircraft. It was specifically designed to meet Canadian requirements for a rugged 'bush' aircraft but found a ready market in other countries and sold in 65 different countries. A total of 1,163 Beavers was built before production ceased. The Royal Canadian Mounted Police are using four Beavers, based at Ottawa, Regina, Edmonton and Kamloops (BC), using wheels, skis or floats as landing gear as necessary. Another police user of the rugged, versatile STOL craft is Dallas City PD in Texas USA.

DHC-2 Mk III Turbo Beaver

De Havilland entered the jet age in 1960 with the development of the Turbo Beaver. A lighter, more powerful gas turbine engine replaced the piston engine fitted to earlier versions of the Beaver, giving greater work efficiency and increased payload. Undercarriage options included wheels, wheels and skis, skis or floats enabling it to be operated from hard-surfaced runways, snow covered fields or water. Sixty examples of the Turbo Beaver were sold, two of these being used by the RCMP based at Prince George BC and Peace River, Alberta. Another one is used by the Ontario Provincial Police to patrol about 28 Indian Reserves in the vast northland of the province.

Below: *De Havilland Turbo Beaver of the Royal Canadian Mounted Police.* RCMP

DHC-3 Otter

Accommodation: 1 pilot and 10 passengers
Engine: One Pratt & Whitney 'Wasp' 600bhp
Wingspan: 58ft
Length: 41ft 10in
Gross weight: 8,000lb
Speed: 144mph (134mph seaplane) (cruising)
Range: 875 miles

The Otter followed the Beaver 'bush' aircraft tradition of the Beaver as a one-ton payload airborne truck. It first flew in 1951 and was sold as an enlarged version of the Beaver. A total of 460 aircraft was built, many being sold to the US and Canadian armed forces. The Royal Canadian Mounted Police took five and fly them out of Thompson and Winnipeg (Manitoba), Goose Bay (Labrador), Yellow Knife

(NWT) and Ottawa. The Ontario Provincial Police use one to supplement their Beaver patrols of the northern parts of the province.

The Otter is fitted with either land, snow or water landing gear and an amphibious version was developed, using retractable wheels in the standard floats.

Special equipment carried in the OPPs Otter includes an axe, a message dropper, first aid kit and resuscitator, flashlight, maps, paddles, distress signal, thermal blanket, emergency flare kit, eight man/day emergency rations, survival kit (matches, compass, etc) and inflatable life vest. Production of the Otter ceased in 1967.

DHC-6 Twin Otter

Accommodation: 1-2 pilots, up to 20 pasengers
Engines: Two Pratt & Whitney turbo props
Wingspan: 65ft
Length: 51ft 9in
Gross weight: 12,500lb
Speed: 210mph (max cruising)
Range: 794 miles
Service ceiling: 28,000ft

The Twin Otter is a twin-engined development of the single-engine Otter, using tubro-prop power units mounted on the high wing. It can carry up to 20 passengers or two tonnes of freight, landing and taking off from short, partially prepared landing strips. The sturdy construction, combined with ease

of maintenance are attractive to many operators, including the police, and the Royal Canadian Mounted Police use eight, based at Thompson (Manitoba), Edmonton (Alberta), Regina and Prince Albert (Saskatchewan), Whitehorse (Yukon), and three in the North West Territories. Introduced in 1966, production of the Twin Otter continues and some 600 have been sold in around 70 countries throughout the world. Twin Otters may be fitted with wheels, skis or floats to choice. Earlier models were fitted with 579ehp engines but current versions use 652ehp motors.

Below: *De Havilland Twin Otter of the Royal Canadian Mounted Police.* RCMP

Enstrom

USA

The Enstrom Helicopter Corporation is one of the smaller specialist manufacturers of helicopters, making up in quality what they lack in quantity.

The first Enstrom helicopter flew in 1960 and three models are now produced which are regularly

used by Police Departments in the United States.

Head Office — the Enstrom Helicopter Corp, PO Box 277, Twin County Airport, Menominee, Michigan 49858.

F-28C/F-28C-2/280C

Accommodation: 3 seats
Engine: Lycoming four-cylinder fuel injected engine giving 205hp and fitted with a Rajay Turbocharger to maintain power at all altitudes and temperatures
Rotor diameter: 32ft
Fuselage length: 29ft 4in
Gross weight: 2,350lb
Speed: 112mph (max)
107mph (cruising)
Range: 270 miles (no reserve)
Operating ceiling: 12,000ft

These three models are essentially the same, all being developments of the original F-28 which first flew in 1962. All are functionally designed three-seat turbocharged helicopters, the F-28C-2 being mainly intended for utility work whilst the other two are designed as business and pleasure machines. All use the same engine and are externally identical save for detail design points.

These helicopters are used by a number of police forces in the United States and also by the Tasmanian Police.

Below: *Enstrom F-28C-2.*

Grumman

USA

Grumman have been well known for many years for their sturdy reliable aircraft, not a few of which served with distinction in World War II. It was one of the last companies to make amphibians of the classic style.

Head Office — Grumman American Aviation Corporation, PO Box 2206, Savannah, Georgia 31402.

Grumman Goose

Accommodation: 8 persons
Engines: Two Pratt & Whitney Wasps Jr, 400hp at 2,300rpm
Wingspan: 49ft
Length: 38ft 4in
Gross weight: 8,000lb
Speed: 185mph (max)
150mph (cruising)
Range: Up to 825 miles
Service ceiling: 18,000ft

Dating from just before the war, the Goose was produced to meet orders from commercial users for a rugged amphibian but most of the 250 plus which were built went to aid the US war effort, especially in the Pacific. After the war many of these found their way on to the civilian market as war surplus and one of these is used by the Royal Canadian Mounted Police, flying out of Prince Rupert, BC.

Helio

USA

The Helio Aircraft Corporation was founded to develop and market a light aircraft with STOL characteristics and high safety margins. The sole product of the company is now the Super Courier which replaced the Courier.

Courier/Super Courier

Accommodation: 6 seats
Engine: One Lycoming 295hp piston engine
Wingspan: 39ft
Length: 31ft
Gross weight: 3,400lb
Speed: 150mph (cruising)
Range: 660/1, 400 miles

The Courier was developed out of a Piper Vagabond and used full-span automatic leading edge slats and high-lift flaps. The versatile landing and take-off characteristics, plus its slow cruising speed make it an ideal light aircraft for airborne patrols and it is used for this purpose by the Los Angeles County Sheriff's Department.

Hughes

USA

One of the small but highly successful American Helicopter manufacturers, Hughes make just two models — the 300 and the 500 — for the general market, plus the YAH-64 advanced attack helicopter for the US Army.

The Hughes Tool Company first entered the helicopter field in 1955 with the Model 269 which eventually became the 300.

Head Office — Hughes Helicopters, Culver City, California 90230.

Hughes 300 (Sky Knight)

Accommodation: 3 seats
Engine: One Lycoming 190hp reciprocating engine
Rotor diameter: 26ft 10in
Length: 30ft 10in
Gross weight: 2,050lb
Speed: 115mph (max)
100mph (cruising)
Range: 260 miles
Service ceiling; 15,000ft
Endurance: 3.5 hours

The 300 began life as the 269 and was put on sale in 1961 after the US Army had carried out evaluation tests and taken some into service. It became a standard military primary trainer and has been bought for military use by a number of countries. So far as police work is concerned the 300 is in use with the Houston City Police Department and the Los Angeles County Sheriff's Department. The Bahrain police also use them and the Hertfordshire Constabulary, the West Yorkshire Metropolitan Police and the Nottinghamshire Constabulary hire them as and when required.

A special, law-enforcement version, known as the Sky Knight is available. This has double exhaust silencing to allow quiet operation at 500ft altitude in urban areas, siren, searchlights, public address system and ballistic fibreglass cabin armour under the seats. The 27ft rotor diameter is small enough to allow the Sky Knight to be put down in a street.

Right: *Hughes 300 Sky Knight of the Los Angeles County Sheriff's Dept Aero Bureau.*
Los Angeles County Sheriff

Hughes 500 (Sky Knight)

Accommodation: 5 seats
Engine: One Allison 317shp engine, derated to 278shp
Rotor diameter: 26ft 6in
Length: 23ft 2in
Gross weight: 3,000lb
Speed: 175mph (max)
155/168mph (cruising)
Range: 350 miles at 160mph
Service ceiling: 15/20,000ft
Endurance: $3\frac{1}{2}$ hours at 80mph

Under the designation OH-GA, the 500 was taken into service by the US Army in 1966 and commercial versions followed soon afterwards. It is the fastest five-seat light turbine in production and can raise one ton in hover.

Like the Model 300, a police version, also known as Sky Knight, is available and is used by a number of forces including the Bahrain Police, the Victoria Police (Australia), the Danish State Police, Houston City Police, Washington (DC) Metropolitan Police Department, Maricopa County Sheriff's Department (Arizona), and the California Highway Patrol.

Below: Hughes 500 Sky Knight of the Los Angeles County Sheriff's Dept emergency services detail with crew of paramedic deputy sheriffs.
Los Angeles County Sheriff

Kamov

USSR

Kamov is one of the smaller aircraft manufacturers in the USSR, concentrating on helicopters and comprising the team which Nikolai Kamov gathered round him before his death. Kamov have been producing helicopters with co-axial rotors for a number of years.

Kamov Ka-26

Accommodation: 2 crew and up to 6 passengers
Engine: 2 Vedeneev 325hp radial engines
Rotor diameter: 42ft 8in
Length: 24ft 5in

Gross weight: 7,165lb
Speed: 56-93mph (cruising)
Range: 745 miles with auxiliary tanks

The Ka-26 is a standard, all-purpose helicopter which is used extensively in Russia and other East European Countries. It first appeared in 1965 and, by podding the two radial engines and mounting them on short stub wings, the whole rear fuselage is made detachable behind the flight deck. The fuselage pod, which normally holds up to six passengers or an equivalent amount of freight, can be left off and the aircraft used as a flying crane or fitted with a cargo platform.

The Ka-26 is known to be in use with the East German Volkspolizei and it is probably used by a number of other police forces behind the 'Iron Curtain'.

Messerschmitt   West Germany

The name of Messerschmitt is synonymous with the fighters and fighter-bombers of the Luftwaffe in World War II and even today, this famous West German firm turns out fine aircraft, although these are now for more peaceful, civilian purposes. The BO105 has, in particular, earned an enviable reputation in the helicopter field.

Head Office — Messerschmitt-Bölkow-Blohm GmbH, Helicopter Division, Postfach 801140, 8000 München 80.

BO105

Accommodation: 5 seats
Engines: Two Allison 317shp or 400shp turbine engines
Rotor diameter: 32ft 3in
Length: 28ft 0.5in
Gross weight: 5,070lb
Speed: 144mph (cruising)
Range: 658 miles (with auxiliary tank)

Below: *Messerschmitt BO105 of the Dutch Rijkspolitie.* Korps Rijkspolitie

The BO105, developed under German government contract, came into production in the late 1960s and, in 1971, the first police model was taken into use by the Bavarian Police. By 1977 more than 50 models were in use with police forces both in West Germany and abroad, covering several of the German forces, the Policia Federal Argentina, the Dutch Rijkspolitie, the Carabineros de Chile, the Philippines Integrated National Police and the Spanish Guardia Civil. For police work the BO105 is fitted with a large searchlight, siren, armoured cabin etc.

Partenavia   Italy

Mainly involved in producing lightweight, high wing monoplanes for pleasure, air-taxi and training work, Partenavia also make the P68 Victor twin-engined light transport.

P68 Victor

Accommodation: 1 pilot and 5 passengers
Engines: Two Lycoming 200hp piston engines
Wingspan: 39ft 4.5in
Length: 30ft 2in
Gross weight: 4,320lb
Speed: 185/190mph (cruising)
Range: 1,045 miles at 9.000ft

The Victor only came into production in 1974 and was very quickly taken into service with the Western Australia Police who use this long-legged transport to reach the furthermost corners of their vast 'constablewick'.

Piper   USA

The Piper Aircraft Corporation has a long and distinguished history as the manufacturer of quality light aircraft at reasonable cost. Not surprisingly, therefore, Piper aircraft find a ready market in police circles.

Head Office — Piper Aircraft Corporation — Lock Haven, Pennsylvania 17745.

Aztec

Accommodation: 6 seats
Engines: Two Lycoming 250hp six-cylinder or two Lycoming turbocharged 250hp engines. Bendix fuel injection
Wingspan: 37ft 2.5in
Length: 31ft 2.75in
Gross weight: 5,200lb
Speed: 220mph (235/260mph Turbo model) (cruising)
Range: 1,135 miles (1,525 with reserve tanks)
Service ceiling: 17,600ft

The Aztec has become something of a legend since its introduction in 1959 with a reputation for rugged reliability, versatility and ease of handling. Over 4,500 are in use throughout the world. Improvements and refinements have been added over the 20 plus years of production, each significant change being recognised by a new model letter; current versions are designated Aztec F.

The Virginia State Police are among the principal police users of this versatile twin-engined aircraft.

Senaca

Accommodation: 6-7 seats
Engines: Two Teledyne Continental Turbo-charged 200hp engines

Below: *Piper Senaca of the South Australia Police.*
South Australia Police

Wingspan: 38ft 10.75in
Length: 28ft 6in
Gross weight: 4,570lb
Speed: 215mph (cruising)
Range: 800 miles
Service ceiling: 25,000ft
Endurance: 290min

Since its introduction in 1971 the Senaca has gained a reputation for size, comfort, quietness, range and economy. It is fully equipped with de-icing equipment, full line of avionics, weather radar, cabin heaters and oxygen package. The propellers are counter rotating for smooth flight and elimination of differential torque. The South Australian Police use the Senaca to cover their vast territory in speed and comfort.

Super Cub

Accommodation: 2 seats in tandem
Engine: One Lycoming 150hp piston engine
Wingspan: 35ft 3.5in
Length: 22ft 6in
Gross weight: 1,750lb
Speed: 130mph (max)
115mph (cruising)
43mph (stalling)
Range: 460 miles
Service ceiling: 19,000ft

The Super Cub with its ability to land and take-off almost anywhere was introduced in 1949 — long before the word STOL was coined. The two seats are

placed in tandem and the aircraft can be flown from either. The hinged right door and window can be opened in flight — a useful feature for police work as well as for photography and hunting purposes. The Super Cub takes-off in 200ft and can clear a 50ft obstacle from a starting point only 500ft away. Although the official ceiling is 19,000ft a Super Cub set up the world's altitude record for piston-engined light aircraft when it climbed to 30,203ft.

The STOL capabilities and its ability to fly low and slow make the Super Cub an ideal aircraft for many police purposes and models are in use in places as far apart as Austria, Virginia (State Police) and Sussex.

Navajo

Accommodation: 1 Pilot and 5-7 passengers
Engines: Two Lycoming 425hp piston engines
Wingspan: 40ft 8in
Length: 34ft 6in
Gross weight: 7,800lb
Speed: 190/266mph (cruising)
Range: 1,335 miles

Below: *Piper Navajo of the Victoria Police.*
Victoria Police

The Navajo came into production in 1967 since when it has represented the largest aircraft in the Piper range. In 1975 the Victoria Police in Australia established the value of using aircraft for police purposes and formed an Air Wing. Its tasks included searches (escapees, offenders, missing persons), traffic control, survey of disaster areas and rapid transport of personnel and equipment. For the latter role a Navajo was used (although this has recently been replaced by a Rockwell Shrike Commander).

Rockwell

USA

The Rockwell-Standard Corporation merged with the North American Aviation Company in 1967, forming part of the Rockwell International Company which has been heavily involved in aerospace work. Aircraft manufacture is under the General Aviation Division.

Head Office — Rockwell International, General Aviation Division, 5001 North Rockwell Avenue, Bethany, Oklahoma 73008.

Shrike Commander

Accommodation: 6 seats
Engines: Two Lycoming six-cylinder, air-cooled, fuel injected engines, 290hp
Wingspan: 49ft 0.5in
Length: 36ft 9.75in
Gross weight: 6,750lb
Speed: 215mph (max)
203 mph (cruising)
Range: Up to 950 miles
Service ceiling: 19,400ft

The Commander was designed in 1946 and a company — Aero Design and Engineering Co — was established to produce it. The Commander was the first light twin to be specifically created for business flying and was simple enough for an owner/pilot to fly. It was also the first light twin to be used as a

Presidential transport when the Eisenhower administration bought several for White House use. President Kennedy used the Commander exclusively.

In 1958 Aero Design became a subsidiary of Rockwells and was renamed Aero Commander. When Rockwell and North American merged in 1967, Aero Commander became the General Aviation Division (and remains so today) and the Commander aircraft became the Shrike Commander.

It is a large aeroplane, the designation 'light' being relative and has a gross weight of 6,750lb.

Police users of the Shrike Commander include the Bahamas Police and the Victoria Police in Australia.

Below: *Rockwell Shrike Commander.*

Saab-Scannia

Sweden

Saab-Scania is Sweden's principal aircraft manufacturer and is also well known for its automobiles. The bulk of Saab's aircraft production is intended for military use but a number of private models are available.

Head Office — Saab-Scania AB, Aerospace Division, S-581 88 Linköping, Sweden.

Supporter

Accommodation: 2-3 seats
Engine: One Lycoming 200hp piston engine
Wingspan: 29ft
Length: 22ft 11.5in
Gross weight: 2,425lb
Speed: 160mph (max)
Endurance: 5hr 10min

Originally a product of the MFI Company, production of the Supporter continued after MFI was taken over by Saab, and developed as a lightweight strike aircraft. It is in use for military purposes with a number of armies, including those in Scandinavia, Pakistan and in Africa. The Danish Army Aviation branch cooperates with the Danish State Police, making Supporters available to them as required. For police missions, these aircraft are usually flown by an Army pilot with a police observer.

Sikorsky   USA

On 14 September 1939, Igor Sikorsky lifted the wheels of his experimental helicopter a few inches off the ground and the age of direct-lift aircraft was born. This fledgling quickly grew up, its unique ability to rise and descend vertically, hover, move backwards and forwards or sideways lending it to a wide variety of tasks. Today, helicopters made by Sikorsky Aircraft, a division of United Technologies

Corporation, are flown by all the US military services and in more than 30 foreign countries.

Sikorsky helicopters are also manufactured under licence in other countries, notably Westland's in the United Kingdom and Sud Aviation in France. They are also built in Japan.

Sikorsky S58

Below: *Sikorsky S-58 of the Los Angeles County Sheriff's Dept search and rescue unit.*
Los Angeles County Sheriff

Accommodation: 16-18 passengers
Engine: One Wright 1,525hp piston engine
Rotor diameter: 56ft
Length: 47ft 3in
Gross weight: 13,000lb
Speed: 127mph (cruising)
Range: 299 miles (with reserves)

The S58 was produced in 1954 under a contract with the US Navy for an anti-submarine helicopter

and a total of 1,821 models was eventually made. It is of an ideal size and design for Coastguard work and Search and Rescue operations on both land and sea.

Although primarily a military aircraft, a number of civilian versions are in use and the Los Angeles County Sheriff's Department uses five S58s for emergency and disaster operations/search and rescue work.

Sikorsky S61/Sea King

Data: S61
Accommodation: 25-30 passengers
Engines: Two General Electric 1,500hp turboshaft engines
Rotor diameter: 62ft
Length: 59ft 4in
Gross weight: 19,000lb
Speed: 138mph (cruising)
Range: 518 miles (with reserves). The Sea King military version is faster and has a still greater range

The S61 is a large, passenger or load carrying version of the military Sea King but with a longer fuselage and certain other differences. Fitted with two turboshaft engines, the S61 has a greater range than the S58 and is therefore more suitable for long distance work. A number are used to service the North Sea oil rigs, for example.

The only police force known to use these large machines is the Danish State Police — probably utilising the fleet acquired by the Danish Air Force for long-range air/sea rescue.

Sikorsky S62

Accommodation: Up to 10 passengers
Engine: One General Electric turboshaft engine, 1,250hp derated to 730hp
Rotor diameter: 53ft
Length: 44ft 6in

Below: *Sikorsky S-62 of the Thailand Police.*

Gross weight: 8,000lb
Speed: 92mph (cruising)
Range: 462 miles

In 1958, Sikorsky unveiled the S62 — the fore-runner of an entirely new generation of production helicopters. The S62 was amphibious, being equipped with a flying boat hull and powered by a single turbine, and was taken into use by the US Coast Guard for search and rescue. When Hurricane Betsy struck New Orleans in 1965, Coast Guard S62s rescued nearly 1,200 people.

The S62 has been taken into use with the Thailand Police Department for general police work and border patrols.

Westland   UK

The Westland Aircraft Company was one of those smaller manufacturers which built up a sound reputation between the wars which it consolidated by stirling work in aircraft production in the 1939/45 conflict. Most of the aeronautical work today is undertaken by its subsidiary, Westland Helicopters Limited, which produces a wide range of helicopters, although the majority of these are built under licence (eg from Sikorsky) or in collaboration with other helicopter manufacturers (eg Aerospatiale). The Scout/Wasp is, however, a fully British product.

Scout

Accommodation: 5-6 seats
Engine: One Rolls-Royce Nimbus turboshaft
Rotor diameter: 32ft 3in
Length: 40ft 4in
Gross weight: 5,500lb
Speed: 130mph (max)
Range: 275 miles
Service ceiling: 12,500ft

Below: *Westland Scout of the Bahrain Police Air Wing.*

The Scout is a general purpose light helicopter, currently in service with the British Army. The Wasp, which is a modified version of the Scout, is designed for sea-going use and is in service with the Royal Navy.

The Scout's small rotor diameter and ease of handling permits operation from very restricted areas. Performance is maintained at high altitudes and in hot climates.

The Bahrain Police use the Scout for general police duties and it is known that the Ugandan Police Air Wing had one but little information is available from that troubled country at the time of writing.

Index

Cars & Vans

Alfa Romeo
  Alfasud 6
  Alfetta 6
  Giulia 7
Alfasud (Alfa Romeo) 6
Alfetta (Alfa Romeo) 6
Allegro (Austin) 9
Alpine (Chrysler) 17
Alpine (Renault) 70
ARO 240 7
Ascona (Opel) 57
Aspen (Dodge) 24
Audi
  80 8
  100 8
Austin Allegro 9
Avenger (Chrysler) 17
Avia 2500 10

Bedford
  HA 10
  CF 11
Beetle (Volkswagen) 84
Bluebird (Datsun) 22
BMW
  3.0S 13
  320 12
  520 11
  525 12
  528 13
  728 13
  730 13
  2000 11
  2002 11
  2500 12
  2800 13
Bobcat (Mercury) 55
Bronco (Ford) 27
Bug (Volkswagen) 84

Capri (Ford) 32
Capri (Mercury) 55
Caprice (Chevrolet) 13
Carina (Toyota) 77
Catalina (Pontiac) 64
Cavalier (Vauxhall) 81
Celica (Toyota) 78
Charger (Chrysler) 16
Cherokee (Jeep) 45
Chevette (Vauxhall) 82
Chevrolet
  Caprice 13
  Impala 13
  Malibu 14
  Nova 14
Chrysler (US)
  Coronet 15
  Satellite 15
  Newport 15
Chrysler (Australia)

Valiant 15
  Charger Coupe 16
Chrysler (Spain) 180/2 litre 16
Chrysler (UK)
  Alpine 17
  Avenger 17
  Sunbeam 18
  Hunter 18
Citivan (Fiat) 26
Citroën
  ID21/Super 19
  DS 23 19
  SM (Maserati) 20
  CX2400 20
  Fourgon 20
City (Opel Kadett) 58
Civic (Honda) 43
CJ (Jeep) 44
Club Wagon (Ford) 28
Coccinelle (Volkswagen) 84
Colt
  Galant/Galant Sigma 21
  Lancer 21
Commodore (Opel) 57
Corolla (Toyota) 78
Corona 2000 (Toyota) 78
Coronet (Chrysler) 15
Cortina (Ford) 32
Cougar (Mercury) 55
Cressida (Toyota) 78
Cross-Country C303 (Volvo) 91
Crown (Toyota) 79
Cruiser (Land) (Toyota) 80
Custom 500 (Ford) 28

Daihatsu FZO 22
Datsun
  160B/180B Bluebird 22
  160J Violet 22
  200GT Skyline 23
  240C/260C/280C 23
Derby (Volkswagen) 88
Dispatcher 100 (Jeep) 45
Dodge
  Aspen 24
  St Regis 24
Dolomite (Triumph) 80
Dune Buggy (Volkswagen) 88

Eagle (Hestair) 37
Econoline (Ford) 28
Emergency One 24
Enforcer, Pontiac Catalina Freeway 64
Enforcer, Pontiac Le Mans 65
Escort (Ford) 33
Escort 35/45 Van (Ford) 34

F100 (Ford) 31
Fairmont (Ford) 28
Falcon (Ford) 31

Fiat
  127   25
  128   25
  131 Mirafiori   25
  132 Supermirafiori   26
  900 Citivan   26
Fiesta (Ford)   34
Ford (US)
  Bronco   27
  Custom 500   28
  Econoline van   28
  Club Wagon   28
  Fairmont   28
  LTD   29
  LTD II   29
  Maverick   30
  Torino   30
Ford (Australia)
  Falcon Sedan   31
  Falcon Wagon/Utility   31
  F100   34
Ford (UK)
  Capri   32
  Cortina   32
  Escort   33
  Escort 35/45 van   34
  Fiesta   34
  Transit   35
Ford (Germany) Granada   36
Fourgon (Citroën)   20
Freeway Enforcer (Pontiac Catalina)   64
Fury (Plymouth)   63

Galant (Colt)   21
Gemini (Holden)   39
Giulia (Alfa Romeo)   7
Golf (Volkswagen)   85
Granada (Ford)   36
Gran Fury (Plymouth)   63
GTS (Holden)   39

Harvester, International D1610   43
Hestair Eagle   37
Hi-Ace (Toyota)   80
Hillman Imp   38
Holden
  GTS   38
  Gemini   39
  Kingswood   40
  Torana   41
  Vans/pick-ups   41
  Kingswood vans/pick-ups   41
  One-tonner   42
Honda Civic   43
Hunter (Chrysler)   18

Imp (Hillman)   38
Impala (Chevrolet)   13
International Harvester D1610   43

J7 (Peugeot)   59
J20 (Jeep)   46
Jaguar XJ6/XJ4.2/XJ3.4   44
Jeep
  CJ Range   44
  Cherokee   45

  Wagoneer   45
  Dispatcher 100   45
  J20   46

Kadett (Opel)   57
Kadett City (Opel)   58
Käfer (Volkswagen)   84
Kever (Volkswagen)   84
Kingswood (Holden)   42
Kingswood van/pick-up (Holden)   42
Kombi (Volkswagen)   86

L 207 (Mercedes-Benz)   53
L 408, L 409 (Mercedes-Benz)   53
L 508D, L608D (Mercedes-Benz)   54
Lada 1500   46
Lancer (Colt)   21
Land Cruiser   80
Land Rover   73
Laurentian (Pontiac)   65
Le Mans (Pontiac)   65
Leyland
  Mini   47
  Maxi   47
  Princess   47
  Sherpa   48
LTD/LTD II (Ford)   29

Magnum (Vauxhall)   82
Malibu (Chevrolet)   14
Manta (Opel)   58
Marina (Morris)   56
Marquis (Mercury)   55
Maverick (Ford)   30
Maxi (Leyland)   47
Mazda
  616   49
  1300   49
  1800   49
  929   49
  RX series   50
Mercedes-Benz
  200   51
  230/250   51
  280/280E   51
  280S/SE   51
  350SL/450SL   52
  L207   53
  L408/409   53
  L508D/608D   54
  1210D   54
  1113   54
Mercury
  Bobcat   55
  Capri   55
  Cougar   55
  Marquis   55
  Monarch   55
  Zephyr   55
MGB GT   56
Mini (Leyland)   47
Mirafiori (Fiat)   25
Mitsubishi see Colt
Monarch (Mercury)   55
Morris Marina   56

Newport (Chrysler)   15
Nova (Chevrolet)   14

One-tonner (Holden)   42
Opel
    Ascona   57
    Commodore   57
    Kadett   57
    Kadett City   58
    Manta   58
    Rekord   58

Passat (Volkswagen)   87
Peugeot
    J7   59
    204   59
    304   60
    305   61
    404   61
    504   62
    604   62
Plymouth
    Fury   63
    Gran Fury   63
    Volaré   64
Princess (Leyland)   47
Police Protection Vehicle   24
Polo (Volkswagen)   88
Pontiac
    Catalina Freeway Enforcer   64
    Laurentian   65
    Le Mans Enforcer   65
Porsche
    911   66
    924   66
Rancho (Simca)   76
Range Rover   74
Rekord (Opel)   58
Renault
    4F   67
    4   67
    5   68
    6   68
    12   69
    14   69
    16   70
    30TS   70
    Alpine A110/A310   70
Rover
    3500 (1968-76)   71
    3500 (1976+)   72
    2600   73
    Land   73
    Range   74
RX Series (Mazda)   50

Saab
    95/96   75
    99   75
St Regis (Dodge)   24
Satellite (Chrysler)   15
Sherpa (Leyland)   48
Sigma (Colt Galant)   21
Simca
    Rancho   76
    1100   76

Skoda 110   77
Skyline (Datsun)   23
Sunbeam (Chrysler)   18
Supermirafiori (Fiat)   26

Torana (Holden)   41
Torino   (Ford)   30
Toyota
    Carina   77
    Celica   78
    Corolla   78
    Corona 2000   78
    Cressida   78
    Crown   79
    Land Cruiser   80
    Hi-Ace   80
Transit (Ford)   35
Triumph
    Dolomite   80
    2500   81
    2000   81

Valiant (Chrysler)   15
Vauxhall
    Cavalier   81
    Chevette   82
    Magnum   82
    Ventora   82
    Victor   82
    Viva   83
    VX Range   82
Ventora (Vauxhall)   82
Victor (Vauxhall)   82
Violet (Datsun)   22
Viva (Vauxhall)   83
Volare (Plymouth)   64
Volkswagen
    Beetle   84
    Bug   84
    Coccinelle   84
    Derby   88
    Dune Buggy   88
    Golf   85
    Käfer   84
    Kever   84
    Kombi   86
    Passat   87
    Polo   88
Volvo
    140/240 Series   89
    160/260 Series   90
    343   90
    C303 Cross Country   91
    66   92
VX Range (Vauxhall)   82

Wagoneer (Jeep)   45

XJ6 (Jaguar)   44
XJ3.4 (Jaguar)   44
XJ4.2   (Jaguar)   44

YLN 803/803SD   92

Zephyr (Mercury)   55

Motorcycles

BMW
   R45 93
   R50 93
   R60 93
   R65 93
   R75 94
   R80 94
   R90 95
   R100 95
Bonneville (Triumph) 119
BSA
   250 Star 96
   A50 Royal Star 96
   A65/A65T 96
Bullet (Enfield) 99

Cardinal (NVT) 114
Ciao (Vespa) 120
Commando (NVT) 113
CZ — see Jawa

DLB/Honda
Ducati
   450/500 97
   750/900 98

Electraglide (Harley-Davidson) 100
Enfield 350 Bullet 99

Florett (Kreidler) 111

Gold Wing (Honda) 105

Harley-Davidson
   45 Servi-car 99
   Electraglide 100
Hercules K125BW 101
Honda
   C90 102
   175/185 102
   CB200 102
   CB250 103
   350/360 103
   400/450/500 104
   500/550/4-cyl 104
   750 105
   1000 Gold Wing 105
   DLB 106

Interpol (NVT) 113

Jawa-CZ
   250 107
   350 107

Kawasaki
   200 108
   250/350 108
   KH400 108

Z400 109
Z900/Z1000 110
Kreidler Florett 111

Moto-Guzzi
   V35/V50 111
   V7-750/850T3 112
   1000 112

Norton — see NVT
Norton Yamaha 125
NVT (Norton) Commando/Interpol 113
NVT (Triumph) Trident/Cardinal 114

Rickman
   125 114
   650 115
Royal Star (BSA) 96

Sanglas 400F 116
Servi-car (Harley-Davidson) 99
Star (BSA) 96
Suzuki
   FR70/FR80 116
   A100 116
   GT185 117
   GT250 117
   GS550 117
   GS750 118

Tiger 750 (Triumph) 120
Trident (NVT) 114
Triumph see also under NVT
Triumph
   T100/5T 119
   650 (TR6 and Bonneville) 119
   750 (Tiger 750 and Bonneville) 120

Vespa
   Ciao 120
   Scooters 120

Yamaha
   V70/75 121
   YB100 121
   RD125 121
   RD200/RD250 122
   RD350 123
   RD400 123
   XS500 124
   XS650 125
   XS1100 126
Yamaha/Norton 125

Zundapp
   ZD40 127
   R50/RS50 127
   KS175 128

Aircraft

Aerospatiale
   Alouette 2 129

Alouette 3 129
Gazelle 130

Puma   131
Alouette 2 (Aerospatiale)   129
Alouette 3 (Aerospatiale)   129
Aztec (Piper)   146

Beaver (De Havilland)   139
Beechcraft
   18   131
   E90 Kingair   132
   Super Kingair   132
   A80 Queenair   133
Bell
   47   133
   UH1B/UH1D/205   134
   206 Jet Ranger   134
   206L Long Ranger   135
   212   136

Centurion (Cessna)   138
Cessna
   150/152   137
   172/Skyhawk   137
   182/Skylane   137
   180/185 Skywagon   137
   206 Stationair   137
   210 Centurion   138
   310   138
   337 Skymaster   138
   401/402/402B   139
   404 Titan   139
Commander (Rockwell)   148
Courier (Helio)   143

De Havilland
   Beaver   139
   Otter   140
   Turbo Beaver   140
   Twin Otter   141

Enstrom F-28C/F-28C-2/280C   142

Gazelle (Aerospatiale)   130
Goose (Grumman)   142
Grumman Goose   142

Helio Courier/Super Courier   143
Hughes
   300 Sky Knight   143
   500 Sky Knight   144

Jet Ranger (Bell)   134

Kamov Ka-26   144
Kingair (Beechcraft)   132

Long Ranger (Bell)   135

Messerschmitt BO105   145

Navajo (Piper)   147

Otter (De Havilland)   140

Partenavia P68 Victor   146
Piper
   Aztec   146
   Senaca   146
   Super Cub   147
   Navajo   147
Puma (Aerospatiale)   131

Queenair (Beechcraft)   133

Rockwell Shrike Commander   148
Saab Supporter   149
Scout (Westland)   151
Sea King (Sikorsky)   150
Senaca (Piper)   146
Shrike Commander (Rockwell)   148
Sikorsky
   S58   149
   S61 Sea King   150
   S62   150
Skyhawk (Cessna)   137
Sky Knight 300 (Hughes)   143
Sky Knight 500 (Hughes)   144
Skylane (Cessna)   137
Skymaster (Cessna)   138
Skywagon (Cessna)   137
Stationair (Cessna)   137
Super Courier (Helio)   143
Super Cub (Piper)   147
Super Kingair (Beechcraft)   132
Supporter (Saab)   149

Titan 404 (Cessna)   139
Turbo Beaver (De Havilland)   140
Twin Otter (De Havilland)   141

Victor (Partenavia)   146

Westland Scout   151